ITZÁ
MAYA
TEXTS

WITH A
GRAMMATICAL OVERVIEW

Charles Andrew Hofling

University of Utah Press
Salt Lake City

Copyright © 1991 University of Utah Press
All rights reserved

Book design by Richard Firmage

∞The paper in this book meets the standards for permanence and durability established by the Committee on Production Guidelines for Book Longevity of the Council on Library Resources

Library of Congress Cataloging-in-Publication Data

Hofling, Charles Andrew.
    Itzá Maya texts with a grammatical overview / Charles A. Hofling.
        p.   cm.
    Includes bibliographical references.
    ISBN 0-87480-359-4 (alk. paper)
    1. Itzá dialect—Texts.   2. Itzá dialect—Grammar.   3. Mayas—
Legends.   4. Mayas—Social life and customs.   I. Title.
PM3969.I89H64   1991
497'.415—dc20   90-52553
                                                                       CIP

ITZÁ MAYA TEXTS

For Lynne and Helen

CONTENTS

ACKNOWLEDGMENTS

This research was supported in part by a Fulbright Fellowship (1979–80) and a University of Kentucky Summer Faculty Research Fellowship (1988), for which I am grateful. I thank the many people of San José, Petén, who assisted me in this work, especially don Fernando Tesucún, don Julian Tesucún, and don Domingo Chayax Suntecún. Don Fernando Tesucún has been a wonderful teacher and friend throughout, and I owe him a special thanks. I am also grateful to Helen Crawford for her assistance in preparing the manuscript, and to Munro S. Edmonson and an anonymous reader for helpful comments. It has been a pleasure to work with the University of Utah Press and I am grateful to its past director, David Catron, and current director, Nana Anderson, for their support. I especially appreciate their very able assistant, Norma B. Mikkelsen, for her careful editing and oversight of the manuscript. My thanks also to Richard Firmage for his excellent book design. Finally, I would like to thank my colleagues at the University of Cincinnati for their continuing support of my research documenting the Itzá Maya language.

ABBREVIATIONS AND SYMBOLS

,	short pause (less than .7 seconds)
…	long pause (more than .7 seconds)
-	morpheme break
=	compound
[ ]	square brackets enclose false starts, slips of the tongue, paralinguistic notes, etc.
[?]	inaudible or uninterpretable speech
( )	parentheses enclose reconstructed or corrected speech
(?)	uncertain as to form; follows questionable portion
{ }	curved brackets enclose backchannels and interruptions
_____	overlapping speech is underlined in conversational text
1	first person
2	second person
3	third person
ABIL	abilitive aspect
ADJ	adjectival
ANIM	animate numeral classifier
ASSUR	assurative aspect
CAUS	causative
CELER	celeritive
CLASS	numeral classifier
COM	completive aspect
COND	conditional
COP	copula
DESID	desiderative aspect
DET	determiner
DETRAN	detransitive
DIST	distal
DPM	distal patient marker
DUB	dubitive
DUR	durative aspect
EMP	emphatic
EXCLAM	exclamation

FEM	feminine noun classifier
HORT	hortative
IMMED	immediative aspect
INAM	inanimate numeral classifier
INC	incompletive aspect
INCHOAT	inchoative
INTENS	intensifier
INTRAN	intransitive
IOpr	indirect object pronoun
Ipr	independent pronoun
LOC	locative
MASC	masculine noun classifier
NEG	negative
NP	noun phrase
OBLIG	obligative aspect
OST	ostensive
PART	participle
PARTIT	partitive
PAS	passive
PERF	perfect
pl	plural
PL	plural (third person)
PM	patient marker
PN	proper noun
PPM	proximal patient marker
Ppr	possessive pronoun
POS	possessive
POSIT	positional
PROX	proximal
REFL	reflexive
REL	relative
REPET	repetitive
REPORT	reportative
REV	reverential
SPM	subordinate patient marker
SUB	subordinator
TEMP	temporal
TERM	terminative aspect
TOP	topic
TRAN	transitive

INTRODUCTION

Linguistic and Cultural History

Itzá Maya is a member of the Yucatecan branch of the Mayan language family. It is a dying language, currently spoken by less than a hundred older adults in Petén, Guatemala. According to glottochronological estimates (Kaufman 1976), the Yucatecan family began to diversify at least ten centuries ago. The other extant members of the Yucatecan family are Mopán Maya, with approximately five thousand speakers in Petén and in Belize (Ulrich and Ulrich 1976); Lacandón, spoken by small groups in Chiápas, Mexico, and in Petén (Bruce 1968); and Yucatec Maya, by far the most robust member of the family with perhaps half a million speakers in the Mexican states of Yucatán, Campeche, and Quintana Roo, and in Belize (Bricker 1981a). As their present proximity suggests, there has doubtless been contact among the members of the family since diversification a millennium ago.

While the history of the Itzá Maya before Spanish contact is far from clear, there are frequent references to them in the Yucatecan Books of Chilam Balam (Edmonson 1982, 1986). According to these sources, the Itzá were a group of wanderers who came to the Yucatan from the west, perhaps from Champoton (Edmonson 1982:6). They claimed to have established Chichén Itzá as a ritual center at the end of the seventh century (this claim is probably mythic and not historically accurate; Edmonson 1982:xvi). During the Postclassic and colonial periods, the Itzá dominated the eastern half of the Yucatan Peninsula and were rivals of the Xiu, who controlled the western half of the peninsula. In the Chilam Balam of Chumayel, written from the Xiu perspective, the Itzá are referred to as stuttering foreigners (Edmonson 1986:3). In the fifteenth century (8 Ahau, 1441–1461) a group of Itzá fleeing local conflicts migrated to the Petén and founded Tayasal on the shores of Lake Petén-Itzá. These are the ancestors of the group referred to as Itzá Maya today. The main body of the Itzás remained in Yucatan and today speak Yucatec Maya.

It is uncertain whether the Itzá settled in largely uninhabited territory along the shores of Lake Petén-Itzá or whether they initially dominated and ultimately absorbed (or were absorbed by) a population already living there. The latter scenario is more probable in light of the archaeological and ethnohistorical evidence of repeated migrations of populations from the north into the Petén, where the immigrant populations mixed with local inhabitants (Chase 1985; Rice 1986; Farriss 1984; Jones 1982, 1989). The Petén Itzá first had contact with the Spanish when Cortés led an expedition through their territory on his way to Honduras in 1524 (Means 1917:26). Spanish contact for the rest of the sixteenth and most of the seventeenth centuries, was intermittent, and it was not until 1697 that the Itzá were finally conquered (Bricker 1981b; Means 1917; Sosa 1970). Tayasal remained a center of Maya culture during the sixteenth and seventeenth centuries, when the Itzá maintained hieroglyphic writing and other traditions that had been suppressed elsewhere. It is clear from colonial records that the Petén Itzá were in contact with their neighbors to the north during this period.

After the conquest, the Itzá were ravaged by disease. Thompson (1976:65) estimates that the population decreased by 90 percent during the eighteenth century, with approximately 800 survivors living in three villages. In the middle of the nineteenth century, C. Berendt visited the Petén and collected a short list of Itzá words and phrases (reproduced in Means 1917). A number of other visitors compiled brief word lists and notes during the nineteenth and early twentieth centuries (Andrade 1976; Armas n.d.; Brasseur de Bourbourg 1865). At the beginning of the twentieth century, a group of Itzá speakers fleeing political repression left San José, Petén, to found San José Soccotz in Belize (Schumann 1971).[1] A repressive language policy during the 1930s, according to which children were forbidden by their teachers to speak Maya, effectively ended the intergenerational transmission of the language (Schumann 1971).

In the 1960s, Otto Schumann conducted linguistic fieldwork among the Itzá in the Petén. At that time, he reports there were two dialects, one spoken in San Andrés and the other in San José, neighboring towns across the lake from the departmental capital city, Flores. He compiled a slim volume, including a brief ethnography, a grammar, word list, and two short texts of the San José dialect (Schumann 1971) and separately published one other Itzá text (Schumann 1964). More recently, unpublished materials (largely textual) have been collected by a number of scholars, including Pierre Ventur, Ortwin Smailus, and Nikolai Grube. The dialect of San Andrés was reportedly more strongly influenced by Yucatec as a result of waves of Yucatec immigrants arriving in San Andrés, particularly during the period of the the Caste Wars of Yucatan in the nineteenth century. It is clear that Yucatec immigrants also arrived in San José, and many inhabitants of San José proudly trace their ancestry to Yucatan or Campeche.

Schumann's description of San José suggests an accelerating acculturation to ladino culture, particularly among the younger generation, who did not speak Maya and often left San José in search of work. Both Schumann (1971) and Sosa (1970) describe town life in the 1960s as largely traditional, but in transition. There was local production of pottery (cf. Text 23), wooden artifacts, such as canoes and washbasins (cf. Text 10), and traditional thatch houses; but only the older generation wore traditional dress. There was heavy reliance on native medicinal treatments, but only remnants of indigenous ritual and religion had survived (cf. Texts 18, 19, and 23). All of the townspeople were

---

[1]Thompson (1977:22) suggests that Schumann was mistaken about Itzá speakers fleeing to Soccotz. Oral tradition in San José, Petén, maintains that a group did go to Soccotz.

at least nominally Catholic. Most men worked as traditional agriculturalists, raising corn, beans, squash, etc., in their milpas (cf. Text 20). Many worked in the chicle industry (cf. Text 22) and collected other forest products for sale in Flores.

Current Status

I conducted fieldwork with the Itzá of San José during 1979–80 and again in the summer of 1988. The pace of acculturation has not slowed. In 1980, San Andrés had only a couple of speakers left, and in 1988, none, so far as I could tell. San José is a smaller and more conservative town, whose inhabitants in 1980 (approximately 500) were almost entirely of Maya ancestry. In 1980, Itzá speakers were all about fifty years old or older and predominately male. On social occasions, older men would often speak Itzá among themselves. However, virtually all speakers of Itzá were also fluent in Spanish.

By 1980 traditional dress had all but disappeared. House construction of cement block and tin roofs was increasingly popular. Pottery was only used for ceremonial purposes, but native woodcrafts were still common. For medical services the people relied almost entirely on a local clinic and the hospital across the lake in San Benito. The chicle industry had collapsed, as had a nearby lumbering operation, and men were increasingly drawn to wage labor away from town.

The changes in San José between 1980 and 1988 were dramatic. Fortunately, it was relatively untouched by the political violence of the 1980s. However, there was large-scale migration into the Petén and the population of San José doubled. Woodcrafts were largely abandoned, and native washbasins were replaced by locally produced concrete ones. The town had reliable electricity as well as not-so-reliable running water. The arrival of cable television was perhaps the most dramatic change, although few households were able to afford the service. There were fewer traces of native ritual, and half the town's inhabitants were pentacostal protestants. Young men continued to leave town in search of work.

Most of those who knew Itzá Maya, now age sixty or over, hardly ever spoke it. There are perhaps several dozen speakers left in San José. They lament the loss of the language and the old ways, but generally recognize that the changes are now irrevocable and that the Itzá Maya language and culture preserved in these texts will soon perish.

Itzá Maya Discourse

Itzá Maya discourse, like that of other Mayan languages, reflects a rich oral tradition based on dialogic verbal performance (Tedlock 1983, 1985; Brody 1986, 1989a, 1989b; Hanks 1989). Repetition and other parallelisms are prominent features of discourse in all of the texts. The circumstances of text collection, in which the native speaker addresses the unusual audience of the anthropologist with tape recorder, at times obscures the essentially interactional nature of Itzá discourse, regardless of genre.

Text Collection

The texts reproduced here were provided by three native speakers of Itzá Maya: Fernando Tesucún, born around 1930; his cousin and contemporary, Julian Tesucún; and Domingo Chayax Suntecún, born in 1914. Fernando Tesucún was my primary consultant. Most of the texts were recorded in his house, where I and other family members who might be present were the audience. This was not the most natural of audiences. With the exception of his aged and not entirely lucid mother, who was sometimes present, none of his audience had native competence in the language. Nevertheless, it is clear from the texts that he was talking to us, and to me in particular, not to a fictional audience.

The narrative texts given by Julian Tesucún (Text 12) and by Domingo Chayax Suntecún (Text 23) were recorded at the house where I lived in San José and were addressed to me. The conversation betweend don Julian and don Domingo (Text 24) was recorded at don Julian's house where other members of his family and I were present. This event was arranged by me. As I noted above, spontaneous Itzá conversation is no longer commonplace. However, the two were old friends and had talked often, and once started, the conversation appeared natural.

Immediately after the texts were tape-recorded, they were transcribed in a practical orthography and translated into Spanish with the assistance of the speakers. I then typed the texts, listening again (and again) to the tapes and adding morphological analysis and English translation. The texts were then checked at least once (and usually twice) more with each of the speakers. Throughout text collection and analysis, I was engaged in grammatical investigations which stimulated ongoing review and revisions of the texts.

Presentational Format

A basic unit in the presentation of the texts is the text line. Word-internal morpheme divisions are indicated in the Itzá line by hyphens, or in the case of compounds, by equal signs. Glosses for each morpheme are provided beneath the Itzá line, followed by a translation into English.

The line is a key unit in Itzá discourse, and corresponds to what Halliday (1967) identified as "information units" and what Chafe (1982) has called "idea units." The line is widely recognized as a fundamental unit in Native American discourse, particularly important in ethnopoetics (Hymes 1981; Tedlock 1983; Burns 1983; Swann 1983; Bright 1984; Sherzer and Woodbury 1987; Hanks 1989). Lines are cognitively based units, marked both intonationally and morphosyntactically, and are roughly equivalent to a grammatical clause (but are often phrasal). Distinctive stress patterns (chapter 2, **1.4.**) and pauses typically signal a line juncture. A set of morphosyntactic markers, described in chapter 2, also regularly signals line boundaries.

Usually intonational and morphosyntactic cues agree in signaling line boundaries. However, at times they do not, and other analysts might scan the texts differently. Pausal and grammatical information is explicit in the texts for use in such reanalysis.

I have included false starts, slips of the tongue, etc., which are marked with square brackets on the text line. This information will be of particular interest to those examining processes of cognition and discourse production. Later corrections or reconstructions are shown in parentheses on the text line. Thus, one may easily compare what was actually said with what the participants and I believe was intended when they differ.

In more formal genres (e.g., folktales), lines often enter into larger verse stuctures of couplets, stanzas, and episodes. These are not marked explicitly in the text, but the interested reader may derive such structures with the information provided.

I chose not to indicate larger poetic or thematic units in the texts for both practical and aesthetic reasons. For example, to add information on rhetorical structure by indenting makes a text with interlinear glosses and translation very difficult to read. A common solution to this dilemma is to abandon interlineal glosses and indicate verse structure in the text and in a translation alongside. However, one thereby loses information on grammatical structure, which makes the texts virtually useless for those interested in linguistic analysis. More complex schemes of multiple versions overcome this shortcoming, but, again, are more difficult for the reader.

Another reason for the present format is that it allows a standard presentation among and within texts. Not all types of texts have a verselike structure, nor need a single text be entirely in verse. The basic unit of the line enters in all genres of discourse. Similarly, the poetic use that is made of the line in parallelisms is present to some degree in all oral discourse and reflects its dialogic base (England 1988; Brody 1989a, 1989b).

Genre and Grammatical Structure

A symptom of language death is the loss of certain genres as the language is used in fewer contexts. For example, I was unable to obtain examples of ritual speech or song, for these genres were not in the repertoire of my linguistic consultants. They prayed and sang in Spanish. Relatedly, I did not discover an elaborate taxonomy of named genres, such as that reported for other Mayan languages (Bricker 1974; Burns 1983). I have divided the texts into four broad categories, which are readily distinguishable in Itzá, and which I would imagine are in most languages: personal narrative, folklore, expository discourse, and conversation.

Personal narrative refers to discourse in which the speaker relates personally experienced events. First-person references to the speaker are frequent and the past events described are asserted to have truly occurred. Linguistic parallelisms occur with variable frequency. Generally, personal narratives are structured according to the natural chronological order of the events described.

Folklore is a more formulaic genre. Folktales typically begin with a standard formula, marking the genre as folktale and signaling a time reference in the distant past. They may have an elaborate thematic structure, with formally marked episodes and stanzas, and they typically end with a précis. The marker of reported speech, *b'in*, regularly occurs, and quoted speech of the protagonists of the tales is a common feature.

Expository discourse refers to speech whose purpose is to explain or describe how things are or how they are done. These texts have nonspecific actors rather than individualized characters. The passive voice and noncompletive aspects are relatively high in frequency in expository discourse.

The distinctive feature of conversation is that two or more speakers are actively participating in constructing the discourse. Conversation is the broadest and most basic of genres. Although it is formally quite flexible, first- and second-person references to the conversational participants are the norm.

A wide range of grammatical structures occur within these texts, some with unceasing regularity, some very rarely. This collection is intended in part as a document of the Itzá language and how it is used. In order to understand the function of a grammatical structure, one must know its discourse context, and it is very useful to know its frequency of occurrence. A text corpus of this kind permits such investigations into discourse function. In chapter 2, I provide a brief overview of the grammatical structure of Itzá Maya. This grammatical sketch relies heavily on examples from the texts and is intended as an aid for interpreting the texts. The texts themselves provide a source of unplumbed depth for future investigations of Itzá discourse.

GRAMMATICAL OVERVIEW

Introduction

This brief grammatical description is intended as an aid in interpreting the grammatical structures and their functions in the texts. References to more complete discussions of many of the constructions described are noted for the interested reader. Most of the examples are drawn from the texts, cited by text and line numbers: for example, (2:11) refers to Text 2, line 11. Certain grammatical elements and processes that do not appear, or are rare in the texts, receive scant or no attention below.

1. Phonology

1.1. Phonemic Inventory

The practical orthography proposed by the Guatemalan Academy of Mayan Languages and adopted by the Guatemalan government is employed throughout this work. The transcription is basically phonemic, but I have attempted to record nonpredictable variation. The phonemic inventory and values of the practical alphabet are indicated in the following chart. Consonants found only in Spanish loanwords are in parentheses.

Phonemic Inventory

Consonants

	Labial	Dental	Alveolar	Palatal	Velar	Glottal
Stops						
Voiceless	p	t			k	'
glottalized	p'	t'			k'	
voiced	b'	(d)			(g)	
Affricates						
voiceless			tz	ch		
glottalized			tz'	ch'		
Fricatives						
voiceless	(f)		s	x		h
voiced	(v)					
Liquid		l				
Vibrants			(r, r̃)			
Nasals	m	n		(ñ)		
Semivowels	w			y		

Vowels

	Front	Central	Back
High	i ii	ä	u uu
Mid	e ee		o oo
Low		a aa	

1.2. Phonological Processes

1) [l] ~ [h] ~ ϕ / _____ #
  Examples: *hun tuul winik* (one ANIM man) → *hun tuuh winik* → *hun tuu winik*. *u-nah-il* (3Ppr-house-POS)→ *u-nah-ih* → *u-nah-i*.

2) [l] → ϕ / _____C[alveolar] (variable)
  Examples: *tal-s-ik* (come-CAUS-PPM) → *ta-s-ik* (obligatory); *chil-tal* (lie-INCHOAT) → *chi-tal* (optional?); *tzikb'al-t-ik* (talk-TRAN-PPM) → *tzikb'a-t-ik* (optional).

3) ['] ~ [h] ~ ϕ / _____ #
  Examples: *he'-lo'* (OST-DIST) → *he'-loh* → *he'-lo*; *a'-winik-e'* (DET-man-TOP) → *a'-winik-eh* → *a'-winik-e*.

4) ['] ~ ϕ /# _____V
  Examples: *'a'-winik-eh* (DET-man-TOP) → *a'-winik-eh*; *'u-hol* (3Ppr-hole) → *u-hol*. In the practical orthography, word-initial vowel symbols represent /'V/.

5) [h] ~ ϕ / _____#
  Examples: *bin-ih* (go-3) → *bin-i*; *chokoh* ('hot') → *choko*.

6) 'V-initial root allomorphy with Set A dependent pronouns.[1]
  6a) -'VC → -wVC (obligatory with 1st and 2nd person)
  Examples: *'il* ('see'): *k-in-wil-ik* (INC-1sg-see-PPM); *k-a-wil-ik* (INC-2-see-PPM); *ki-wil-ik* (INC/1pl-see-PPM); *'ätan* ('wife'): *in-wätan* (1sgPpr-wife); *a-wätan*: (2Ppr-wife).

  6b) -'VC → yVC (obligatory with 3rd person)
  Examples: -*'il* ('see'): *k-u-yil-ik* (INC-3-see-PPM); *'ätan* ('wife'): *u-yätan* (3Ppr-wife).

7) Nasal assimilation (optional).
  /n/ → [m] / _____ [labial]
     → [ŋ] / _____ [velar]
  Examples: *k-in-bin* (INC-1sg-go) → *k-im-b'in*; *in-paal* (1sgPpr-child) → *im-paal*; *k-u-män-b'-äl* (INC-3-buy-PAS-INTRAN) → *k-u-mäm-b'-äl*; *in-k'a't-ih* (1sg-want-3) → *iŋ-k'a't-ih*.

8) Vowel Harmony: CV_iC-VC → CV_iC-V_iC (obligatory)

---

[1] Alternatively, one might consider the Set A dependent pronouns to be allomorphic with 'V-initial roots (cf. Blair 1964; Bricker 1981a).

The vowels of the intransitive suffix (-*Vl*), the irrealis (subjunctive) suffix (-*Vk*), and the subordinate patient marker (-*V'*) harmonize with the preceding vowel.

Examples: *uk'-ul* (drink-INTRAN), *uk'-uk* (drink-IRREAL), uk'-u' (drink-SPM); *han-al* (eat-INTRAN), *han-ak* (eat-IRREAL); *tz'on* (shoot), *tz'on-o'* (shoot-SPM).

9)   [ä] ~ [a]

Several verbal morphosyntactic processes involving voice and transitivity show alternations of [ä] and [a]. For one class of verbs with roots of the form *CaC*, the harmonic suffixes described in 8) (except the SPM) appear as -*äC*.

Examples: *k-in-pa'-ik* (INC-3-break-PPM), *k-u-pa'-äl* (INC-3-break-INTRAN), *pa'-äk* (break-IRREAL), buy *im-paa'* (1sg-break/SPM).

For transitive roots of the form *CäC*, the antipassive and intransitive (mediopassive) appear as *CaC*.

Examples: *k-u-tz'äk-ik* (INC-3-cure-PPM), *k-u-tz'ak* (INC-3-cure [antipassive]); *k-u-p'ät-ik* (INC-3-leave-PPM), *k-u-p'at* (INC-3-leave [antipassive]), *k-u-p'at-äl* (INC-3-leave-INTRAN [mediopassive]); *k-in-män-ik* (INC-3-buy-PPM), *k-in-man-al* (INC-3-buy-INTRAN [antipassive]). Note that if it occurs, the -*Vl* intransitive suffix appears as -*al* on antipassive forms, but as -*äl* on mediopassive forms.

For all verbs with either *CaC* or *CäC* roots, *CäC* appears in harmonic suffixes on passives.

Examples: *k-in-han-al* (INC-1sg-eat-INTRAN), *k-in-han-t-ik* (INC-3-eat-TRAN-PPM), *han-b'-äk* (eat-PAS-IRREAL), *han-t-äb'-äl* (eat-TRAN-PAS-INTRAN); *k-u-kän-ik* (INC-3-learn-PPM), *k-u-kän-b'-äl* (INC-3-learn-PAS-INTRAN), *u-kän-ä'* (3-learn-SPM), *kän-b'-äk* (learn-PAS-IRREAL).

The masculine noun classifier also shows [a] ~ [ä] alternation with the allomorph [ah] appearing in unpossessed forms and [wäh] or [yäh] in possessed forms.

Examples: *ah kax* (MASC chicken), *in-wäh kax* (1sgPpr-MASC chicken); *u-yäh kax* (3Ppr-MASC chicken).

10)   Reduplication: $C_1V_1C_2 \rightarrow C_1V_1(C_2)C_1V_1C_2$ (obligatory)

With adjectives, reduplication functions to mark intensity.

Examples: *kän* ('red') → *känkän* ('very red'); *chich* ('hard') → *chichich* ('very hard').

11)   V'C ~ V'VC

Examples: *wa'l-ik* (say-PPM) → *wa'al-ik*; *he'-lo'* (OST-DIST) → *he'e-lo'*; *te'-lo'* (LOC-DIST) → *te'e-lo'*.

1.3 Spanish Loanwords

In Spanish words with stress preceding the final syllable, the stressed vowel is lengthened. /h/ is added to Spanish words ending in a vowel. Examples: Sp. *mésa* > *a'-meesah-oo'* (DET-table-PL); Sp. *abuela* > *abweela*(*h*) ('aunt'). Spanish loans that are common discourse markers, such as *como*, 'as', are often pronounced as in Spanish.

1.4. Lexical Stress

There is considerable variation in word stress patterns in discourse as Schumann (1971:31) notes. He reports as the general rule that stress falls on the final syllable of a word. When the last syllable is a particle, stress is variable, falling either on the last or on the penultimate syllable. Overriding this rule (contrary to Schumann), stress falls on long vowels—or on V'(V)—anywhere in a word. For verbs, stress falls on the first syllable of the root when phrase medial, but on the last syllable of the verb when phrase final. If two or more syllables follow the root, stress falls both on the root and the last syllable.

2. Nominal Morphosyntax

2.1. Unmodified Nouns

Nouns lacking morphological modification generally signal indefinite or generic information (1–3). Exceptions are cases where definite reference is made by virtue of specific shared cultural information, as when *kah* 'town' or *nah* 'house' refer to the "town" or "house" of the speaker (4–5). Examples:

1. (2:11)   in-wil-a' wa yan, *keeh* ich a'-kol-eh. …
             1sg-see-SPM COND COP deer in DET-milpa-TOP
             (for me) to see if there were deer in the milpa.

2. (5:3)   tumen hach yaab' *k'oxol*. …
             because very much mosquito
             because there are so many mosquitos.

3. (6:4)   B'el in-k(a'a) in-ch'äk-ä' yaab' *si'*
             go 1sg-go-1sg-cut-SPM much wood
             I am going to cut a lot of wood

4. (3:3)   I p'at-een ich *kah* …
             and remain-1sg in town
             And I stayed in town,

5. (3:29)   ka' t-u-yok-s-ah-een-oo' ich *nah*. …
             then COM-3-enter-CAUS-DPM-1sg-PL inside house
             and they brought me inside the house.

2.2. Noun Classifiers

Some nouns require a preceding noun classifier, either the masculine noun classifier, *ah*, or the feminine noun classifier, *ix*, regardless of definiteness (also see **2.5.** and **7.5.**). Examples:

1. (2:91)   Ma tan-u-käy *ah kax*. …
             already DUR-3-sing MASC chicken
             The roosters were already crowing.

2. (10:21)   Ii, ka' t-u-tz'ah ten hun tuul *ah wach* …
             and then COM-3-give/DPM 1sgIOpr one ANIM MASC Mexican
             And then he gave me a Mexican,

3. (13:110) ya hun tuul noxi' *ah koh*. …
             already one ANIM big MASC lion
             he's already a big lion.

4. (13:139) *ah koh-eh* tun-hum u-yakan
             MASC lion-TOP DUR/3-sound 3Ppr-roar
             the lion, his roar was sounding

5. (16:52) *Ix nok'ol* he'-loh …
             FEM worm OST-DIST
             That worm,

6. (21:51) k-u-top'-ol u-*yix nok'ol*-il a'-xa'an-eh. ,
             INC-3-hatch-INTRAN 3Ppr-FEM worm-POS DET-thatch-TOP
             the worm of the thatch is hatched.

7. (17:152) ka' t-u-ya'al-ah ti' *ix ch'up-eh*: …
             then COM-3-say-DPM to FEM woman-TOP
             then he said to the woman:

2.3. Numerals and Numeral Classifiers

Numeral classifiers are present whenever a noun is modified by a numeral. The numeral classifiers indicate such features as animacy, shape, and measure. Numerals and numeral classifiers precede the modified noun in this order: Numeral + Numeral Classifier + Noun. Indefinite-referential marking is frequently signaled by numeral modifiers, and is commonly employed when introducing significant characters or context into a discourse (1–5) (Hofling 1982, 1989). Possessive marking preceding the numeral distinguishes ordinal from cardinal numerals (6). Occasionally, numeral + numeral classifier serves pronominal functions (7). Examples:

1. (1:15) tumen yan *hun tuul* im-paal k'oh-a'an …
            because COP one ANIM 1sgPpr-child sick-PART
            because I have a sick child

2. (2:17) te' wa'an *hun tuul* keeh-i'ih. …
            LOC stand/PART one ANIM deer-LOC
            there was standing a deer.

3. (2:81) tu'ux yan *hum p'e* che', lub-al-eh,
            where COP one INAM tree fall-PART-REL
            where there is a big fallen tree,

4. (3:1) Yan-ah-ih *hum p'e* k'in …
           COP-DIST-3sg one INAM day
           There was a day,

5. (12:2) u-tzikb'al-il *hun tuul* winik,
            3Ppr-talk-POS one ANIM man
            (is) the story of a man,

6. (12:68) t-u-*ox p'e* k'in k-u-b'el
in-3Ppr-three INAM day INC-3-go
it's going into the third day

7. (13:99) Ka' t-u-ya'l-ah b'in *hun tuul*
then COM-3-say-DPM REPORT one ANIM
Then one said

t-u-yet'ok-eh: ,
to-3Ppr-companion-TOP
to his companion:

2.4. Plurals

Plurals are formed with the suffix *-oo'*, and are typically definite (1–3). Certain inanimate nouns are marked by the plural suffix *-tak* (4–5). Examples:

1. (7:3) I a'-mehen-pek'-*oo'*-eh,
and DET-small-dog-PL-TOP
And the small dogs,

2. (4:11) t-u-kaal-*oo'*-eh. ,
to-3Ppr-town-PL-TOP
to their towns.

3. (13:165–66) I mentäk-eh, a'-b'a'al=che'-*oo'* he'-lo',
and therefore-TOP DET-animal-PL OST-DIST
And therefore, those animals,

4. (16:49) u-may-*tak* a'-keeh-eh. …
3Ppr-hoof-PL DET-deer-TOP
the hooves of the deer.

5. (21:35) k-u-chäk-ik a'-b'a'ax-*tak* mum. …
INC-3-cook-PPM DET-thing-PL tender
it cooks the tender things.

2.5. Adjectives

Descriptive adjectives generally precede the noun they modify (1–2). Occasional exceptions, where the adjective follows, may be due to Spanish influence (3–4). Predicate adjectives may precede or follow the noun they modify (5–7). Intensification of predicate adjectives may be marked with reduplication of the first syllable and the suffix *-ki* (8–9). Noun classifiers may also appear when the adjective precedes the modified noun (10–12). Examples:

1. (7:3) I a'-*mehen* pek'-oo'-eh,
and DET-small dog-PL-TOP
And the small dogs,

2. (12:132) Ka' t-u-kuch-ah u-si' a'-*nohoch* winik-eh
then COM-3-load-DPM 3Ppr-firewood DET-great man-TOP
Then the great man loaded his firewood

3. (22:118)   sum *polok*. ...
                rope thick
                (is) thick rope.

4. (18:44)   T-u-män-ah hum p'e lak *tu'umb'en*. ...
                COM-3-buy-DPM one INAM plate new
                He bought a new clay plate.

5. (5:10)   B'ayoritah-eh hach *k'as* a'-b'eh-eh. ,
                now-TOP very bad DET-road-TOP
                Now the road is very bad.

6. (2:65)   Im-pol-eh, *al*, *al*. ...
                1sgPpr-head-TOP heavy heavy
                My head, it was heavy, heavy.

7. (20:103)   yok' u-p'at-äl *säk* a'-ixi'im-eh,
                SUB 3-remain-INTRAN white DET-corn-TOP
                so that the corn remains white,

8. (5:4–6)   A'-beh, tu'ux k-im-b'el ti meyah-eh
                DET-road where INC-1sg-go SUB work-REL
                The road where I go to work is

                tz'o-tz'op-ki ...
                INTENS-swampy-ADJ
                very swampy

9. (22:313)   porke *tä'-täk'-'ki*. ...
                because INTENS-sticky-ADJ
                because it's very sticky.

10. (12:30)   Ka' lub'-ih *ah tikin* che'-eh. ...
                then fall-3sg MASC dry tree-TOP
                Then the dry tree fell.

11. (15:19)   T-u-yil-ah *ah noh* b'a'al=che',
                COM-3-see-DPM MASC big animal
                He saw the big animal

12. (20:83)   et-el *ix kuxu'* ixi'im-eh. ...
                with-POS FEM tender corn-REL
                with tender corn.

2.6. The Determiner *a'*-

Definite reference is typically marked by the determiner prefix *a'*- in conjunction with a series of postposed elements including the topic-marking suffix and demonstrative adjectives (Hofling 1982, 1987). The determiner precedes adjectival modifiers. Examples:

1. (5:19)   tulakal t-*a'*-b'eh-eh. ...
                all on-DET-road-TOP
                all along the road.

2. (11:5)   t-*a*'-yax kol-oo' ...
              to-DET-first milpa-PL
              to the first milpas

3. (10:30)   "*A*'-che' he'-la'-eh,"
              DET-tree OST-PROX-TOP
              "This tree,"

2.7. The Topic Marker -*e*'

The topic marker -*e*' frequently occurs in conjunction with the determiner *a*'- to mark given, topical noun phrases, often in topic-shift constructions where the nominal is fronted (1–2) (Hofling 1987, 1989). The same frame marks relative clauses (3–4). The topic marker also enters into certain other subordinate constructions (cf. **14.**, **15.**, **16.**, **17.2.**; Hofling 1982, 1987). It also frequently appears on independent pronouns (5) and possessed nouns (6), and on occasion marks topical indefinites (7). Examples:

1. (1:33)   tumen *a*'-che'-*eh*,
              because DET-wood-TOP
              because the wood,

2. (22:94)   U-yitz *a*'-che' he'-lo'-*eh*,
              3Ppr-resin DET-tree OST-DIST-TOP
              The resin of those trees,

3. (2:3–4)   B'in-een tulakal t-*a*'-noh b'eh tu'ux k-in-meyah-*eh*. ...
              go-1sg all on-DET-big road where INC-1sg-work-REL
              I went all along the big road where I work.

4. (3:7)   *a*'-ha' t-in-wuk'-ah-*eh* ...
              DET-water COM-1sg-drink-DPM-REL
              the water that I drank,

5. (1:12)   In-ten-*eh* t-in-wa'al-ah ti'ih,
              EMP-1sgIpr-TOP COM-1sg-say-DPM 3IOpr
              Me, I said to him,

6. (2:65)   Im-pol-*eh*, al, al. ...
              1sgPpr-head-TOP heavy heavy
              My head, it was heavy, heavy.

7. (21:95)   mak-*eh* pwes ...
              person-TOP well
              a person, well,

2.8. The Partitive Marker -*i'ih*

The partitive marker -*i'ih* is used to refer to a part of a previously mentioned (or otherwise given) nominal referent. It is most common as a suffix to numeral classifers and quantifiers, but may also be suffixed to nouns, pronouns, verbs, and certain adverbials (Hofling 1982). Examples:

1. (4:9) patal-u-p'ät-ik ten-*i'ih*. …
   ABIL-3-leave-PPM 1sgIOpr-PARTIT
   he could leave me some of them.

2. (10:43) He'-u-hok'-ol hum p'e ma'lo' chem-*i'ih*-eh. …
   ASSUR-3-leave-INTRAN one INAM good canoe-PARTIT-TOP
   A good canoe will come out of it.

3. (12:31) Ka' t-u-p'is-ah hun yuul-*i'ih*. …
   then COM-3-measure-DPM one piece-PARTIT
   Then he measured a piece of it.

4. (12:78) K-in-si'-ik tech hun tuul-*i'ih*. …
   INC-1sg-donate-PPM 2sgIOpr one ANIM-PARTIT
   I'll give you one of them.

2.9. Demonstrative Adjectives

Demonstrative adjectives are composed of the ostensive marker *he'-* and either the proximal marker *la'* or the distal marker *lo'*. They may precede or follow the noun they modify. When they precede, they highlight their ostensive nature and occur in conjunction with the determiner and the topic (or relative) marker in the construction OST-DIST/PROX + DET-N- (relative clause)-TOP (1–2) (Hofling 1982). More frequently the demonstratives follow the modified noun in the construction DET-N + OST-DIST/PROX([-relative clause]-TOP) (3–6). Examples:

1. *He'-loh* a'-pek'-eh.
    OST-DIST DET-dog-TOP
    That (/there) is the dog.

2. *He'-la'* a'-winik t-u-yok-l-ah
    OST-PROX DET-man COM-3-steal-?-DPM
    Here is the man that stole

    in-ta' = k'in-eh.
    1sgPpr-money-REL
    my money.

3. (11:11) "a'-kol *he'-la'*-eh." …
   DET-milpa OST-PROX-TOP
   "this milpa."

4. (14:67) T-u-chi' a'-noh ha' *he'-lo'* yan-eh …
   at-3Ppr-edge DET-big water OST-DIST COP-REL
   At the edge of that big lake there,

5. (8:20–21) Mia' tulakal a'-k'in-oo' *he'-la'*
   DUB all DET-day-PL OST-PROX
   I think all these days

   tan-u-b'et-ik ha'-eh …
   DUR-3-make-PPM water-REL
   that it was raining,

6. (13:73)   ma' = ta'ax u-yil-ik-oo' a'-b'a'al = che' *he'-lo'*.
                never 3-see-PPM-PL DET-animal OST-DIST
                they had never seen that animal.

2.10. Possession

2.10.1. Ppr-Possessed NP (+ Possessor NP)

Possession is minimally marked by Set A (ergative) dependent pronominal prefixes referencing the possessor attached to the possessed noun phrase:
Ppr-NP (1–2). The possessor may also be referenced by a full NP, regularly
following the possessed NP in the order: Ppr-NP + Possessor NP (3–5). Most
frequently in discourse, the possessor is animate, topical information, and the
possessor NP is absent. Possessed NPs commonly refer to body parts, kin, and
personal property. Inanimate part-whole relationships are commonly marked
by possessive constructions in which the possessor NP is present and are often
locative. See Hofling (1990) for more detailed information on possessive constructions. Examples:

1. (1:1)   Ho'leh-ih, tal-ih *im-b'al* …
                yesterday-3sg come-3sg 1sgPpr-brother-in-law
                Yesterday my brother-in-law came,

2. (1:5)   U-ka'ah u-b'et-eh *u-yotoch* …
                3-go 3-make-SPM 3Ppr-home
                He is going to make his home(s)

3. (12:127)   ka' p'at-ih *u-yaal u-k'ab' a'-b'alum-eh*,
                then remain-3sg 3Ppr-child 3Ppr-hand DET-jaguar-TOP
                and the fingers of the jaguar's paws remained,

4. (3:19)   T-u-heb'-ah-oo' *u-hol a'-nah-eh* …
                COM-3-open-DPM-PL 3Ppr-door DET-house-TOP
                She opened the door of the house,

5. (18:7)   t-*u-haal a'-ha'* …
                on-3Ppr-shore DET-water
                on the shore of the lake,

2.10.2. Ppr-Possessed NP-*Vl* (+ Possessor NP)

A possessive suffix, usually *-el*, appears on a set of "inalienably" or
inherently possessed body parts (1–2). An *-il* suffix also occurs on the possessed NP when the possessor is inanimate, indefinite, or collective in constructions other than the part-whole type described in **2.10.1.** (3–5), and in deriving
abstract nouns from adjectival forms (6–7). Examples:

1. (3:25)   Chawak *u-tzo'otz-el u-pol.* …
                long 3Ppr-hair-POS 3Ppr-head
                Long is the hair of her head.

2. (3:26)   K-u-lub'-ul tak t-*u-b'ak-el u-yit.* …
                INC-3-fall-INTRAN till to-3Ppr-bone-POS 3Ppr-rump
                It falls to the bone of her rump.

3. (2:71)   Mia *u-yum-il k'aax*,
               DUB 3Ppr-lord-POS forest
               I think it's the lord of the forest,

4. (20:137)   yan-u-b'et-ik mak *u-nah-il*. …
               OBLIG-3-make-PPM person 3Ppr-house-POS
               one has to make its (the milpa's) house.

5. (22:320–21) yan hun tuul … *u-nohoch-il*
               COP one ANIM 3Ppr-big-POS
               there is one, who is the chief (the big one of the group)

6. (22:244)   ke a'-winik hach, yah *u-k'oh-a'an-il*-eh,
               SUB DET-man very bad 3Ppr-sick-PART-POS-REL
               the man, whose sickness is very bad,

7. (22:337)   *U-'al-il a'-chiikleh*-eh …
               3Ppr-heavy-POS DET-chicle-TOP
               The weight of the chicle,

2.11. Relational Nouns

Relational nouns are a special class of possessed forms that typically signal oblique, often locative, case relations. They are composed of a possessive pronoun, the root, and (usually) a -*Vl* suffix, frequently in prepositional phrases. Examples:

1. (12:2–3)   hun tuul winik, *yet-el* hun tuul b'alum. …
               one ANIM man 3Ppr/with-POS one ANIM jaguar
               a man and a jaguar.

2. (17:12)   "b'el in-ka'a ti muk-b'-ul ket t-*a-wet-el*" …
               go 1sg-go SUB bury-PAS-INTRAN together to-2Ppr-with-POS
               "I am going to be buried together with you."

3. (17:142)   "B'a'ax u-ka'a ma' tan-b'el ti *ki-wet-el*?" …
               what 3-go NEG DUR/2-go to 1plPpr-with-POS
               "Why don't you come with us?"

4. (13:101–2) "Ko'ox ki-wil-a' wa chuk-a'an t-*in-wok'-ol*."
               HORT 1pl-see-SPM COND fit-PART to-1sgPpr-over-POS
               "Let's see if it fits over me."

2.12. Reflexives

Reflexives are composed of possessive pronouns and the reflexive pronoun, *b'ah* (Ppr-*bah*). When functioning as direct objects, they typically appear immediately after the verb. Examples:

1. (2:37)   te' k-u-hil-t-ik *u-b'ah*-i'ih. …
               LOC INC-3-throw-TRAN-PPM 3Ppr-REFL-SCOPE
               there it throws itself.

2. (9:52)   I ki-mol-ik *ki-b'ah* a'-k'in,
            and INC/1pl-collect-PPM 1plPpr-REFL DET-day
            And we meet (collect ourselves) the day,

3. (17:81) kap-ih u-pek-es *u-b'ah* u-yätan-eh. …
            begin-3sg 3-move-CAUS/SPM 3Ppr-REFL 3Ppr-wife-TOP
            his wife began to move herself.

4. (17:95) wa'ye muk-a'an *ki-b'ah*. …
            here bury-PART 1plPpr-REFL
            here we ourselves are buried.

3. Pronouns

3.1. Dependent Pronouns

In Mayan linguistics dependent pronouns are traditionally divided into two sets: Set A, which are prefixes; and Set B, which are suffixes.

3.1.1. Set A Dependent Pronouns

The Set A dependent pronouns are as follows:

	Singular		Plural		
1st person	in-	excl.	ki-		
		incl.	ki-	…	-e'ex
2nd person	a-		a-	…	-e'ex
3rd person	u-		u-	…	-oo'

As noted in **2.10.**, Set A (ergative) dependent pronouns appear on nouns in possessive constructions, referencing the possessor. They also are verbal prefixes, signaling agreement with the transitive agent regardless of aspect or mode (and thus, are the ergative set) (1–2), and with intransitive subjects in noncompletive aspects (3). In the completive aspect and in the subjunctive, intransitive subjects are marked by Set B dependent pronouns (cf. **3.1.2.**), resulting in a split-ergative verb-agreement system (Hofling 1982). The system is ergative in the completive aspect and in the subjunctive, where transitive agents are marked by Set A pronouns, but intransitive subjects and transitive objects are marked by Set B pronouns. The system is nominative in the noncompletive aspects, where Set A pronouns mark both transitive and intransitive subjects, whereas transitive objects are marked by Set B pronouns. Examples:

1. a. K-*in*-wil-ik.   b. K-*a*-wil-ik.   c. K-*u*-yil-ik.
      INC-1sg-see-PPM   INC-2-see-PPM   INC-3-see-PPM
      I see it.   You see it.   He sees it.

   a. *Ki*-wil-ik.   b. K-*a*-wil-ik-*e'ex*.   c. K-*u*-yil-ik-*oo'*.
      INC/1pl-see-PPM   INC-2-see-PPM-2pl   INC-3-see-PPM-PL
      We (excl.) see it.   You (pl.) see it.   They see it.

2. a. T-*in*-wil-ah.   b. T-*a*-wil-ah.   c. T-*u*-yil-ah.
      COM-1sg-see-DPM   COM-2-see-DPM   COM-3-see-DPM
      I saw it.   You saw it.   He saw it.

3. a. K-*in*-tal.   b. K-*a*-tal.   c. K-*u*-tal.
    INC-1sg-come   INC-2-come   INC-3-come
    I come.   You come.   He comes.

3.1.2. Set B Dependent Pronouns

The Set B dependent pronouns are as follows:

	Singular		Plural
1st person	-(e)en	excl.	-o'on
		incl.	-o'on-e'ex
2nd person	-(e)ech		-e'ex
3rd person	-ø, -ih		-oo'

Set B (absolute) dependent pronouns are suffixed to adjectives and nouns in stative constructions. Examples: *wi'ih-en*, 'I am hungry'; *winik-ech*, 'you are a man'; *chokoh-ø*, 'he is hot.'

They also mark verb agreement of the transitive object, regardless of tense/aspect or mode (1–3). The ø allomorph of the third-person-singular pronoun marks direct-object agreement. The lengthened vowels of the first- and second-person singular appear when they mark direct objects in the subjunctive (3), but not when they mark direct objects elsewhere. Examples:

1. a. K-u-yil-ik-*en*.   b. K-u-yil-ik-*ech*.   c. K-a-wil-ik-*ø*.
    INC-3-see-PPM-1sg   INC-3-see-PPM-2sg   INC-2-see-PPM-3sg
    He sees me.   He sees you.   You see him.

2. a. T-u-yil-ah-*en*.   b. T-u-yil-ah-*ech*.   c. T-a-wil-ah-*ø*.
    COM-3-see-DPM-1sg   COM-3-see-DPM-2sg   COM-2-see-DPM-3sg
    He saw me.   He saw you.   You saw him.

3. a. U-ka'a u-yil-a'-*eech*.   b. U-ka'a u-yil-a'-*een*.
    3-go 3-see-SPM-2sg   3-go 3-see-SPM-1sg
    He is going to see you.   He is going to see me.

Set B pronouns also mark intransitive subjects in the completive aspect, where the lengthened vowels of the first- and second-person singular also appear and where the -*ih* allomorph of the third-person singular occurs (4).

4. a. Tal-*een*.   b. Tal-*eech*.   c. Tal-*ih*.
    come-1sg   come-1sg   come-3sg
    I came.   You came.   He came.

3.2. Independent Pronouns

The independent pronouns are as follows:

	Singular		Plural
1st person	ten	excl.	to'on
		incl.	to'on-e'ex
2nd person	tech		te'ex
3rd person	layti', ti'ih		layti'-oo', ti'ih-oo'

Independent pronouns signal discourse highlighting and are commonly fronted in topic-shift and contrastive-focus constructions (1–6) (Hofling 1982).

Except when marking indirect objects, they are typically redundant, for their reference is additionally and obligatorily marked by dependent pronouns. Indirect-object pronouns commonly appear after the verb, but are identical to the independent pronouns in other functions except in the third person, where the forms *ti'ih* and *ti'ihoo'* occur (7–8).

First- and second-person independent pronouns (but not indirect-object pronouns or third-person pronouns of any kind) may also have the emphatic prefix *in-* (1, 4–5), reflecting additional discourse highlighting. Examples:

1. (2:68)   I *in-ten*-eh, ya
                and EMP-1sgIpr-TOP already
                And me, then

                ma' pat-ah-ih in-xi'mal. ...
                NEG ABIL-DIST-3sg 1sg-walk
                I couldn't walk.

2. (4:12-13)   *Layti'-oo'*-eh käh-a'an-oo' tak Chal,
                3Ipr-PL-TOP live-PART-PL till PN
                Them, they live over at Chal,

3. (10:31)   *layti'* a'-ki' t-in-wich-eh
                3Ipr DET-good to-1sgPpr-eye-REL
                it is the one I like

4. (11:53-4)   I *in-to'on*-eh nak'-a'an-o'on t-u-ni'
                and EMP-1plIpr-TOP climb-PART-1pl at-3Ppr-top
                And as for us, we were up at the top

                a'-witz-eh,
                DET-hill-TOP
                of the hill,

5. (17:15-16) Wa *tech* k-a-kim-il taan-il-eh ...
                COND 2sgIpr INC-2-die-INTRAN front-POS-TOP
                If you die first,

                in-ten k-im-b'el,
                EMP-1sgIpr INC-1sg-go
                I am going

6. (15:204-5) *layti'* a'-miismo k'in he'-lo'
                3Ipr DET-same day OST-DIST
                it was that same day

                sut-k'-ah-ih-eh.
                return-CELER?-DIST-3sg-REL
                that he returned.

7. (15:118-19) a'-nohoch winik-eh, k-u-ya'al-ik b'in *ti'ih*-eh:
                DET-great man-TOP INC-3-say-PPM REPORT 3IOpr-TOP
                the old man says to him, they say:

8. (1:2)   i t-u-ya'al-ah *ten* …
             and COM-3-say-DPM 1sgIOpr
             and he told me

There is also a set of independent possessive pronouns formed from Set A dependent pronominal prefixes and the stem *ti'a'al* (e.g., *in-ti'a'al*, 'mine'; *a-ti'a'al*, 'yours,' *u-ti'a'al*, 'his').

3.3. Demonstrative Pronouns

Demonstrative pronouns are composed of the determiner and the demonstrative adjectives in the form DET-(OST)-DIST/PROX-(PL). Like the independent pronouns described in **3.2.**, demonstrative pronouns mark discourse highlighting in topicalization and contrastive-focus constructions. Examples:

1. (2:70)   "*A'-la'*-eh ma' ma'lo' b'a'ax-i'ih."
             DET-PROX-TOP NEG good thing-SCOPE
             "This is not a good thing."

2. (11:58)   "*a'-lah* keeh." …
             DET-PROX deer
             "this is a deer."

3. (15:15)   porke chen *a'-lo'* u-meyah-eh
             because only DET-DIST 3Ppr-work-TOP
             because only that is his work,

4. (22:168) *A'-lo'*-oo'-eh,
             DET-DIST-PL-TOP
             All of that (those things),

5. (12:1)   *He'el-a'* k-im-b'el in-tzikb'al-t-eh tech-eh,
             OST-PROX INC-1sg-go 1sg-tell-TRAN-SPM 2sgIOpr-REL
             This that I am going to tell you

4. Locatives: *te'-lo'*; *te'* … -*i'ih*

The locative system is analogous to the demonstrative system outlined in **2.9.** and **3.3.**. Like demonstrative adjectives, locatives play an important role in discourse highlighting and cohesion (Hofling 1987). Locative morphology involves the locative *te'*, the distal marker -*lo'*, and the scope marker -*i'ih*. When the distal marker appears, it is always suffixed to the locative. *Te'lo'* is a deictic that often depends on the physical context of discourse for its interpretation in conversation. In narrative discourse, it often appears at the front of a sentence after a conjunction and serves a cohesive function marking the beginning of a new scene. Examples:

1. (14:61–62) Ii, *te'-lo'*-eh,
               and LOC-DIST-TOP
               And there,

               ka' t-u-yil-ah b'in u-b'ah a'-och-eh
               then COM-3-see-DPM REPORT 3Ppr-REFL DET-fox-TOP
               then the fox met

2. (17:134–35)   Ii, *te'-loh*,
                  and LOC-DIST
                  And there,

                  ka' tal-ih hum p'e noh chem. …
                  then come-3sg one INAM big canoe
                  then came a large canoe.

3. (18:77–78)   I *te'e-loh*,
                  and LOC-DIST
                  And there,

                  k-u-yil-ik ma' patal-u-hok'-ol-eh
                  INC-3-see-PPM NEG ABIL-3-leave-INTRAN-TOP
                  it sees it can't get out

Te' … *-i'ih* are framing particles that mark locative scope, and are used to highlight locations that are shared information, generally from prior discourse. They often appear after prepositional phrases or relative clauses identifying the locative reference. *Te'* occurs clause-initially, and *-i'ih* is a clause-final suffix. They are very common in narrative discourse and often form parallel series (5). Examples:

4. (2:16–17)   I chumuk t-a'-kol-eh,
                  and mid of-DET-milpa-TOP
                  And in the middle of the milpa,

                  te' wa'an hun tuul keeh-*i'ih*. …
                  LOC stand/PART one ANIM deer-SCOPE
                  there was standing a deer.

5. (2:34–37)   Tulakal a'-k'aax tu'ux mas sup'-eh,
                  all DET-forest where more overgrown-REL
                  All around the forest where it's more overgrown,

                  te' k-u-käx-t-ik-*i'ih*
                  LOC INC-3-seek-TRAN-PPM-SCOPE
                  there it seeks it

                  te' k-u-b'el,
                  LOC INC-3-go
                  there it goes,

                  te' k-u-hil-t-ik u-b'ah-*i'ih*. …
                  LOC INC-3-throw-TRAN-PPM 3Ppr-REFL-SCOPE
                  there it throws itself.

Te' may occur alone, when the locative information is provided in immediately following discourse (6). *-i'ih* may also stand alone as a locative marker when the location is shared, but not highlighted information (7). For detailed discussion of locatives, see Hofling (1982).

6. (16:47–48) I *te'* in-ch'uy-kin-m-ah
and LOC 1sg-hang-CAUS-PERF-DPM
And there I have hung them

yok' u-k'aak' in-wätan,
over 3Ppr-fire 1sgPpr-wife
over the fire of my wife,

7. (5:13) mia, b'el in-ka'a ti wen-el-*i'ih*,
DUB go 1sg-go SUB sleep-INTRAN-LOC
I think maybe I'll sleep there

5. Prepositions

Itzá Maya is prepositional. The preposition *ti'*, 'to,' 'at,' 'on,' is very common and typically forms contractions with the determiner and possessive pronouns (1–3). Other common prepositions appear in 4–8. Examples:

1. (1:17) *ti* Peten. …
in PN
in Flores.

2. (9:2) ka' nak'-äk-en *t*-a'-noh nah,
SUB climb-IRREAL-1sg to-DET-big house
(for me) to climb to the big house (town hall),

3. (10:109) ka' b'in-een ti chi-tal *t*-in-k'aan. …
then go-1sg SUB lie-POSIT in-1sgPpr-hammock
and I went to lie down in my hammock.

4. (1:25) *ich* a'-k'in-oo' he'-la',
within DET-day-PL OST-PROX
within the next few days,

5. (5:1) B'ayorita, *ich* k'aax-eh,
now inside forest-TOP
Now, in the forest,

6. (10:36) Ten-eh ka', nak'-een *yok'* a'-che'-eh
1sgIpr-TOP then climb-1sg over DET-tree-TOP
Me, then I climbed on top of the tree,

7. (11:28) ko'ox *tak* ka'nal. …
HORT up to top
let's go up to the top.

8. (12:42) *kan* a'-winik-eh. …
with DET-man-TOP
to the man.

9. (15:20) wa'an *chumuk* kol-eh,
stand/PART mid milpa-REL
standing in the middle of the milpa,

6. Adverbials

Adverbs are not a large class in Itzá Maya, but they play an important role in framing discourse units in narrative discourse (Hofling 1987). Temporal adverbs frequently mark the start of scenes and episodes. As seen in the examples below, forms serving adverbial functions may be morphologically complex. For convenience and economy, I include in this section examples of the reportative evidential, *b'in*, (11), the dubitive, *mia*, (12), and the possibilitive, *wal*, (13). Examples:

1. (2:7)   *Ka'* k'och-een,
               when arrive-1sg
               When I arrived,

2. (1:22)   *t-u-mas-seeb'.* ...
               to-3Ppr-more-quick
               more quickly.

3. (1:36)   *hach* chokoh.
               very hot.

4. (6:1)   *Samal-*eh ma' tan-ki-b'el ti meyah ...
               tomorrow-TOP NEG DUR-1pl-go SUB work
               Tomorrow we aren't going to work,

5. (7:12)   I *b'a-lah san=samal* yan-ki-känän-t-ik ...
               and TEMP-PROX every day OBLIG-1pl-guard-TRAN-PPM
               And now every day we have to care for them,

6. (8:1)   *Sam-ih hatska',*
               while-3sg early
               A while ago, in the morning,

7. (9:33)   *b'ay-lo'* ti-ki-b'et-ah-eh
               like-DIST COM-1pl-do-DPM-REL
               it is thus that we did it

8. (11:50)   Ma' t-in-wil-ik *ma'lo',*
               NEG DUR-1sg-see-PPM well
               I'm not seeing it well

9. (22:267)   *ka'ax* kim-en-eh
               although die-NOM-TOP
               although he's a corpse

10. (24:462)   *He-tu'ux-ak-eh.* ,
               OST-where-IRREAL?-TOP
               Wheresoever.

11. (13:1–2)   *Uch-ih* ... yan-ah-ih *b'in* ka' tuul winik ...
               happen-3sg COP-DIST-3sg REPORT two ANIM man
               Long ago, there were, they say, two men

12. (2:71)   *Mia* u-yum-il k'aax,
              DUB 3Ppr-lord-POS forest
              I think it's the lord of the forest,

13. (8:23)   te' k-u-ch'i'-ik-oo' *wal* u-che'-il
              LOC INC-3-take-PPM-PL perhaps 3Ppr-wood-POS
              they took the wood there, perhaps,

7. Verbal Morphosyntax

7.1. Aspect

Tense/aspect is generally marked on verbs in the indicative mood by a rich set of aspectual prefixes. In addition, certain adverbs may also function in place of aspect markers (13–14). The noncompletive vs. completive aspectual distinction is of major importance in verbal morphosyntax and is described in **7.2.** and **7.3.**. As may be seen in 3, 4, and 6, certain aspect markers are clearly derived from intransitive verbs and may have intransitive inflection (cf. **7.2.1.1.**, **7.2.1.2.**).[2] The topic marker -*e'* appears clause-finally with the aspect markers *he'* (assurative) and *kil* ('when') (9–11) (cf. **15.**). Examples:

1. (1:2)   i *t*-u-ya'al-ah ten …
            and COM-3-say-DPM 1sgIOpr
            and he told me

2. (2:4)   tu'ux *k*-in-meyah-eh. …
            where INC-1sg-work-REL
            where I work.

3. (1:14)   wa *pat-al*-in-hok'-s-ik …
            COND ABIL-INTRAN-1sg-leave-CAUS-PPM
            if it's possible for me to take it out,

4. (2:68)   I in-ten-eh, ya ma' *pat-ah-ih* in-xi'mal. …
            and EMP-1sgIpr-TOP already NEG ABIL-DIST-3sg 1sg-walk
            And me, then I couldn't walk.

5. (1:16)   ii *yan*-im-b'is-ik ti tz'äk-b'-äl …
            and OBLIG-1sg-go/CAUS-PPM SUB cure-PAS-INTRAN
            and I have to carry him to be cured

6. (2:42)   *Ho'm-ih* in-lah-man t-u-b'aak' tulakal a'-kol-eh
            TERM-3sg 1sg-all-pass at-3Ppr-perimeter all DET-milpa-TOP
            I finished walking completely around all of the milpa

7. (2:91)   Ya *tan*-u-käy ah kax. …
            already DUR-3-sing MASC chicken
            The roosters were already crowing.

---

[2] With aspects, there is a continuum from phonologically reduced forms that are clearly bound prefixes to forms that are inflected intransitive verbs (Bricker 1981c; more generally, see Givón 1984). In the transcription, aspectual forms with pronominal inflection appear as free lexical items, whereas those lacking it appear as prefixes to verb stems.

8. (3:30)   I *tantoh*-in-wok-ol ich nah,
               and IMMED-1sg-enter-INTRAN inside house
               And I just entered inside the house

9. (5:20)   *Kil*-u-mäch-ik mak a'-b'eh-*eh*,
               when-3-take-PPM person DET-road-TOP
               When one takes the road,

10. (10:43)   *He'*-u-hok'-ol hum p'e ma'lo' ch'em-i'ih-*eh*. …
               ASSUR-3-leave-INTRAN one INAM good canoe-PARTIT-TOP
               A good canoe will come out of it.

11. (13:43)   *He-b'ix* u-tz'on-ik-oo'-*eh*,
               OST-how 3-shoot-PPM-PL-TOP
               Just as they shot them,

12. (13:71)   i *tak*-u-pul-ik u-b'ah yok'
               and DESID-3-throw-PPM 3Ppr-REFL over
               and wanted to throw itself on top

               a'-winik-oo'-eh. ,
               DET-man-PL-TOP
               of the men.

13. (15:139)   "*Asta* in-wa'al-ik tech"
               until 1sg-say-PPM 2sgIOpr
               "(Not) until I tell you"

14. (16:81)   *chen* u-man-tz'on-ik. …
               only 3-mis-shoot-PPM
               he only wounded them.

7.2. Intransitive Verbs

7.2.1. Root Intransitives

7.2.1.1. Noncompletive Aspects: ASP-Dpr-ROOT(-*Vl*)

In the noncompletive aspects, intransitive roots are inflected with an aspect marker, a Set A dependent pronoun, and often a harmonic -*Vl* suffix. Examples:

1. (1:11)   k-u-b'el
               INC-3-go
               he is going

2. (1:27)   k-u-yok-ol
               INC-3-enter-INTRAN
               it enters

3. (3:13)   t-in-wen-el
               DUR-1sg-sleep-INTRAN
               I was sleeping

4. (3:24)   tan-u-tal-el
            DUR-3-come-INTRAN
            (she was) coming

5. (3:26)   K-u-lub'-ul
            INC-3-fall-INTRAN
            It falls

6. (3:42)   k-u-nak'-äl
            INC-3-rise-INTRAN
            (it) rises

7. (5:9)   k-u-k'och-ol
            INC-3-arrive-INTRAN
            (it) arrives

8. (10:12) k-u-sut
            INC-3-return
            it (re)turns

7.2.1.2. Completive Aspect: ROOT-Dpr

The completive aspect is unmarked (or marked by ∅) for intransitive verbs. In the completive, verb agreement is marked by Set B dependent pronouns. Examples:

1. (1:1)   tal-ih
            come-3sg
            he came

2. (2:2)   hok'-een
            leave-1sg
            I left

3. (2:7)   k'och-een
            arrive-1sg
            I arrived

4. (2:9)   kap-een
            begin-1sg
            I began

5. (2:22)   lub'-ih
            fall-3sg
            it fell

6. (2:29)   b'in-ih
            go-3sg
            it went

7. (2:32)   tzay-een
            follow-1sg
            I followed

7.2.1.3. Subjunctive (Optative) and Imperative

In the subjunctive, intransitive verbs are inflected with the irrealis (subjunctive) harmonic -*Vk* suffix and Set B dependent pronouns.

Examples:

1. (12:66) ma' han-ak-en
            NEG eat-IRREAL-1sg
            I haven't eaten

2. (16:37) ka' hok'-ok-ech
            SUB leave-IRREAL-2sg
            that you go out

3. (17:11) ka' kim-ik-en
            SUB die-IRREAL-1sg
            that I die

Affirmative imperatives are marked with the suffix -*en*. Negative imperatives have second-person noncompletive inflection. Examples:

4. a. Nak'-en!   b. Ma' a-nak'-äl!
        climb-IMP   NEG 2-climb-INTRAN
        Climb!   Don't climb!

5. a. Ok-en!   b. Ma' a-wok-ol!
        enter-IMP   NEG 2-enter-INTRAN
        Enter!   Don't enter!

6. a. Wen-en!   b. Ma' a-wen-el!
        sleep-IMP   NEG 2-sleep-INTRAN
        Sleep!   Don't sleep!

7. a. Hok'-en!   b. Ma' a-hok'-ol!
        leave-IMP   NEG 2-leave-INTRAN
        Leave!   Don't leave!

7.2.2. Positional Verbs

Positional verbs are a class of intransitives that commonly refer to positions of a body or object such as "sitting," "standing," or "lying." They are marked by the suffix -*tal* in the noncompletive aspects. In the completive aspect they are marked by the positional suffix -*l*- and the distal marker -*ah*.[3] The positional suffix -*l*- is also present in the affirmative imperative and in the subjunctive form, where the irrealis marker -*ak* occurs. Examples:

1. a. k-u-wa'-tal   b. wa'-l-ah-ih
        INC-3-stand-POSIT   stand-POSIT-DIST-3sg
        he stands   he stood

---

[3] For discussion of the distal marker -*ah* and patient markers -*ah* and *ik*, see Hofling (1982) and Durbin and Ojeda (1982).

c. Wa'-l-en!
  stand-POSIT-IMP
  Stand!

d. ka' wa'-l-ak-ø
  SUB stand-POSIT-IRREALIS-3sg
  that he stand

2. a. k-a-t'uch-tal
  INC-2-squat-POSIT
  you squat

  b. t'uch-l-ah-eech
  squat-POSIT-DIST-2sg
  you squatted

c. T'uch-l-en
  squat-POSIT-IMP
  Squat!

c. ka' t'uch-l-ak-ech
  SUB squat-POSIT-IRREAL-2sg
  that you squat!

7.2.3. Stative and Inchoative (Versive) Intransitives

Statives are formed from adjectival or nominal stems with Set B pronominal suffixes. Like positionals, the completive aspect is marked by the distal marker -*ah*. Examples:

1. a. saak-en
  afraid-1sg
  I am afraid

  b. saak-ah-een
  afraid-DIST-1sg
  I was afraid

2. a. winik-ech
  man-2sg
  you are a man

  b. winik-ah-eech
  man-DIST-2sg
  you were a man

Inchoative (versive) intransitives also have adjectival or nominal stems and have the meaning of "becoming X." In the noncompletive aspects they are marked for aspect by Set A dependent pronouns and by the suffix -*tal*. In the completive aspect they are marked by the distal marker -*ah* and Set B dependent pronouns. The irrealis suffix -*ak* appears in the subjunctive. Examples:

3. a. k-u-tikin-tal
  INC-3-dry-INCHOAT
  it dries

  b. tikin-ah-ih
  dry-DIST-3sg
  it dried

  c. ka' tikin-ak-ø
  SUB dry-IRREALIS-3sg
  that it dry

4. a. k-a-polok-tal
  INC-2-fat-INCHOAT
  you get fat

  b. polok-ah-eech
  fat-DIST-2sg
  you got fat

  c. ka' polok-ak-ech
  SUB fat-IRREAL-2sg
  that you get fat

7.3. Transitive Verbs

Transitive verbs are marked for aspect, subject-verb agreement (by Set A dependent pronouns), direct-object agreement (by Set B dependent pronouns) and have patient markers.

7.3.1. Root Transitives

7.3.1.1. Noncompletive aspects: ASP-Dpr-ROOT-*ik*-Dpr

In the noncompletive aspects, transitive roots are marked by an aspectual prefix followed by a Set A dependent pronoun marking agreement with the agent and the proximal patient marker suffix -*ik* followed by a Set B dependent pronoun marking agreement with the direct object. Examples:

1. k-in-wil-ik-ech
    INC-1sg-see-PPM-2sg
    I see you

2. tan-u-tz'on-ik-∅
    DUR-3-shoot-PPM-3sg
    he is shooting it

3. k-a-mäch-ik-o'on
    INC-2-grab-PPM-1pl
    you grab us

7.3.1.2. Completive Aspect: COM-Dpr-ROOT-*ah*-Dpr

In transitive verbs in the completive aspect, the distal patient marker *-ah* occurs.[4] Examples:

1. t-in-wil-ah-ech
    COM-1sg-see-DPM-2sg
    I saw you

2. t-u-tz'on-ah-∅
    com-3-shoot-DPM-3sg
    he shot it

3. k-a-mäch-ah-o'on
    INC-2-grab-DPM-1pl
    you grabbed us

7.3.1.3. Perfect: Dpr-ROOT-*m*-*ah*-Dpr

In perfect forms, the suffix *-m-* appears before the distal patient marker *-ah*. Generally there is no prefixed aspect marker, but the completive aspect marker may occur. Examples:

1. in-wil-m-ah-ech
    1sg-see-PERF-DPM-2sg
    I have seen you

2. u-tz'on-m-ah-∅
    3-shoot-PERF-DPM-3sg
    he has shot it

3. a-mäch-m-ah-o'on
    2-grab-PERF-DPM-1pl
    you have grabbed us

---

[4] See note 3.

7.3.1.4. Subjunctive and Imperative

In the subjunctive and imperative, root transitives regularly have the subordinate patient marker suffix (SPM) -*V* '.[5] The SPM is often deleted when a Set B pronoun follows. No agent-verb agreement marking appears in the imperative. Examples:

1. a. Il-a'-ø!
      see-SPM/IMP-3sg
      See it!

   b. ka' in-wil-(a')-eech
      SUB 1sg-see-(SPM)-2sg
      that I see you

2. a. Tz'on-o'-ø!
      shoot-SPM/IMP-3sg
      Shoot it!

   b. ka' u-tz'on-(o')-eech
      SUB 3-shoot-(SPM)-2sg
      that he shoot you

3. a. Mäch-ä'-ø!
      grab-SPM/IMP-3sg
      Grab it!

   b. ka' a-mäch-(ä')-o'on
      SUB 2-grab-(SPM)-1pl
      that you grab us

7.3.2. Transitivized Verbs with -*t*-

A major class of transitive verbs are derived from intransitives and marked with the suffix -*t*-. Like root transitives, they are marked with the proximal patient marker -*ik* in noncompletive aspects (1a, 2a), and the distal patient marker -*ah* in the completive aspect (1b, 2b). Subjunctive and imperative forms are marked by the subordinate patient marker -*eh* (1c, d; 2c, d). In the perfect, the transitive marker -*t*- is replaced by the perfective -*m* (1e). Examples:

1. a. k-in-han-t-ik
      INC-1sg-eat-TRAN-PPM
      I eat it

   b. t-in-han-t-ah
      COM-1sg-eat-TRAN-DPM
      I ate it

   c. Han-t-eh!
      eat-TRAN-SPM/IMP
      Eat it!

   d. ka' in-han-t-eh
      SUB 1sg-eat-TRAN-SPM
      that I eat it

   e. in-han-m-ah
      1sg-eat-PERF-DPM
      I have eaten it

2. a. k-a-pak'-t-ik-en
      INC-2-wait-TRAN-PPM-1sg
      you await me

   b. t-a-pak'-t-ah-en
      COM-2-wait-TRAN-DPM-1sg
      you awaited me

   c. Pak'-t-een!
      wait-TRAN-1sg
      Wait for me!

   d. ka' a-pak'-t-eh
      SUB 2-wait-TRAN-SPM
      that you await him

---

[5] The subordinate patient marker for *il* 'see' is irregular. It appears as -*a*' rather than harmonizing with the root vowel.

7.3.3. Causative Verbs
7.3.3.1. *-s-* Causatives

Another major class of transitive verbs are causatives marked by the suffix *-s-*. Causatives may also be formed from certain stems with the *-t-* transitive marker, where the causative allomorph *-es* appears (2). Subjunctive and imperative forms are also marked by the allomorph *-es* (1c, d). In the perfect, the allomorph *-äm-* appears (1e). Examples:

1. a. k-in-kin-s-ik
        INC-1sg-die-CAUS-PPM
        I kill it

    b. t-in-kin-s-ah
       COM-1sg-die-CAUS-DPM
       I killed it

    c. Kim-es!
       die-CAUS/IMP
       Kill it!

    d. ka' in-kim-es-eech
       SUB 1sg-die-CAUS/SPM-2sg
       that I kill you

    e. in-kin-s-äm-ah
       1sg-die-CAUS-PERF-DPM
       I have killed it

2. a. k-in-han-t-es-ik
        INC-1sg-eat-TRAN-CAUS-PPM
        I feed him

    b. t-in-han-t-es-ah
       COM-1sg-eat-TRAN-CAUS-DPM
       I fed him

7.3.3.2. *-kUn-t-(es)* Causatives

Less frequent in occurrence is a class of causative verbs marked by the suffix *-kUn-*. *-kUn-* is a disharmonic suffix, regularly appearing as *-kun* when following a syllable with the vowels *a*, *e*, or *i* and as *kin* when following *u* or *o*. The transitive *-t-* also appears and, for certain stems, the causative marker *-es* as well. If the causative marker is absent, they are inflected like *-t-* transitives (**7.3.2.**); if it is present, like other causatives (**7.3.3.1.**). Examples:

1. a. k-in-much'-kin-t-ik
        INC-1sg-pile-CAUS-TRAN-PPM
        I pile it

    b. t-in-much'-kin-t-ah
       COM-1sg-pile-CAUS-TRAN-DPM
       I piled it

2. a. k-a-wa'-kun-t-ik
        INC-2-stand-CAUS-TRAN-PPM
        you raise it

    b. t-a-wa'-kun-t-ah
       COM-2-stand-CAUS-TRAN-DPM
       you raised it

3. k-in-k'oh-a'an-kun-t-es-ik
    INC-1sg-sick-PART-CAUS-TRAN-CAUS-PPM
    I make it sick

7.4. Passive

Passives function in discourse to highlight the semantic patient and background the semantic agent and to lower transitivity in the process (Hofling 1982). Generally the semantic agent is deleted (4–7), but it may be expressed obliquely (8). Passives are marked by the suffix *-b'* (causatives with the allomorph *-äb'*). Like intransitive roots, in the noncompletive aspects they are marked with Set A dependent pronouns and the intransitive *-Vl* suffix; in the completive with Set B dependent pronouns; and in the subjunctive with the irrealis suffix -*Vk* and Set B pronouns. Examples:

1. a. k-u-tz'on-b'-ol   b. tz'on-b'-ih
        INC-3-shoot-PAS-INTRAN   shoot-PAS-3sg
        it is shot   it was shot

    c. ka' tz'on-b'-ok
        SUB shoot-PAS-IRREAL
        that it be shot

2. a. k-u-han-b'-äl   b. han-b'-ih
        INC-3-eat-PAS-INTRAN   eat-PAS-3sg
        it is eaten   it was eaten

    c. ka' han-b'-äk
        SUB eat-PAS-IRREAL
        that it be eaten

3. a. k-u-kin-s-äb'-äl   b. kin-s-äb'-ih
        INC-3-die-CAUS-PAS-INTRAN   die-CAUS-PAS-3sg
        it is killed   it was killed

    c. ka' kin-s-äb'-äk
        SUB die-CAUS-PAS-IRREAL
        that it be killed

4. (3:46)   tu'ux k-u-muk-b'-ul a'-kim-en-oo'-eh. ...
              where INC-3-bury-PAS-INTRAN DET-die-NOM-PL-REL
              where the dead are buried.

5. (17:240) ka' hup-b'-ih ich-il. ...
              then put-PAS-3sg inside-POS
              and she was put inside.

6. (10:47)   b'ix u-men-b'-el. ...
              how 3-do-PAS-INTRAN
              how it is done.

7. (17:37)   ka' ok-s-äb'-ih xan,
              then enter-CAUS-PAS-3sg also
              then he was entered also (in the tomb)

8. (15:166) k'ub'en-b'-ih ti'ih men a'-chämach-eh,
              recommend-PAS-3sg 3IOpr by DET-old man-TOP
              it was recommended to him by the old man

7.5. Antipassive and Object Incorporation

The antipassive and object incorporation function to highlight the semantic agent and background the semantic patient (Hofling 1982).

7.5.1. Noncompletive Aspects

In the noncompletive aspects, both intransitive and stative object-demoted forms can be constructed. In the intransitive antipassive forms, aspect marking is present, but the proximal patient marker (-*ik*) and object-verb agreement suffixes are absent. In object-incorporated forms, the object noun immediately follows the verb and cannot be modified. Transitive roots generally have no patient-marking suffix whether or not an object noun is present (1). For some roots the vowel is lengthened (or in the case of *ä*, shifts to *a*) in the antipassive (2). Verbs that may be transitivized with -*t*- are inflected like intransitives (3). Causatives are marked by the distal patient marker -*ah* (reduced to -*ä* in object-incorporated forms) (4). Examples:

1. a. Tan-in-huch'   b. Tan-in-huch'=ixi'im
      DUR-1sg-grind   DUR-1sg-grind=corn
      I am grinding   I am corn grinding

2. a. tan-in-tz'ak   b. tan-in-tz'äk=yah
      DUR-1sg-cure   DUR-1sg-cure=pain
      I am curing   I am pain curing (I am a healer)

3. a. tan-in-han-al   b. tan-in-han-ä=b'äk'
      DUR-1sg-eat-INTRAN   DUR-1sg-eat-INTRAN?=meat
      I am eating   I am meat eating

4. a. tan-in-kin-s-ah   b. tan-in-kin-s-ä=b'alum
      DUR-1sg-die-CAUS-DPM   DUR-1sg-die-CAUS-DPM=jaguar
      I am butchering   I am jaguar killing (hunting)

In the stativized antipassive, a masculine or feminine noun classifier is present and Set B dependent pronouns mark agreement. Examples:

5. a. ah (/ix) huch'-en   b. ah (/ix) huch'=ixi'im-en
      MASC (/FEM) grind-1sg   MASC (/FEM) grind=corn-1sg
      I am a grinder   I am a corn grinder

6. a. ah han-al-en   b. ah han-ä=b'u'ul-en
      MASC eat-INTRAN-1sg   MASC eat-INTRAN?=bean-1sg
      I am an eater (glutton)   I am a bean eater

7. a. ah kin-s-ah-en   b. ah kin-s-ä=b'alum-en
      MASC die-CAUS-DPM-1sg   MASC die-CAUS-DPM=jaguar-1sg
      I am a killer   I am a jaguar killer

7.5.2. Completive, Perfect, and Subjunctive

Antipassive and object-incorporated forms are marked by the detransitive suffix -*n* in the completive, perfect, and subjunctive. In the completive and perfect, the detransitive suffix is followed by a distal marker (-*ah*), signaling past tense, and Set B dependent pronouns. In the subjunctive, the detransitive marker is followed by the irrealis marker -*ak* and pronominal agreement markers. Noun classifiers are optional in completive object-incorporated forms, but do not appear elsewhere. Examples (compare with **7.3.1.3.** and **7.5.1.**):

1. a. huch'-n-ah-een
        grind-DETRAN-DIST-1sg
        I ground

    b. (ah/ix) huch'=ixi'im-n-ah-een
        (MASC/FEM) grind-corn-DETRAN-DIST-1sg
        I was a corn grinder

    c. huch'-m-ah-n-ah-een
        grind-PERF-DPM-DETRAN-DIST-1sg
        I have ground

    d. huch'-m-ah=ixi'im-n-ah-een
        grind-PERF-DPM-corn—DETRAN-DIST-1sg
        I have been a corn grinder

    e. ka' huch'-n-ak-en
        SUB grind-DETRAN-IRREAL-1sg
        that I grind

2. a. han-al-n-ah-een
        eat-INTRAN-DETRAN-DIST-1sg
        I ate (/have eaten/was an eater)

    b. (ah/ix) han-ä=b'äk'-n-ah-een
        (MASC/FEM) eat-INTRAN=meat-DETRAN-DIST-1sg
        I was a meat eater

    c. han-m-ah-(b'äk')-n-ah-een
        eat-PERF-DPM-(meat)-DETRAN-DIST-1sg
        I have been an eater (a meat eater)

    d. ka' han-(al)-n-ak-en
        SUB eat-INTRAN-DETRAN-IRREAL-1sg
        that I eat

3. a. kin-s-ah-n-ah-een
        die-CAUS-DPM-DETRAN-DIST-1sg
        I butchered

    b. (ah/ix) kin-s-ä-b'alum-n-ah-een
        (MASC/FEM) die-CAUS-DPM-jaguar-DETRAN-DIST-1sg
        I was a jaguar hunter

    c. kin-s-äm-ah-(b'alum)-n-ah-een
        die-CAUS-PERF-DPM-(jaguar)-DETRAN-DIST-1sg
        I have been a (jaguar) killer

    d. ka' kin-s-ah-n-ak-en
        that die-CAUS-DETRAN-IRREAL-1sg
        that I butcher

7.6. Participles

7.6.1. The Participle *-a'an*

The past participle *-a'an* is by far the most common participial marker and may attach to both transitive and intransitive stems, including antipassive forms. When attached to transitive stems, the meaning is passive. Such participles lack aspect marking and are inflected with Set B pronouns. Examples:

1. (3:9)   I hach k'äl-*a'an*-en
              and very drunk-PART-1sg
              And I was very drunk

2. (10:69)   chil-*a'an* ti lu'um. ,
              lie-PART on earth
              laid on the ground.

3. (8:6)   k'ub'en-*a'an* ten. …
              recommend-PART-1sgIOpr
              (it is) entrusted to me

4. (14:53)   k-im-p'ät-ik te' pul-*a'an*-i'ih. ,
              INC-1sg-leave-PPM LOC throw-PART-SCOPE
              I leave him thrown there.

5.   huch'-n-ah-*a'an*-en
              grind-DETRAN-DIST-PART-1sg
              I have been a grinder

7.6.2. The Passive Participle *-b'il*

The participle *-b'il* only attaches to transitive stems (including -*t*- transitive roots) and is always passive in meaning. Examples:

1. (22:105–6) toh k'ax-*b'il* . . . i b'om-*b'il* ma'lo'
               well tie-PART and paint-PART well
               well tied, and painted well

2. (22:255)   kuch-*b'il* a'-k'oh-a'an-eh
               haul-PART DET-sick-PART-TOP
               the sick(ened) one is hauled

3. a. han-*b'il*   b. kin-s-*äb'il*
       eat-PART   die-CAUS-PART
       eaten   killed

7.6.3. The Participle *-al*

The participial suffix *-al* attaches to both intransitive and transitive roots and has a medio passive or agentless passive sense. Examples:

1. (10:55–56) u-ni' a'-che'-eh, ma' tak'-*al* tak ti lu'um. …
               3Ppr-tip DET-tree-TOP NEG stick-PART down to on earth
               the top of the tree isn't stuck down to earth.

2. (20:50)   I ya lah-el-*al* tulakal u-che'-il-eh …
                and already all-burn-PART all 3Ppr-tree-POS-TOP
                And when all of its trees are completely burned,

3. (20:129)   ma' hat-*al*
                NEG break-PART
                it's not broken

4. (21:102)   ya lub'-*al* ti lu'um
                already fall-PART on earth
                (she) is already fallen on the ground

7.7. Adverbial Incorporation

A set of adverbial elements including *ka'*, the repetitive marker; *hach* and *sen(kech)*, intensifiers; *lah* 'completely'; and *seeb'* 'quickly' are commonly incorporated into the verb, appearing before the root. Examples:

1. (2:42)   Ho'm-ih in-*lah*-man t-u-b'aak' tulakal a'-kol-eh
                TERM-3sg 1sg-all-pass at-3Ppr-perimeter all DET-milpa-TOP
                I finished walking completely around all of the milpa,

2. (2:60)   I ka' *ka'*-wa'-l-ah-een
                and then REPET-stand-POSIT-DIST-1sg
                And then I stood again

3. (14:55)   "tu'ux t-in-*sen*-lox-ah." …
                where COM-1sg-INTENS-hit-DPM
                "where I hit him so much."

4. (14:102)   u-*hach*-'il-a'-eh. …
                3-much-see-SPM-TOP
                to see it well.

5. (12:80)   "ki-*seeb'*-b'el." …
                INC/1pl-quick-go
                "we'll go soon (quickly)."

8. Equational Constructions

Verbless equational constructions are common in Itzá discourse. They are formed simply by the paratactic juxtaposition of constituents. Examples:

1. (2:65)   Im-pol-eh, al, al. …
                1sgPpr-head-TOP heavy heavy
                My head, it was heavy, heavy.

2. (2:77)   Mia layti' u-pixan,
                DUB 3Ipr 3Ppr-spirit
                I think it is a spirit,

3. (3:25)   Chawak u-tzo'otz-el u-pol. …
                long 3Ppr-hair-POS 3Ppr-head
                Long is the hair of her head.

4. (5:10)   B'ayoritah-eh hach k'as a'-b'eh-eh. ,
              now-TOP very bad DET-road-TOP
              Now the road is very bad.

5. (10:31)   layti' a'-ki' t-in-wich-eh
              3Ipr DET-good to-1sgPpr-eye-REL
              it is the one I like,

6. (12:26)   "A'-la' ma'lo', tikin" …
              DET-PROX good dry
              "This is good, dry"

7. (12:58)   "In-tech nohoch winik?"
              EMP-2sgIpr great man
              "You are a great man?"

8. (22:56)   A'-oox-eh hum p'e che' …
              DET-ramon-TOP one INAM tree
              The ramon is a tree,

9. The Copula *yan*

Existential constructions with the copula *yan* are frequently employed to introduce important new information into discourse (1–4) and to form predicates of possession (5–7). In these constructions, the nominal subject regularly follows the copula. Folktales typically begin with a formulaic existential construction to introduce the main characters of the story (3–4). Examples:

1. (2:5)   I yan hum p'e noh kol,
              and COP one INAM big milpa
              And there is a big milpa

2. (9:35)   tumen . . . yan-ah-ih pax …
              because COP-DIST-3sg music
              because there was music

3. (13:2)   yan-ah-ih b'in ka' tuul winik …
              COP-DIST-3sg REPORT two ANIM man
              there were, they say, two men

4. (14:1–2) Yan-ah-ih b'in, hun tuul nohoch ko'lel. . . .
              COP-DIST-3sg REPORT one ANIM great lady
              There was, they say, a great lady.

5. (11:37)   In-ten-eh yan in-b'en-il
              EMP-1sgIpr-TOP COP 1sgPpr-path-POS
              Me, I have my path

6. (13:13)   A'-che' he'-lo'-eh yan u-hol, hob'on. …
              DET-tree OST-DIST-TOP COP 3Ppr-hole hollow
              That tree has a hole, hollow.

7. (14:14)   hach yan u-na'at. …
              much COP 3Ppr-idea
              (he) has a lot of ideas.

10. Order of Major Constituents

The order of the verb (V), nominal subject (S), and nominal object (O) reflects processes of discourse highlighting. Although sentences with two nominal arguments are low in frequency in natural discourse (Du Bois 1987), all six possible word orders occur. More commonly one or both nominal mentions are omitted and reference is signaled by verb agreement alone. The positions of the arguments and their morphosyntactic marking signal if they are highlighted as topics, in contrastive focus, or not pragmatically marked.

The least marked orders in Itzá are VOS and SVO. In both orders, the subject is typically marked as topic, a usual pragmatic role for subjects. In the examples below (except perhaps 1) the subjects are also examples of topic shift, where one expects a nominal subject (Hofling 1989). Examples:

```
              V            O        S
```
1. (12:123)   Ka' t-u-mäch-ah u-maskab' a'-winik-eh
              then COM-3-grab-DPM 3Ppr-machete DET-man-TOP
              Then the man grabbed his machete

```
              V            O       S
```
2. (12:132)   Ka' t-u-kuch-ah u-si' a'-nohoch winik-eh
              then COM-3-load-DPM 3Ppr-firewood DET-great man-TOP
              Then the great man loaded his firewood

```
              S                V           O
```
3. (6:13)   Layti'-oo'-eh yan-u-b'et-ik-oo' han-al
              3Ipr-PL-TOP OBLIG-3-make-PPM-PL eat-NOM
              They have to make food

```
              S                       V              O
```
4. (13:70)   porke a'-b'a'al=che'-eh tan-u-han-t-ik a'-ch'iich'-eh,
              because DET-animal-TOP DUR-3-eat-TRAN-PPM DET-bird-TOP
              because the animal was eating the bird

Highlighted positions for NPs are preverbal, both as topics and in contrastive focus. Out of discourse context, marked orders are often ambiguous regarding case role (9). If both NPs precede the verb, the first is typically topic and the second is in contrastive focus. These principles account for the following occurring orders: S[topic] VO, S[focus]VO, O[focus]VS, S[topic] O[focus] V, O[topic] S[focus] V. See Hofling (1982, 1984b) for more detail on word order. Examples:

```
              S[focus]       V         O
```
5. (22:179)   pwes, layti'-oo' yan-u-chäk-ik-oo' u-b'u'ul
              well 3Ipr-PL OBLIG-3-cook-PPM-PL 3Ppr-bean
              well, *they* have to cook their beans

```
              O [focus] V              S
```
6. (15:218–19) A'-loh k-u-tzikb'al-t-ik to'on ki-noolah
              DET-DIST INC-3-say-TRAN-PPM 1plIOpr 1plPpr-grandmother
              That, our grandmother told us

                              O[topic]   V
7. (22:94–95) U-yitz a'-che' he'-lo'-eh, k-u-ch'i-ik-oo'-eh,
               3Ppr-resin DET-tree OST-DIST-TOP INC-3-take-PPM-PL-TOP
               The resin of those trees, they take it,

                           S[topic] O[focus] V
8. (16:115–16) "In-tech-eh b'a'ax k-a-käx-t-ik wa'yeh?"
                EMP-2sgIpr-TOP what INC-2-seek-TRAN-PPM here
                "You, what are you seeking here?"

                          S /O[topic] O/S[focus]   V
9.   A'-winik-eh a'-b'alum he'-lo' k-u-kin-s-ik.
               DET-man-TOP DET-jaguar OST-DIST INC-3-die-CAUS-PPM
               The man, he kills *that jaguar*.
        or The man, *that jaguar* kills him.

11. Interrogation

Interrogation processes are not fully in evidence in the text corpus since most of the texts are narrative, where interrogatives are generally limited to passages in direct quotation. Interrogation is commonly marked intonationally by a final rise in pitch. Examples:

1. (12:62)   "In-tech nohoch b'alum?"
             EMP-2sgIpr big jaguar
             "You are a big jaguar?"

2. (24:26)   "Ma' wach'-äk?"
             NEG tassel-IRREAL
             "It hasn't tasseled?"

Interrogation is also marked by a set of clause-initial interrogative words including *tu'ux* 'where', *b'a'ax* 'what', *max* 'who', *b'ix* 'how', *b'oon* 'how much', and *b'ik'in* 'when'. The scope marker *-i'ih* may also appear with the interrogative words, or suffixed to a constituent in interrogative focus, which is frequently a noun marked with the possessive suffix *-il* (7b). For more details, see Hofling (1982). Examples:

3. (12:60)   "*B'a'ax* k-a-men-t-ik?"
                what INC-2-do-TRAN-PPM
                "What are you doing?"

4. (15:186–88) "*B'ix* ma' ki-wok'-ol si tech-eh, sat-al-ech? ..."
                how NEG 1pl-cry-INTRAN if 2sgIpr-TOP lose-PART-2sg
                "Why wouldn't we be crying if you, you are lost?"

5. (17:91)   "*tu'ux* yan-en wa'yeh?"
                where COP-1sg here
                "where am I here?"

6. (14:110)   "kien sa' *max-i'ih*,"
                who know who-SCOPE
                "who knows who it is,"

7. a. *B'a'ax-i'ih?*
   what-SCOPE
   What is it?

b. *B'a'ax* pek'-il-*i'ih?*
   what dog-POS-SCOPE
   Which of the dogs?

12. Negation

The two primary markers of negation are *ma'* and *mix*. *Ma'* is a general negative marker of variable scope ranging from the sentence to a single constituent. *Mix* may be glossed as 'no' 'neither', 'nor', or 'not even' according to context, and generally negates constituents below clause level with contrastive force. Both *ma'* and *mix* appear before negated constituents, and the scoping suffix -*i'ih* may appear as a terminal framing particle with both to mark negative contrastive focus. When verbs in the incompletive aspect are negated, the aspect marker *k-* is replaced by *t-*. For extended discussion, see Hofling (1982). Examples:

1. (2:38) I *ma'* pat-ah-ih in-mäch-ik. ...
   and NEG ABIL-DIST-3sg 1sg-grab-PPM
   And I couldn't grab it.

2. (2:43) *ma'* t-in-wil-ah *mix* b'a'al. ...
   NEG COM-1sg-see-DPM NEG thing
   I didn't see anything.

3. (2:70) "A'-la'-eh *ma'* ma'lo' b'a'ax-*i'ih*."
   DET-PROX-TOP NEG good thing-SCOPE
   "This is not a good thing."

4. (5:18) *ma'* an *mix* tu'ux u-wa'-tal ma'lo'
   NEG/COP NEG where 3-stand-POSIT well
   there isn't anywhere to stand well

5. (19:21) wa *ma'* ah kax-*i'ih*-eh kutz. ...
   COND NEG MASC chicken-SCOPE-TOP turkey
   if not a chicken, a turkey.

6. (21:119) I *ma'* ha'-*i'ih*
   and NEG water-SCOPE
   And it's not rain,

7. (16:17) *ma'* *t*-in-tz'on-ik *mix* b'a'al. ...
   NEG INC-1sg-shoot-PPM NEG thing
   I don't shoot anything.

13. Coordination

Coordinate constructions may be formed paratactically, simply by juxtaposition (1). Common conjunctions include *ih* 'and' (apparently, but not certainly, a Spanish borrowing), *(tu)men* 'because' (a relational noun: *t-u-men*, at-3Ppr-do?; cf. **2.11.**), and *wa* 'either', 'or'. The relational noun *yet-el* (3Ppr/with-POS) 'with' may also mark nominal coordination (7). Conjunctions are important cohesive devices linking the constituents that follow them to previous discourse. *ih* frequently (and *tumen* occasionally) marks topic and scene shifts, where it often appears sentence-initially in conjunction with adverbs or locatives (8, 9, 10) (Hofling 1987, 1989). It also commonly marks parallelisms (10). Examples:

1. (23:105–6)   K-u-päk'-ik-oo' a'-che'-eh
                 INC-3-plant-PPM-PL DET-tree-TOP
                 They plant the tree,

                 k-u-tz'ik u-yich. …
                 INC-3-give/PPM 3Ppr-fruit
                 it gives its fruit.

2. (1:15–16)   *tumen* yan hun tuul im-paal k'oh-a'an …
                 because COP one ANIM 1sgPpr-child sick-PART
                 because I have a sick child

                 ii yan-im-b'is-ik ti tz'äk-b'-äl …
                 and OBLIG-1sg-go/CAUS-PPM SUB cure-PAS-INTRAN
                 and I have to take him to be cured

3. (1:33–34)   *tumen* a'-che'-eh, u-k'a't-ih ti'ih
                 because DET-wood-TOP 3-want-PM? SUB
                 because the wood, he wants it for

4. (6:8)   In-na' *ih* in-wätan-eh,
                 1sgPpr-mother and 1sgPpr-wife-TOP
                 My mother and my wife,

5. (2:71–72)   Mia u-yum-il k'aax,
                 DUB 3Ppr-lord-POS forest
                 I think it's the lord of the forest,

                 wa u-yum-il witz. …
                 or 3Ppr-lord-POS hill
                 or the lord of the hills.

6. (23:270–71)   *wa* t-u-laak' tinaahah *wa* ti kuum. …
                 either in-3Ppr-other jar or in pot
                 either in another jar or in a pot.

7. (12:2–3)   hun tuul winik, *yet-el* hun tuul b'alum. …
                 one ANIM man 3Ppr/with-POS one ANIM jaguar
                 a man and a jaguar.

8. (15:39)   *Ii*, ah tz'on-eh
                 and MASC shoot-TOP
                 And the hunter, (topic shift)

9. (15:61)   *I* ka' wa'-l-ah-ih b'in-eh
                 and then stand-POSIT-DIST-3sg REPORT-TOP
                 And then he stood, they say, (scene shift)

10. (15:9–12)   *I* b'aay-loh, *i* b'aay-loh,
         and like-DIST and like-DIST
         And thus, and thus,

         kap-ih ti tz'on, *i* ti tz'on. …
         begin-3sg SUB shoot and SUB shoot
         he began to shoot and to shoot.

14. Conditional Clauses

Conditional clauses are marked by the conditional *wa* clause-initially and the topic marker *-eh* clause-finally. Conditional clauses generally precede consequent clauses. Examples:

1. (1:18)   Wa ma' tan-u-mas-k'oh-a'an-tal-eh …
         COND NEG DUR-3-more-sick-PART-INCHOAT-TOP
         If he doesn't get sicker,

2. (1:8)   ke *wa* patal-in-hok'-s-ik tulakal a'-che'-*eh*
         SUB COND ABIL-1sg-leave-CAUS-PPM all DET-wood-TOP
         that if I can take out all of the wood,

3. (4:8)   *wa* ma'an u-b'a'al in-tz'on-*eh*
         COND NEG/COP 3Ppr-bullet 1sgPpr-gun-TOP
         if there aren't any bullets for my gun

4. (13:114)   *Wa* ma' tan-a-b'el-*eh* …
         COND NEG DUR-2-go-TOP
         If you don't go,

15. Adverbial Clauses

As mentioned in **6.**, clause-initial adverbs play an important role in framing discourse chunks and providing discourse cohesion. The adverb *ka'* 'then', 'when', is a ubiquitous discourse marker that provides a temporal grounding for discourse (Hofling 1987). When it occurs alone (or with a conjunction), it serves a cohesive role as a connective indicating the natural chronological sequence of events (1–4). It occurs with verbs in the completive aspect and with the subjunctive, and thus is associated with ergative verb agreement marking (cf. **3.1.**, **7.**). Clauses with intransitive verbs may be additionally marked by the marker *ti*, (4), which often serves as an intransitive subordination marker (cf. **17.**). Examples:

1. (2:9)   *Ka'* kap-een ti xi'mal,
         then begin-1sg SUB walk
         Then I began to walk

2. (2:18)   *Ka'* t-in-tz'on-ah. …
         then COM-1sg-shoot-DPM
         Then I shot it.

3. (2:50–51)   *Ka'* wa'-l-ah-een
         then stand-POSIT-DIST-1sg
         Then I stood,

                        ka' t-in-sut-ah in-k'aak'-eh,
                        then COM-1sg-turn back-DPM 1sgPpr-fire-TOP
                        then I turned my light back

4. (12:48)   *Ka' ti* näk-l-ah-ih u-cha'an-t-eh. …
                        then SUB sit-POSIT-DIST-3sg 3-watch-TRAN-SPM
                        Then it sat to watch him.

    The frame (*a'-*)*ka'* … *-e'* is a common marker of subordinate temporal adverbial clauses in the completive aspect and may appear in the subjunctive (5–8). In noncompletive aspects, the frame *kil* … *-e'* appears (9) (cf. aspect and ergativity in **7.**). These subordinate adverbial clauses generally refer to information previously given in the discourse and provide contextual background for new information in the main clause that follows. This structure may be manipulated to provide dramatic tension as in 5 and 8, where information crucial to the interpretation of the adverbial clause appears in the following main clause rather than in prior discourse. Examples:

5. (2:19)   *A'-ka'* wak'-ih in-tz'on-*eh*,
                DET-when explode-3sg 1sgPpr-gun-TOP
                When my gun fired,

6. (2:92)   *Ka'* k'och-een-*eh*
                when arrive-1sg-TOP
                When I arrived

7. (14:36)   I ka' tak a'-och-eh …
                and when come/IRREAL DET-fox-TOP
                And when the fox comes,

8. (2:47–48) Chen *a'-ka'* t-in-wu'y-ah-*eh*,
                only DET-when COM-1sg-hear-DPM-TOP
                Only then I heard it,

                tan-u-hum u-tal …
                DUR-3-sound 3-come
                it was making noise, coming,

9. (16:68)   *kil*-u-hok'-ol mak ti tz'on-*eh* …
                when-3-leave-INTRAN person SUB shoot-TOP
                when one goes out to hunt,

    The comparative adverbials *he-b'ix* 'just as', 'so' and *b'ay* 'like' also function as framing particles with the topic marker *-e'* (10–13). *B'ix* generally marks verb phrases, whereas *b'ay* marks noun phrases. When these adverbials function as aspect markers, verbs are inflected as in noncompletive aspects (cf. **7.2.**, **7.3.**). *Ich* 'in' may also appear in this construction, indicating past-time reference (11). Examples:

10. (13:43–45)   *He-b'ix* u-tz'on-ik-oo'-*eh*,
                     OST-how 3-shoot-PPM-PL-TOP
                     Just as they shot them,

he-b'ix u-lub'-ul a'-b'a'al=che'-oo'
OST-how 3-fall-INTRAN DET-animal-PL
thus the animals fell

t-u-yaam a'-witz-*eh*. …
in-3Ppr-clearing DET-hill-TOP
in the clearing of the hill.

11. (14:82)   *he-b'ix* ich u-b'et-ik tech-*eh*. ,
OST-how in 3-do-PPM 2sgIOpr-TOP
just as he did to you.

12. (15:56–57) yan hun p'eel noh aktun,
COP one INAM big cave
(there) was a big cave,

b'ay u-hol hun kuul nah-*eh*. …
like 3Ppr-entrance one CLASS house-TOP
like the door of a house.

13. (21:113–14) k-u-yub'-ik mak u-hum
INC-3-hear-PPM person 3Ppr-sound
one hears the sound

b'ay u-hum chaak-*eh*. …
like 3Ppr-sound thunder-TOP
like the sound of thunder.

16. Relative Clauses

As noted in **2.7.**, relative clauses are generally marked by the *a'-* … *-e'* frame, as are topicalized definite nouns (1–8). Relative clauses generally contain supplementary information to aid in the identification of the head noun. Relative pronouns of the interrogative series noted in **11.** may follow or replace the head noun (1, 3, 4) or both head noun and relative pronoun may be absent (5, 6). Relative clauses also often follow contrastively focused NPs as in (5–7). The Spanish borrowing *ke* also appears as a relative marker (8). Examples:

1. (2:3–4)   t-*a'*-noh b'eh *tu'ux* k-in-meyah-*eh*. …
on-DET-big road where INC-1sg-work-REL
along the big road where I work.

2. (3:7)   *a'*-ha' t-in-wuk'-ah-*eh* …
DET-water COM-1sg-drink-DPM-REL
the (fire)water that I drank,

3. (3:14–15)   Lub'-een *a'-tu'ux* lub'-een-*eh*
fall-1sg DET-where fall-1sg-REL
I fell where I fell

4. (2:100)   *a'-b'a'ax* t-in-wu'y-ah ich k'aax-*eh*. …
DET-what COM-1sg-hear-DPM inside forest-REL
what (the thing that) I heard inside the forest.

5. (2:77–78)   u-pixan, *a'*-k-u-tal t-im-pach-*eh*. …
                 3Ppr-spirit DET-INC-3-come at-1sgPpr-back-REL
                 a spirit, that which is coming behind me.

6. (10:31)   layti' *a'*-ki' t-in-wich-*eh*
                 3Ipr DET-good to-1sgPpr-eye-REL
                 it is the one I like,

7. (15:204–5)   layti' *a'*-miismo k'in he'-lo' sut-k'-ah-ih-*eh*.   ,
                 3Ipr DET-same day OST-DIST return-CELER?-DIST-3sg-REL
                 it was that same day that he returned.

8. (22:205–6)   *a'*-mees-oo', *ke* yan a'-winik ich k'aax-*eh*,
                 DET-month-PL SUB COP DET-man in forest-REL
                 the months that the man is in the forest,

17. Complements

17.1. Verbs of Motion and Modal Controllers

Subordinate complements commonly follow verbs of motion and modal-controlling verbs such as *k'a't* 'want'.

17.1.1. Cross-Reference

17.1.1.1. Intransitive Complements

When the subject of an intransitive subordinate complement cross-references the intransitive subject or the transitive object of the main verb, the subordinator *ti* appears and the subordinate verb is not inflected for verb agreement (1–3). With the modal verb *k'a't* 'want', no subordination marker appears for cross-referential intransitive subordinate verbs (4) (Hofling 1984a). Examples:

1. (1:28)   layti', k-u-b'el *ti* tal
                 3Ipr INC-3-go SUB come
                 he is going to come

2. (2:9)   Ka' kap-een *ti* xi'mal
                 then begin-1sg SUB walk
                 then I began to walk

3. (1:16)   yan-im-b'is-ik *ti* tz'äk-b'-äl …
                 OBLIG-1sg-go/CAUS-PPM SUB cure-PAS-INTRAN
                 I have to take him to be cured

4. (18:64)   Ii, u-k'a't-ih hok'-ol t-a'-aktun-eh.
                 and 3-want-PM? leave-INTRAN from-DET-cave-TOP
                 And it wants to leave the cave.

17.1.1.2. Transitive Complements

When the transitive subject of a transitive subordinate verb cross-references an argument (subject or direct object) of the main verb, the subordinate patient marker may appear (cf. **7.3.**) and verb-agreement is fully marked. Examples:

1. (1:13)   b'el in-ka'a in-wil-a'
                go 1sg-go 1sg-see-SPM
                I am going to see (something)

2.   in-k'a't-ih in-wil-(a')-eech.
                1sg-want-PM? 1sg-see-(SPM)-2sg
                I want to see you.

3. (2:14)   ka' kap-een in-tich=k'ak'-t-eh
                then begin-1sg 1sg-illuminate-TRAN-SPM
                then I began to illuminate (it)

4. (15:126) waye' k-in-b'el in-pak'-t-eech
                here INC-1sg-go 1sg-await-TRAN-2sg
                it's here I'm going to await you

17.1.2. Switch Reference

When the subject of the subordinate verb is different from arguments on the main verb, the subordination marker *ka'* appears (1–4) (Hofling 1984a). Intransitives are additionally marked by the irrealis suffix *-Vk* and Set B dependent pronouns (2–4). Transitives are marked for subject- and object-verb agreement and with the subjunctive subordinate patient marker, as shown in **17.1.1.2.** and in examples 1 and 4. *Ka'* may contract with the Set A pronoun as in 4. Examples:

1. (1:3–4)   u-k'a't-ih *ka'* in-hok'-es … u-che'-il
               3-want-PM? SUB 1sg-leave-CAUS/SPM 3Ppr-wood-POS
               (that) he wants me to take out the wood

2. (22:161) u-k'a't-oo' *ka'* xi'ik hun tuul ix ch'up,
               3-want-PL SUB go/IRREAL one ANIM FEM woman
               (they) want a woman to go

3. (15:196–97) "B'ix a-wohel-e'ex *ka'* kim-ik-en"
               how 2-know-2pl SUB die-IRREAL-1sg
                "How do you know that I would die"

4. (8:12–14) T-in-wa'al-ah ti'ih,
               COM-1sg-say-DPM 3IOpr
               I told him,

               ka' meyah-n-ak ka' p'e k'in,
               SUB work-DETRAN-IRREAL two INAM day
               to work two days,

               k(a')-u-paak-t-eh
               SUB-3-clear-TRAN-SPM
               that he clear it

17.2. Quotation and Sensory Verbs

In constructions of direct quotation, the topic marker *-e'* appears at the end of the main clause, followed by quoted speech (1–2). Similarly, the topic marker appears at the end of clauses with sensory verbs when followed by object complements containing new, unexpected information (3, 4) (Hofling 1984a, 1987). Examples:

1. (10:29–30) ka' t-u-ya'al-ah ten-*eh*: "A'-che' he'-la'-eh,
   then COM-3-say-DPM 1sgIOpr-TOP DET-tree OST-PROX-TOP
   then he told me: "This tree,

2. (12:44–45) Ka' t-u-ya'al-ah b'in-*eh*: "B'a-lah si,
   then COM-3-say-DPM REPORT-TOP TEMP-PROX yes
   Then it said, they say: "Now, yes, . . .

3. (2:47–48) Chen a'-ka' t-in-wu'y-ah-*eh*, tan-u-hum u-tal …
   only DET-then COM-1sg-hear-DPM-TOP DUR-3-sound 3-come
   Only then I heard it, it was making noise coming,

4. (15:90–91) I k-u-yil-ik-*eh* te' wa'an a'-noh keeh …
   and INC-3-see-PPM-TOP LOC stand/PART DET-big deer
   And he sees that there is standing the big deer,

Indirect quotation is generally additionally marked by the subordinator *ke* (5–8). Verbs of speech may also function as modal-controlling verbs with the subordinator *ka'* and the subjunctive, as in **17.1.2.**(4) and 7 and 8 below. Object complements of sensory verbs not marked as nonexpectative (examples 3 and 4 above) are generally marked with the subordinator *ke* (9, 10). Aspectless object complements without subordination markers also occur (11). Examples:

5. (1:7–8) Ii t-u-ya'al-ah ten-*eh*
   and COM-3-say-DPM 1sgIOpr-TOP
   And he told me

   ke wa patal-in-hok'-s-ik
   SUB COND ABIL-1sg-leave-CAUS-PPM
   that if I can take out

6. (18:27–28) K-u-ya'al-ik-oo'-*eh kee*, u-ka'a ti k'och-ol
   INC-3-say-PPM-PL-TOP SUB 3-go SUB arrive-INTRAN
   They say that perhaps (the day) will come

7. (10:4–5) t-u-ya'al-ah ten-*eh ke ka'* im-b'et-eh
   COM-3-say-DPM 1sgIOpr-TOP SUB SUB 1sg-make-SPM
   he told me that I should make

8. (10:18–19) t-u-ya'al-ah ten-*eh ke ka'*
   COM-3-say-DPM 1sgIOpr-TOP SUB SUB
   he told me that

   xik-en
   go/IRREAL-1sg
   I should go

9. (2:39–40)   A'-ka' t-in-wil-ah
DET-when COM-1sg-see-DPM
When I saw

ke ma' pat-ah-ih in-mäch-ik-eh,
SUB NEG ABIL-DIST-3sg 1sg-grab-PPM-TOP
that I couldn't grab it,

10. (17:208–9)   A'-ka' t-u-yil-ah a'-r̃ey
DET-when COM-3-see-DPM DET-king
When the king saw

ke kux-l-ah-ih u-paal-eh,
SUB live-POSIT-DIST-3sg 3Ppr-child-TOP
that his child revived,

11. (8:31–32)   Mix mak t-u-yil-ah u-ch'äk-b'-äl
NEG person COM-3-see-DPM
No one saw

a'-che'-eh. …
3-cut-PAS-INTRAN DET-wood-TOP
the wood being cut.

18. Purpose Clauses

The subordinators *yok'(ol)* and *ti'ih* often mark purpose clauses in which the subordinate verb lacks aspect but is otherwise inflected like noncompletive verbs (1–6) (cf. **7.**). The suffix *-al* may also be attached to these subordinators (*yok'olal, ti'a'al*) (3, 6) or appear as a suffix after the proximal patient marker on a subordinate transitive verb (2, 4). Occasionally subordinate purpose clauses with *ti'ih* are in the subjunctive (5), and clauses with *ti'a'al* may be additionally marked by *ka'* and the subjunctive (6). Examples:

1. (7:8–9)   Ho'leh-ih b'in-een ti Peten
yesterday-3sg go-1sg to PN
Yesterday I went to Flores

chen *yok'* in-män-ik hum p'e uuleh. …
only SUB 1sg-buy-PPM one INAM nipple
just to buy a nipple.

2. (1:34–35)   U-k'a't-ih *ti'ih* u-men-t-ik-*al* ka'
3-want-PM? SUB 3-make-TRAN-PPM-SUB
He wants it in order to make

kuul nukuch nah …
two CLASS big house
two big houses

ti'ih u-käh-tal et-el u-paal-oo' …
SUB 3-live-POSIT with-POS 3Ppr-child-PL
for him to live with his children,

3. (14:74–75) nich-i' a-koh *yok'ol-al* u-yok-ol
                bare-SPM/IMP 2Ppr-tooth SUB-SUB 3-enter-INTRAN
                bare your teeth so that it enters

                t-u-ho'ol
                in-3Ppr-head
                his head

4. (19:15)   *yok'* u-päk'-ik-*al*-oo' ma'lo' a'-ixi'im-eh. …
                SUB 3-plant-PPM-SUB-PL well DET-corn-TOP
                in order to plant the corn well.

5. (2:51–53)   ka' t-in-sut-ah in-k'aak'-eh
                then COM-1sg-turn back-DPM 1sgPpr-fire-TOP
                then I turned my light back

                ti'ih in-tich' =k'ak'-t-*eh*, a'-b'eh
                SUB 1sg-illuminate-TRAN-SPM DET-road
                in order to illuminate the road

6. (21:9–10)   yan-ki-käx-t-ik ma'lo' u-k'in-il,
                OBLIG-1pl-seek-TRAN-PPM good 3Ppr-day-POS
                we have to seek a good day

                ti'a'al ka' pat-*ak* u-b'et-ik. …
                SUB SUB ABIL-IRREAL 3-do-PPM
                so that we can do it.

TEXTS

I. PERSONAL NARRATIVE

1. Wood for Houses

Told by Fernando Tesucún on September 12, 1979

1. Ho'leh-ih, tal-ih im-b'al …
   yesterday-3sg come-3sg 1sgPpr-brother-in-law
   Yesterday my brother-in-law came,

2. i t-u-ya'al-ah ten …
   and COM-3-say-DPM 1sgIOpr
   and he told me

3. u-k'a't-ih ka' in-hok'-es …
   3-want-PM? SUB 1sg-leave-CAUS/SPM
   that he wants me to take out (of the forest)

4. [che'] u-che'-il ka' ku(ul) nah. …
   [wood] 3Ppr-wood-POS two CLASS house
   the wood for two houses.

5. U-ka'ah u-b'et-eh u-yotoch …
   3-go 3-make-SPM 3Ppr-home
   He is going to make his home(s)

6. San B'eniito. …
   PN
   in San Benito.

7. Ii t-u-ya'al-ah ten-eh
   and COM-3-say-DPM 1sgIOpr-TOP
   And he told me

8. ke wa patal-in-hok'-s-ik tulakal a'-che'-eh
   SUB COND ABIL-1sg-leave-CAUS-PPM all DET-wood-TOP
   that if I can take out all of the wood,

9. ka' in-hok'-es ti'ih …
   SUB 1sg-leave-CAUS/SPM 3IOpr
   that I take it out for him,

10. i ka' in-much'-kin-t-eh t-u-chi'
    and SUB 1sg-mound-CAUS-TRAN-SPM at-3Ppr-edge
    and that I pile it on the edge

    a'-noh b'eh-eh. …
    DET-big road-TOP
    of the big road.

11. Layti' k-u-b'el ti tal [u-,] u-b'en-es. …
    3Ipr INC-3-go SUB come [3-] 3-go-CAUS/SPM
    He is going to come to carry it.

12. In-ten-eh t-in-wa'al-ah ti'ih,
    EMP-1sgIpr-TOP COM-1sg-say-DPM 3IOpr
    Me, I said to him,

13. pwes, kee, b'el in-ka'a in-wil-a'
    well SUB go 1sg-go 1sg-see-SPM
    well, that I am going to see

14. wa patal-in-hok'-s-ik ...
    COND ABIL-1sg-leave-CAUS-PPM
    if it's possible for me to take it out,

15. tumen yan hun tuul im-paal k'oh-a'an ...
    because COP one ANIM 1sgPpr-child sick-PART
    because I have a sick child

16. ii yan-im-b'is-ik ti tz'äk-b'-äl ...
    and OBLIG-1sg-go/CAUS-PPM SUB cure-PAS-INTRAN
    and I have to take him to be cured

17. ti Peten. ...
    in PN
    in Flores.

18. Wa ma' tan[-u...]-u-mas-k'oh-a'an-tal-eh ...
    COND NEG DUR[-3]-3-more-sick-PART-INCHOAT-TOP
    If he doesn't get sicker,

19. b'el in-ka'a in-käxän-t-eh u-laak' in-wet'ok,
    go 1sg-go 1sg-seek-TRAN-SPM 3Ppr-other 1Ppr-companion
    I'm going to look for another companion,

20. yok'ol a'-b'ay-lo'-eh,
    SUB DET-like-DIST-TOP
    so that in that way,

21. patal-ki-hok'-s-ik,
    ABIL-1pl-leave-CAUS-PPM
    we can take it out

22. t-u-mas-seeb'. ...
    to-3Ppr-more-quick
    more quickly.

23. I layti' t-u-ya'al-ah ten-eh kee ...
    and 3Ipr COM-3-say-DPM 1sgIOpr-TOP SUB
    And he asked me

24. wa patal-in-hok'-s-ik,
    COND ABIL-1sg-leave-CAUS-PPM
    if I can take it out

25. ich a'-k'in-oo' he'-la',
    within DET-day-PL OST-PROX
    within the next few days,

26. wa ma' k-in-pak'-t-eh [u-…]
    COND NEG INC-1sg-wait-TRAN-SPM
    if not, that I wait until

    u-laak' a'-semaanah-eh …
    [3Pr] 3Ppr-other DET-week-TOP
    the next week

27. k-u-yok-ol-eh. …
    INC-3-enter-INTRAN-REL
    that's coming.

28. I layti', k-u-b'el ti tal [u-,] u-b'en-es. …
    and 3Ipr INC-3-go SUB come [3-] 3-go-CAUS/SPM
    And he is going to come and carry it away.

29. Chen hach t-u-k'ub'en-t-ah ten …
    only much COM-3-recommend-TRAN-DPM 1sgIOpr
    Only he strongly recommended to me

30. ka' in-hok'-es, ti'ih chen ma'lo' che',
    SUB 1sg-leave-CAUS/SPM 3IOpr only good wood
    that I take out only good wood for him,

31. ma' in-hok'-s-ik …
    NEG 1sg-leave-CAUS-PPM
    not to take

32. che' ma' ki' ti'ih,
    wood NEG good 3IOpr
    wood that isn't good for him,

33. tumen a'-che'-eh,
    because DET-wood-TOP
    because the wood,

34. u-k'a't-i(h) ti'ih u-men[,]-t-ik-al, ka' ku(ul) nukuch nah …
    3-want-PM? SUB 3-make-TRAN-PPM-SUB two CLASS big house
    he wants it in order to make two big houses

35. ti'ih u-käh-tal et-el u-paal-oo' …
    SUB 3-live-POSIT with-POS 3Ppr-child-PL
    for him to live with his children,

36. tumen a'-nah tu'ux, käh-a'an-il-eh hach chokoh.
    because DET-house where live-PART-POS?-TOP very hot
    because the house where he lives is very hot.

2. Deer Hunting

Told by Fernando Tesucún on September 13, 1979

1. Hum p'e k'in … domiingo …
   one INAM day Sunday
   One Sunday

2. hok'-een ti tz'on. …
   leave-1sg SUB shoot
   I went to shoot.

3. B'in-een tulakal t-a'-noh b'eh
   go-1sg all on-DET-big road
   I went all along the big road

4. tu'ux k-in-meyah-eh. …
   where INC-1sg-work-REL
   where I work.

5. I yan hum p'e noh kol,
   and COP one INAM big milpa
   And there is a big milpa

6. chumuk a'-b'eh-eh. …
   mid DET-road-TOP
   along the road.

7. Ka' k'och-een,
   then arrive-1sg
   When I arrived,

8. ya tan-u-yok-ol k'in. …
   already DUR-3-enter-INTRAN sun
   the sun was already setting.

9. Ka' kap-een ti xi'mal,
   then begin-1sg SUB walk
   Then I began to walk

10. tulakal, t-u-b'aak' a'-kol-eh,
    all on-3Ppr-perimeter DET-milpa-TOP
    all around the milpa

11. in-wil-a' wa yan, keeh ich a'-kol-eh. …
    1sg-see-SPM COND COP deer in DET-milpa-TOP
    to see if there were deer in the milpa.

12. Ya ak'ä',
    already night
    It was already night

13. ka' k'och-een t-u-chi' a'-kol-eh,
    when arrive-1sg to-3Ppr-edge DET-milpa-TOP
    when I arrived at the edge of the milpa,

14. ka' kap-een [in-,] in-tich=k'ak'-t-eh tulakal u-b'aak'
    then begin-1sg [1sg-] 1sg-illuminate-TRAN-SPM all 3Ppr-perimeter
    then I began to illuminate all its perimeter

15. a'-tu'ux k-in-b'el t-im-man-eh. …
    DET-where INC-1sg-go DUR-1sg-pass-REL
    where I was walking.

16. I chumuk t-a'-kol-eh,
    and mid of-DET-milpa-TOP
    And in the middle of the milpa,

17. te' wa'an hun tuul keeh-i'ih. …
    LOC stand/PART one ANIM deer-SCOPE
    there was standing a deer.

18. Ka' t-in-tz'on-ah. …
    then COM-1sg-shoot-DPM
    Then I shot it.

19. A'-ka' wak'-ih in-tz'on-eh,
    DET-when explode-3sg 1sgPpr-gun-TOP
    When my gun fired,

20. chen t-in-wil-ah,
    just COM-1sg-see-DPM
    I just saw

21. tu'ux lik'-ih u-siit' …
    where rise-3sg 3Ppr-jump
    where it jumped up

22. i lub'-ih. …
    and fall-3sg
    and it fell.

23. A-ka' k'och-een,
    DET-when arrive-1sg
    When I arrived

24. a'-tu'ux t-in-wil-ah u-lub'-ul-eh …
    DET-where COM-1sg-see-DPM 3-fall-INTRAN-REL
    where I saw it fall,

25. a'-b'a'al=che'-eh,
    DET-animal-TOP
    the animal

26. ma'an t-u-kuuch-il. …
    NEG/COP in-3Ppr-place-POS
    wasn't in its place.

27. Chen a'-ka' t-in-wu'uy-ah-eh,
    only DET-when COM-1sg-hear-DPM-REL
    Only then I heard it,

28. u-hum a'-[ ]-pok=che',
    3Ppr-sound DET-foliage
    the sound of the foliage

29. tu'ux b'in-ih,
    where go-3sg
    where it went,

30. tu'ux k-u-b'el tun-hil-t-ik u-b'ah …
    where INC-3-go 3/DUR-throw-TRAN-PPM 3Ppr-REFL
    where it goes hurling itself,

31. i b'in-een t-u-pach,
    and go-1sg to-3Ppr-back
    and I went behind it,

32. tzay-een t-u-pach. …
    follow-1sg to-3Ppr-back
    I followed behind it.

33. I nak-ih in-wool ti sen=kech xi'mal.
    and tire-3sg 1sgPpr-self SUB INTENS walk
    And my body was tired from so much walking.

34. Tulakal a'-k'aax tu'ux mas sup'-eh,
    all DET-forest where more overgrown-REL
    All around the forest where it's more overgrown,

35. te' k-u-käx-t-ik-i'ih
    LOC INC-3-seek-TRAN-PPM-SCOPE
    there it seeks it,

36. te' k-u-b'el [u-],
    LOC INC-3-go [3-]
    there it goes,

37. te' k-u-hil-t-ik u-b'ah-i'ih. …
    LOC INC-3-throw-TRAN-PPM 3Ppr-REFL-SCOPE
    there it throws itself.

38. I ma' pat-ah-ih in-mäch-ik. …
    and NEG ABIL-DIST-3sg 1sg-grab-PPM
    And I couldn't grab it.

39. A'-ka' t-in-wil-ah
     DET-when COM-1sg-see-DPM
     When I saw

40. ke ma' pat-ah-ih in-mäch-ik-eh,
     SUB NEG ABIL-DIST-3sg 1sg-grab-PPM-TOP
     that I couldn't grab it,

41. ka' bin-een t-u-laak' kol. …
     then go-1sg to-3Ppr-other milpa
     then I went to the other milpa.

42. Ho'm-ih in-lah-man t-u-b'aak' tulakal a'-kol-eh
     TERM-3sg 1sg-all-pass at-3Ppr-perimeter all DET-milpa-TOP
     I finished walking completely around all of the milpa,

43. ma' t-in-wil-ah mix b'a'al. …
     NEG COM-1sg-see-DPM NEG thing
     I didn't see anything.

44. Nak-ih in-wool t-in-[,]-xi'mal-eh,
     tire-3sg 1sgPpr-self from-1sgPpr-walk-TOP
     My body was tired from walking,

45. ka' sut-k'-ah-een t-u-ka'ye'. …
     then return-CELER?-DIST-1sg to-3Ppr-again
     then I returned again.

46. Ya t-in-tal-el chumuk b'eh-eh. …
     already DUR-1sg-come-INTRAN mid road-TOP
     And I was already coming in the middle of the road.

47. Chen a'-ka' t-in-wu'y-ah-eh,
     only DET-when COM-1sg-hear-DPM-TOP
     Only then I heard it,

48. tan-u-hum u-tal …
     DUR-3-sound 3-come
     it was making noise, coming,

49. u-xi'mal mak t-in-pach. …
     3Ppr-walk person at-1sgPpr-back
     the step of a person behind me.

50. Ka' wa'-l-ah-een
     then stand-POSIT-DIST-1sg
     Then I stood,

51. ka' t-in-sut-ah in-k'aak'-eh,
     then COM-1sg-turn back-DPM 1sgPpr-fire-TOP
     then I turned my light back

52. ti'ih in-tich' = k'ak'-t-eh,
    SUB 1sg-illuminate-TRAN-SPM
    in order to illuminate

53. [hach?] a'-b'eh tu'ux, tal-een-eh. …
    [much?] DET-road where come-1sg-REL
    the road where I came.

54. Ma'an mix maak. …
    NEG/COP NEG person
    There wasn't anyone.

55. A'-ka' t-in-wil-ah
    DET-when COM-1sg-see-DPM
    When I saw

56. ke ma'an mix maak-eh
    SUB NEG/COP NEG person-TOP
    that there wasn't anyone,

57. ka' … xi'ma-n-ah-een t-u-ka'ye'. …
    then walk-DETRAN-DIST-1sg to-3Ppr-again
    then I walked again.

58. [stumble] He-b'ix, t-im-b'el ti xi'mal-eh …
    OST-how DUR-1sg-go SUB walk-TOP
    As I was walking,

59. tan-in-wu'uy-ik u-hum u-tal a'-ok t-in-pach-eh. …
    DUR-1sg-hear-PPM 3Ppr-sound 3-come DET-foot at-1sgPpr-back-TOP
    I was hearing the sound of the footstep coming behind me.

60. I ka' ka'-wa'-l-ah-een
    and then REPET-stand-POSIT-DIST-1sg
    And then I stood again

61. in-ka'-il-a'. ,
    1sg-REPET-see-SPM
    to see it again.

62. I ma'an mix b'a'al. …
    and NEG/COP NEG thing
    And there wasn't anything.

63. Chen a'-ka' t-in-wu'y-ah-eh,
    only DET-when COM-1sg-hear-DPM-TOP
    Only when I heard it,

64. xi'il = ke'el-n-ah-een. …
    chill-DETRAN-DIST-1sg
    I felt chills.

65. Im-pol-eh, al, al. …
    1sgPpr-head-TOP heavy heavy
    My head, it was heavy, heavy.

66. I tak in-wak …
    and to 1sgPpr-tongue
    And even my tongue,

67. siis=pomeen-ah-ih. …
    numb-DIST-3sg
    was numb.

68. I in-ten-eh, ya ma' pat-ah-ih in-xi'mal. …
    and EMP-1sgIpr-TOP already NEG ABIL-DIST-3sg 1sg-walk
    And me, then I couldn't walk.

69. Ka' t-in-wa'l-ah-eh: ,
    then COM-1sg-say-DPM-TOP
    Then I said:

70. "A'-la'-eh ma' ma'lo' b'a'ax-i'ih." ,
    DET-PROX-TOP NEG good thing-SCOPE
    "This is not a good thing."

71. Mia u-yum-il k'aax,
    DUB 3Ppr-lord-POS forest
    I think it's the lord of the forest,

72. wa u-yum-il witz. …
    or 3Ppr-lord-POS hill
    or the lord of the hills.

73. Wa mia layti' a'-keeh
    or DUB 3Ipr DET-deer
    Or maybe it's the deer

74. t-in-wil-ah
    COM-1sg-see-DPM
    that I saw

75. t-in-tz'on-ah,
    COM-1sg-shoot-DPM
    and shot

76. i ma' kim-ih-eh. …
    and NEG die-3sg-REL
    and it didn't die.

77. Mia layti' u-pixan,
    DUB 3Ipr 3Ppr-spirit
    I think it is a spirit,

78. a'-k-u-tal t-im-pach-eh. ...
    DET-INC-3-come at-1sgPpr-back-REL
    that which is coming behind me.

79. Ka' tal-een ...
    then come-1sg
    Then I came,

80. ka' k'och-een
    then arrive-1sg
    then I arrived

81. tu'ux yan hum p'e noh che', lub'-al-eh,
    where COP one INAM big tree fall-PART-REL
    where there is a big fallen tree,

82. ka' näk-l-ah-een,
    then sit-POSIT-DIST-1sg
    and I sat down

83. im-pak'-t-eh
    1sg-wait-TRAN-SPM
    to wait

84. asta ka' man-ih u-k'as-il in-wool,
    until when pass-3sg 3Ppr-bad-POS 1sgPpr-self
    until my weakness passed,

85. tu'ux al-ah-i(h) im-pol-eh. ...
    where heavy-DIST-3sg 1sgPpr-head-REL
    where my head hurt.

86. Ka' kap-een ti xi'mal,
    then begin-1sg SUB walk
    Then I began to walk

87. i xi'mal,
    and walk
    and walk

88. aasta ka' k'och-een way t-in-wotoch-eh. ...
    until when arrive-1sg here at-1sgPpr-home-TOP
    until I arrived here at my home.

89. A'-ka' k'och-een way-e', t-in-wotoch-eh
    DET-when arrive-1sg here-TOP at-1sgPpr-home-TOP
    When I arrived here, at my home,

90. ya ak'ä' u-sas-tal. ...
    already night 3-light-INCHOAT
    it was already dawning.

91. Ya tan-u-käy ah kax. …
     already DUR-3-sing MASC chicken
     The roosters were already crowing.

92. Ka' k'och-een-eh
     when arrive-1sg-TOP
     When I arrived

93. ma' t-in-tzikb'al-t-ah mix b'a'al t-in-wätan,
     NEG COM-1sg-say-TRAN-DPM NEG thing to-1sgPpr-wife
     I didn't say anything to my wife,

94. chen ten in-wohel a'-b'a'ax [t-in- …]
     only 1sgIpr 1sg-know DET-what [COM-1sg-]
     only I know what

95. t-in-wil-ah ich k'aax-eh. …
     COM-1sg-see-DPM inside forest-REL
     I saw in the forest.

96. Aasta [t-u-laak' stumble,] a'-ka' sas-ah-ih-eh,
     until [to-3Ppr-other] DET-when light-DIST-3sg-TOP
     Until it dawned,

97. hatz' = ka'-eh,
     early-TOP
     early,

98. tan-ki-han-al-eh
     DUR-1pl-eat-INTRAN-TOP
     we were eating

99. ka' kap-een in-tzikb'al-t-eh ti'ih …
     when begin-1sg 1sg-tell-TRAN-SPM 3IOpr
     when I began to tell it to them,

100. a'-b'a'ax, t-in-wu'y-ah ich k'aax-eh. …
     DET-what COM-1sg-hear-DPM inside forest-REL
     what I heard inside the forest.

101. T-u-hak'-s-ah in-wool. …
     COM-3-frighten-CAUS-DPM 1sgPpr-self
     It frightened me.

102. I a'-k'in he'-lo'-eh tak b'a-he'-la'-eh,
     and DET-day OST-DIST-TOP until TEMP-OST-PROX-TOP
     And from that day until now,

103. ma' ka'-xik-en t-u-ka'ye'
     NEG REPET-go/IRREAL-1sg to-3Ppr-again
     I haven't returned again

t-a'-kol he'-lo'-eh
to-DET-milpa OST-DIST-TOP
to that milpa,

104. ya saak-en ti'ih.
already afraid-1sg 3IOpr
I'm still afraid of it.

3. Ix Tabay[1]

Told by Fernando Tesucún on September 14, 1979

1. Yan-ah-ih hum p'e k'in …
COP-DIST-3sg one INAM day
There was a day

2. ke … kal-een. …
SUB get drunk-1sg
that I got drunk.

3. I p'at-een ich kah …
and remain-1sg in town
And I stayed in town,

4. ya chumuk ak'ä'. …
already mid night
it was already the middle of the night.

5. A'-ka' tal-een ti chi-tal t-in-wotoch-eh …
DET-when come-1sg SUB lie-POSIT to-1sgPpr-home-TOP
When I came to lie down in my home,

6. ya … ak'ä' u-sas-tal. …
already night 3-light-INCHOAT
it was already dawning.

7. Ii, komo hach yaab' … a'-ha' t-in-wuk'-ah-eh …
and as very much DET-water COM-1sg-drink-DPM-REL
And, as it was a lot of the (fire)water that I drank,

8. t-u-kal-t-es-ah-en. …
COM-3-get drunk-TRAN-CAUS-DPM-1sg
it made me drunk.

9. I hach käl-a'an-en
and very drunk-PART-1sg
And I was very drunk

---

[1] Ix Tabay is a female demon who is infamous for luring men to their deaths.

10. a'-ka' k'och-een waye'. …
    DET-when arrive-1sg here
    when I arrived here.

11. Ya ma' pat-ah-ih mix in-wok-ol t-in-wotoch,
    already NEG ABIL-DIST-3sg NEG 1sg-enter-INTRAN in-1sgPpr-home
    Already I couldn't even get in my home,

12. ka' p'at-een …
    then remain-1sg
    so then I stayed,

13. t-in-wen-el taan=ka'. …
    DUR-1sg-sleep-INTRAN outside
    sleeping outside.

14. Lub'-een
    fall-1sg
    I fell

15. a'-tu'ux lub'-een-eh
    DET-where fall-1sg-REL
    where I fell,

16. te' p'at-een t-in-wen-el-i'ih. …
    LOC remain-1sg DUR-1sg-sleep-INTRAN-SCOPE
    there I stayed sleeping.

17. Ya tan-u-käy ah kax,
    already DUR-3-sing MASC chicken
    The roosters were already crowing,

18. ka' lik'-ih [in-…] in-wätan. …
    then get up-3sg [1sgPpr-] 1sgPpr-wife
    then my wife got up.

19. T-u-heb'-ah-oo' u-hol a'-nah-eh …
    COM-3-open-DPM-PL 3Ppr-door DET-house-TOP
    She opened the door of the house,

20. et-el in-na'. …
    with-POS 1sgPpr-mother
    with my mother.

21. Lik'-oo' [u-,] u-yok-es-een-oo' ich nah. …
    get up-PL [3-] 3-enter-CAUS-1sg-PL inside house
    They got up to bring me inside the house.

22. I a'-ka' t-u-heb'-ah-oo' u-hol a'-nah-eh …
    and DET-when COM-3-open-DPM-PL 3Ppr-door DET-house-TOP
    And when they opened the door of the house,

23. t-u-yil-ah-oo' hun tuul noxi' ix ch'up ...
    COM-3-see-DPM-PL one ANIM big FEM woman
    they saw a big woman (Ix Tabay)

24. tan-u-tal-el. ...
    DUR-3-come-INTRAN
    coming.

25. Chawak u-[,]-tzo'otz-el u-pol. ...
    long 3Ppr-hair-POS 3Ppr-head
    Long is the hair of her head.

26. K-u-lub'-ul [tak t-u-...] tak t-u-b'ak-el u-yit. ...
    INC-3-fall-INTRAN [till to-3Ppr] till to-3Ppr-bone-POS 3Ppr-rump
    It falls to the bone of her rump.

27. Ii ho'm-ih u-man ix ch'up-eh. ...
    and TERM-3sg 3-pass FEM woman-TOP
    And the woman finished passing by.

28. Ka' t-u-t'än-ah-een-oo',
    then COM-3-talk-DPM-1sg-PL
    Then they talked to me

29. ka' t-u-yok-s-ah-een-oo' ich nah. ...
    then COM-3-enter-CAUS-DPM-1sg-PL inside house
    and they brought me inside the house.

30. I tantoh-in-wok-ol ich nah,
    and IMMED-1sg-enter-INTRAN inside house
    And I just entered inside the house

31. a'-ka', (t-u-)chema'-t-ah-oo',
    DET-when (COM-3)-spy-TRAN-DPM-PL
    when they spied

32. u-yil-a'-oo' u-ix ch'up-eh
    3-see-SPM-PL 3Ppr-FEM woman-TOP
    to see the woman,

33. tu'ux b'in-ih. ...
    where go-3sg
    where she went.

34. Ka' t-u-yil-ah-oo'-eh ...
    then COM-3-see-DPM-PL-TOP
    Then they saw

35. ke ix ch'up-eh b'in-ih tulakal, t-a'-b'eh,
    SUB FEM woman-TOP go-3sg all on-DET-road
    that the woman went all along the road

36. k-u-b'el ich kah-eh. …
     INC-3-go into town-REL
     that goes into town.

37. Te' b'in-ih-i'ih. …
     LOC go-3sg-SCOPE
     There she went.

38. I ma' sam-ih k-u-b'el-eh,
     and NEG while-3sg INC-3-go-REL
     And it was a little while after she went,

39. ka' t-u-yil-ah-oo' b'in-eh,
     when COM-3-see-DPM-PL REPORT-TOP
     when they saw it, they say,

40. ka' ka'-sut-n-ah-ih. …
     then REPET-return-DETRAN-DIST-3sg
     then she returned again.

41. Ka' tal-ih-eh
     when come-3sg-TOP
     When she came

42. wa'-l-ah-ih waye' uk=taan [t-a'-…] t-in-wotoch-eh …
     stand-POSIT-DIST-3sg here front [of-DET-] of-1sgPpr-home-TOP
     she stood here in front of my home,

43. ka' t-u-ch'a'-ah, a'-b'eh he'-la'
     then COM-3-take-DPM DET-road OST-PROX
     then she took this road (in front of house)

44. k-u-nak'-äl,
     INC-3-rise-INTRAN
     that rises,

45. tu'ux, k-u-b'el tak,
     where INC-3-go till
     where it goes up to

46. tu'ux [a'-,] k-u-muk-b'-ul a'-kim-en-oo'-eh. …
     where [DET-] INC-3-bury-PAS-INTRAN DET-die-NOM-PL-REL
     where the dead are buried (the cemetery).

47. Te' b'in-ih-i'ih.
     LOC go-3sg-SCOPE
     There she went.

48. Ii, yalam a'-che'-oo', päk'-aal-oo'
     and below DET-tree-PL plant-PART-PL
     And below the planted trees

49. yan, waye' t-u-chi' a'-b'eh-eh …
    COP here at-3Ppr-edge DET-road-REL
    that are here along the edge of the road,

50. ek' =hoch'e'en, te' … haw-ih-i'ih
    darkness LOC disappear-3sg-SCOPE
    (in the) darkness, there she disappeared,

51. i a'-ka' t-u-yil-ah-oo'-eh,
    and DET-when COM-3-see-DPM-PL-TOP
    and when they looked,

52. ya ma'an mix b'a'al
    already NEG/COP NEG thing
    there wasn't anything,

53. ya [b'ay] b'ay chen ik'-eh. …
    already [like] like just air-TOP
    it was already like, just air.

54. Ya ma' t-u-ka'-sut-n-ah-ih u-yil-a'-oo'.
    already NEG to-3Ppr-REPET-return-DETRAN-DIST-3sg 3-see-SPM-PL
    Then they didn't return to see her again.

4. The Gun

Told by Fernando Tesucún on November 5, 1979

1. T-in-män-t-ah in-tz'on ti hun tu winik. …
   COM-1sg-lend-TRAN-DPM 1sgPpr-gun to one ANIM man
   I lent my gun to a man.

2. Yan u-kol wa'ye' pach kah-eh. …
   COP 3Ppr-milpa here behind town-TOP
   He has his milpa here behind town.

3. I a'-ka' tal-ih-eh …
   and DET-when come-3sg-TOP
   And when he came,

4. b'a-he'-la' tal-ih,
   TEMP-OST-PROX come-3sg
   now he came,

5. t-u-k'ub'-ah in-tz'on-eh. ,
   COM-3-deliver-DPM 1sgPpr-gun-TOP
   he delivered my gun.

6. Ii, ka' t-u-ya'al-ah ten-eh ke,
   and then COM-3-say-DPM 1sgIOpr-TOP SUB
   And then he told me that,

7. ya'al-ah ten …
   3/say-DPM 1sgIOpr
   he told me

8. wa ma'an u-b'a'al in-tz'on-eh
   COND NEG/COP 3Ppr-bullet 1sgPpr-gun-TOP
   if there aren't any bullets for my gun

9. layti', patal-u-p'ät-ik ten-i'ih. …
   3Ipr ABIL-3-leave-PPM 1sgIOpr-PARTIT
   he could leave me some of them.

10. Ii, komo ya tan-u-b'el-oo' b'a-he'-la',
    and as already DUR-3-go-PL TEMP-OST-PROX
    And, (like) they were already going now

11. t-u-kaal-oo'-eh. ,
    to-3Ppr-town-PL-TOP
    to their towns.

12. Layti'-oo'-eh
    3Ipr-PL-TOP
    Them,

13. käh-a'an-oo' tak Chal,
    live-PART-PL till PN
    they live over at Chal,

14. u-b'en-il Poktun. …
    3Ppr-way-POS PN
    on the road to Poctun.

15. I t-u-p'ät-ah ten yaab' u-b'a'al tz'on,
    and COM-3-leave-DPM 1sgIOpr lot 3Ppr-shell gun,
    And he left me a lot of shotgun shells

16. t(i'ih)-in-tz'on-ik a'-b'a'al=che'. ,
    SUB-1sg-shoot-PPM DET-animal
    for me to shoot animals.

17. B'a-lah hach ki' in-wool
    TEMP-PROX very good 1sgPpr-spirit
    Now I am very happy

18. tumen, ya ma'an-in-män-ik. ,
    because already NEG/OBLIG-1sg-buy-PPM
    because now I don't have to buy them.

19. Si-b'il t-u-b'et-ah ten.
    give-PART COM-3-make-DPM 1sgIOpr
    He made it a gift.

5. The Rainy Season

Told by Fernando Tesucún on October 16, 1979

1. B'ayorita, ich k'aax-eh,
    now inside forest-TOP
    Now, in the forest,

2. ma' patal-u-wen-el mak ma'lo'
    NEG ABIL-3-sleep-INTRAN person well
    a person can't sleep well

3. tumen hach yaab' k'oxol. …
    because very much mosquito
    because there are so many mosquitos.

4. A'-b'eh,
    DET-road
    The road

5. tu'ux k-im-b'el ti meyah-eh …
    where INC-1sg-go SUB work-REL
    where I go to work

6. tz'o-tz'op-ki et-el luk'. …
    INTENS-swampy-ADJ with-POS mud
    is very swampy with mud.

7. K-u-pul-ik mak u-yok [ti xi'm,] ti xi'mal-eh. …
    INC-3-stick-PPM person 3Ppr-foot [SUB] SUB walk-TOP
    A person gets his foot stuck walking.

8. K-u-lah-ts'op-ol ich a'-luk'-eh.
    INC-3-all-sink-INTRAN into DET-mud-TOP
    Everything sinks into the mud.

9. K-u-k'och-ol a'-luk' tak
    INC-3-arrive-INTRAN DET-mud till
    The mud comes up

    t-u-ho'ol u-piix mak-eh. ,
    to-3Ppr-head 3Ppr-knee person-TOP
    to a person's kneecap.

10. B'ayoritah-eh hach k'as a'-b'eh-eh. ,
    now-TOP very bad DET-road-TOP
    Now the road is very bad.

11. Tan-in-tuk-l-ik,
    DUR-1sg-think-?-PPM
    I am thinking,

12. a'-k'in-oo' he'-la'-eh
     DET-day-PL OST-PROX-TOP
     these days

13. mia, b'el in-ka'a ti wen-el-i'ih,
     DUB go 1sg-go SUB sleep-INTRAN-LOC
     I think maybe I'll sleep there

14. yok' ma' [in-,] in-tal t-u-ka' = sut. …
     SUB NEG [1sg-] 1sg-come to-3Ppr-again
     so I don't have to come back again.

15. Tumen k-u-nak-s-ik u-yool mak
     because INC-3-tire-CAUS-PPM 3Ppr-spirit person
     Because it tires a person

16. ti xi'mal ich a'-luk'-il-eh i ha'. …
     SUB walk in DET-mud-POS-TOP and water
     to walk in the mud and water.

17. Po-potz'-ki',
     INTENS-slippery-ADJ
     It's slippery,

18. ma'an mix tu'ux u-wa'-tal ma'lo'
     NEG/COP NEG where 3-stand-POSIT well
     there isn't anywhere to stand well

19. tulakal t-a'-b'eh-eh. …
     all on-DET-road-TOP
     all along the road.

20. Kil-u-mäch-ik mak a'-b'eh-eh,
     when-3-take-PPM person DET-road-TOP
     When one takes the road,

21. puuro chen luk'! , luk'! ,
     pure only mud mud
     it's only mud! mud!

22. I aasta u-k'och-ol mak tak
     and till 3-arrive-INTRAN person till
     And until a person arrives

     t-u-xul [a'-…a'-,] a'-b'eh,
     to-3Ppr-end [DET- DET-] DET-road
     at the end of the road,

23. u-tam-il tu'ux k-u-'äk-tal a'-ha'-eh,
     3Ppr-deep-POS where INC-3-puddle-INCHOAT DET-water-TOP
     the low parts where the water puddles,

24. aasta u-k'och-ol mak, t-u-[,]-näk' a'-witz-oo'-eh,
    till 3-arrive-INTRAN person to-3Ppr-belly DET-hill-PL-TOP
    until one arrives at the foot of the hills,

25. k-u-haw-äl u-xi'ma-t-ik mak luk'.
    INC-3-end-INTRAN 3-walk-TRAN-PPM person mud
    one finishes walking in mud.

6. Preparations for All Souls' Day

Told by Fernando Tesucún on October 23, 1979

1. Samal-eh ma' tan-[,]-ki-b'el ti meyah …
   tomorrow-TOP NEG DUR-1pl-go SUB work
   Tomorrow we aren't going to work

2. tumen b'el in-ka'a ti si',
   because go 1sg-go SUB cut wood
   because I'm going to go to cut wood

3. haal ha'. …
   shore water
   on the lakeshore.

4. B'el in-k(a'a)-in-ch'äk-ä' yaab' si'
   go 1sg-go-1sg-cut-SPM much wood
   I'm going to cut a lot of wood

5. tumen, waye' t-in-wotoch-eh,
   because here in-1sgPpr-home-TOP
   because here in my home

6. b'el u-ka'a ti k'och-ol,
   go 3-go SUB arrive-INTRAN
   it's going to arrive,

7. u-k'in a'-[,]-pixan-ooh-eh. …
   3Ppr-day DET-spirit-PL-TOP
   the day of the spirits.

8. In-na' ih in-wätan-eh,
   1sgPpr-mother and 1sgPpr-wife-TOP
   My mother and my wife

9. yan-u-men-t-ik-oo' pay=chi',
   OBLIG-3-make-TRAN-PPM-PL devotion
   have to make devotions

10. t(i'ih)-u-pak'-t-ik-al-oo' a'-pixan-oo' [k'im]
    SUB-3-await-TRAN-PPM-SUB-PL DET-spirit-PL [die]
    to await the spirits

kim-en-oo'-eh. …
die-NOM-PL-TOP
of the dead.

11. Men kim-en in-noolah,
because die-NOM 1sgPpr-grandmother
Because my grandmother is dead,

12. kim-en [in-,] u-suku'un in-na'. …
die-NOM [1sgPpr-] 3Ppr-older brother 1sgPpr-mother
my mother's brothers are dead.

13. Layti'-oo'-eh yan-u-b'et-ik-oo' han-al
3Ipr-PL-TOP OBLIG-3-make-PPM-PL eat-NOM
They have to make food

14. t(i'ih)-u-pak'-t-ik-al-oo' a'-[,]-pixan-oo'
SUB-3-await-TRAN-PPM-SUB-PL DET-spirit-PL
to await the spirits

15. k-u-b'el-oo' ti tal t-a'-k'in he'-lo'-eh. …
INC-3-go-PL SUB come on-DET-day OST-DIST-REL
that are going to come on that day.

16. Mentäk-eh,
therefore-TOP
Therefore,

17. k-in-wa'al-ik tech,
INC-1sg-say-PPM 2sgIOpr
I tell you

18. b'a-he'-la'-eh,
TEMP-OST-PROX-TOP
now

19. ke samal-eh,
SUB tomorrow-TOP
that tomorrow

20. ma' a-tal,
NEG 2-come
don't come

21. tumen ma' tan-ki-b'el ti meyah.
because NEG DUR-1pl-go SUB work
because we aren't going to work.

7. Puppies

Told by Fernando Tesucún on November 6, 1979

1. Kab'eh-ih kim-ih in-pek'. …
    two days-3sg die-3sg 1sgPpr-dog
    Day before yesterday my dog died.

2. I t-u-p'ät-ah … u-yal. …
    and COM-3-leave-DPM 3Ppr-young
    And it left its young.

3. I a'-[,]-mehen pek'-oo'-eh,
    and DET-small dog-PL-TOP
    And the small dogs

4. tan-kuchi-u-chu'uch-oo'. …
    DUR-before-3-suckle-PL
    were suckling.

5. I b'a-lah,
    and TEMP-PROX
    And now,

6. kim-ih u-na'-eh. …
    die-3sg 3Ppr-mother-TOP
    their mother died.

7. Yan-ki-tz'ik, uk'-ul u-yuk'-u'. …
    OBLIG-1pl-give/PPM drink-NOM 3-drink-SPM
    We have to give them drink to drink.

8. Ho'leh-ih b'in-een ti Peten,
    yesterday-3sg go-1sg to PN
    Yesterday I went to Flores

9. chen yok' in-män-ik, hum p'e uuleh. …
    only SUB 1sg-buy-PPM one INAM nipple
    just to buy a nipple.

10. I ki-tz'ik, t-u-hol hum p'eel b'oteeya,
    and INC/1pl-give/PPM on-3Ppr-hole one INAM bottle
    And we put it on the mouth of a bottle

11. ti'a'al pat-ak u-yuk'-ul. …
    SUB ABIL-IRREAL 3-drink-INTRAN
    so that they could drink.

12. I b'a-lah san=samal yan-ki-känän-t-ik …
    and TEMP-PROX every day OBLIG-1pl-guard-TRAN-PPM
    And now every day we have to care for them

13. tumen a'-mehen pek'-oo'-eh,
    because DET-small dog-PL-TOP
    because the small dogs,

14. u-na'-eh hach ma'lo'
    3Ppr-mother-TOP very good
    their mother was very good,

15. u-yohel=b'äk',
    3-know=meat
    it knew to hunt,

16. i mia [,] u-yal-oo'-eh,
    and DUB 3Ppr-young-PL-TOP
    and perhaps her young

17. he'-u-hok'-ol-oo' xan,
    ASSUR-3-leave-INTRAN-PL also
    will also come out

18. ma'lo' he-b'ix u-na'-eh. ,
    good OST-like 3Ppr-mother-TOP
    well like their mother.

19. Mentäk-eh tan-ki-tan-l-ik,
    therefore-TOP DUR-1pl-attend-?-PPM
    Therefore we are caring for them

20. yok' ma' u-kim-il-oo'. ...
    SUB NEG 3-die-INTRAN-PL
    so that they don't die.

21. Ko'ox ki-kil-a'
    HORT 1pl-see-SPM
    Let's see

22. wa u-ch'iil-oo'. ...
    COND 3-grow-PL
    if they grow.

23. Chen b'a'ax-(i')ih
    only thing-SCOPE
    The only thing is

24. ke yan-in-lik'-il tak et-e ak'ä'
    that OBLIG-1sg-rise-INTRAN till with-POS night
    that I have to get up even at night

25. in-tz'ah u-yuk'-ul-oo',
    1sg-give/SPM 3Ppr-drink-NOM-PL
    to give them their drinks

26. tumen k-u-pa'-ik-oo' in-wen-el.
    because INC-3-break-PPM-PL 1sgPpr-sleep-NOM
    because they interrupt my sleep.

8. Guarding a House

Told by Fernando Tesucún on November 7, 1979

1. Sam-ih hatzka',
   while-3sg early
   A while ago, in the morning,

2. nak'-een in-wil-a' u-yotoch ...
   climb-1sg 1sg-see-SPM 3Ppr-house
   I went up to see the house of

3. ah Paablo Riveera. ... (pseudonym)
   MASC PN
   Pablo Rivera.

4. A'-nah-eh,
   DET-house-TOP
   The house

5. p'ät-a'an,
   leave-PART
   was left,

6. k'ub'en-a'an ten. ...
   recommend-PART 1sgIOpr
   entrusted to me.

7. In-ten yan-in-wil-ik. ...
   EMP-1sgIpr OBLIG-1sg-see-PPM
   I have to watch it.

8. B'a-he'-la'-eh hach, tz'o'k-ih u-sup'-ul,
   TEMP-OST-PROX-TOP very TERM-3sg 3-be overgrown-INTRAN
   Now it has gotten very overgrown,

9. i nak'-een in-wil-a' hun tu(ul) winik,
   and climb-1sg 1sg-see-SPM one ANIM man
   and I went up to see a man

10. t-u-k'a't-ah ten meyah,
    COM-3-ask-DPM 1sgIOpr work
    that asked me for work

11. i tak-u-paak-t-ik. ...
    and DESID-3-clear-TRAN-PPM
    and wants to clear it.

12. T-in-wa'al-ah ti'ih,
    COM-1sg-say-DPM 3IOpr
    I told him

13. ka' meyah-n-ak ka' p'e k'in,
    SUB work-DETRAN-IRREAL two INAM day
    to work two days,

14. k(a')-u-paak-t-eh ka'ax chen u-b'aak'
    SUB-3-clear-TRAN-SPM although only 3Ppr-perimeter
    that he clear it, even if only the perimeter

    a'-nah-eh. …
    DET-house-TOP
    of the house.

15. I ka' k'och-een
    and when arrive-1sg
    And when I arrived

16. sam-ih hatska' in-wil-a'-eh,
    while-3sg early 1sg-see-SPM-TOP
    a while ago in the morning to see it,

17. tulakal u-koloh=che'-il,
    all 3Ppr-house posts-POS
    all the house posts

18. tu'ux, kot-a'an a'-nah-eh …
    where enclose-PART DET-house-REL
    where the house is walled in,

19. lah-okol-a'an. …
    all-steal-PART
    are all stolen.

20. Mia', tulakal a'-k'in-oo' he'-la'
    DUB all DET-day-PL OST-PROX
    I think all these days

21. tan-u-b'et-ik, ha'-eh …
    DUR-3-make-PPM water-REL
    that it was raining,

22. a'-mak-oo' käh-a'an-oo' nats'-i'ih-eh,
    DET-person-PL live-PART-PL close-LOC-REL
    the people that live close to there,

23. te' k-u-ch'i'-ik-oo' [wal] wal u-che'-il
    LOC INC-3-take-PPM-PL [perhaps] perhaps 3Ppr-wood-POS
    they took the wood there, perhaps,

24. t(i'ih)-u-si'-in-t-oo'. …
    SUB-3-firewood-CAUS-TRAN-PL
    for making firewood.

25. Lah-ch'äk-a'an u-ak'-il
    all-cut-PART 3Ppr-vine-POS
    All of the vines were cut

26. a'-[,]-tu'ux k'äx-a'an-il a'-koloh=che'. …
    DET-where tie-PART-POS DET-house posts
    where the house posts are tied.

27. I kap-een in-k'a't-eh,
    and begin-1sg 1sg-ask-SPM
    And I began to ask

28. wa ma' u-yohel-oo'. ,
    COND NEG 3-know-PL
    if they didn't know (who did it).

29. Mix mak …
    NEG person
    No one,

30. mix mak u-yohel. ,
    NEG person 3-know
    no one knows.

31. Mix mak t-u-yil-ah
    NEG person COM-3-see-DPM
    No one saw

32. [u-,] u-ch'äk-b'-äl a'-che'-eh. …
    [3-] 3-cut-PAS-INTRAN DET-wood-TOP
    the wood being cut.

33. B'a-la b'el in-ka'a ti tz'iib ti'ih,
    TEMP-PROX go 1sg-go to write 3IOpr
    Now I am going to write him

34. yok' u-yohel-t-ik b'ix yan-il.
    SUB 3-know-TRAN-PPM how COP-POS?
    so that he knows how it is.

9. The Town Fiesta

Told by Fernando Tesucún on December 6, 1979

1. Tal-een ti t'äm-b'-äl …
   come-1sg SUB call-PAS-INTRAN
   I came to be called

2. ka' nak'-äk-en t-a'-noh nah,
   SUB climb-IRREAL-1sg to-DET big house
   to climb to the big house (town hall)

3. tu'ux yan a'-nohoch winik …
   where COP DET-great man
   where the great man (mayor) is,

4. u-nohoch-il a'-kah-eh. …
   3Ppr-great-POS DET-town-TOP
   the great one (mayor) of the town.

5. I b'in-een in-wu'y-i b'a'ax ti'a(')al-en-oo' ti'ih. …
   and go-1sg 1sg-hear-SPM? what for-1sg-PL 3IOpr
   And I went to hear why they needed me.

6. Ka' k'och-een-eh,
   when arrive-1sg-TOP
   When I arrived,

7. ka' t-u-ya'l-ah-oo' ten-eh …
   then COM-3-say-DPM-PL 1sgIOpr
   then they told me

8. ke yan-u-lah-t'än-ik-oo' u-yum-il-oo' a'-kah-eh,
   SUB OBLIG-3-all-call-PPM-PL 3Ppr-owner-POS-PL DET-town-TOP
   that they have to call all of the owners of the town

9. yok'ol-al b'aay-lo',
   SUB-SUB thus-DIST
   so that in that way

10. [patal- …] patal-[,]-ki-wil-ik,
    [ABIL-] ABIL-1pl-see-PPM
    we can see

11. max ich-il-o'on …
    who in-POS-1pl
    who among us

12. patal-ki-meyah-t-ik …
    ABIL-1pl-work-TRAN-PPM
    can work

13. tulakal a'-k'in-oo' he'-la'-eh …
    all DET-day-PL OST-PROX-TOP
    all of these days

14. [yok',] yok' ki-wil-ik
    [SUB] SUB 1pl-see-PPM
    in order for us to see

15. wa patal-[kii-…]-ki-mol-ik ta' =k'in. …
    COND ABIL-[1pl-]-1pl-collect-PPM money
    if we can collect money.

16. I tulakal a'-ta' =k'in he'-lo' b'el u-ka'a ti,
    and all DET-money OST-DIST go 3-go SUB
    And all of that money is going to

17. k'ab'eet-tal to'on …
    need-INCHOAT 1plIOpr
    to be needed by us

18. ti'ih a'-ki'mak-'ol-al k-u-tal,
    SUB DET-happy-spirit-POS INC-3-come
    for the fiesta that comes

19. t-u-mes-i(l) maarso. ,
    in-3Ppr-month-POS March
    in the month of March.

20. [Layti' u-…] Layti' u-ki'mak-'ol-al a'-[,]-kah he'-la'-eh …
    [3Ipr 3Ppr-] 3Ipr 3Ppr-happy-spirit-POS DET-town OST-PROX-TOP
    The fiesta of this town,

21. u-k'ab'a' u-saantoh-il-eh,
    3Ppr-name 3Ppr-saint-POS-TOP
    the name of its saint

22. San Hoseh. …
    PN
    is San José.

23. Ii u-hach-k'in a'-San Hoseh-eh,
    and 3Ppr-very day DET-PN-TOP
    And the very day of San José

24. diesinweeve ti'ih maarso. …
    nineteen of March
    is the nineteenth of March.

25. I b'a-he'-la'-eh,
    and TEMP-OST-PROX-TOP
    And now,

26. b'el ki-ka'a ki-wil-a'
    go 1pl-go 1pl-see-SPM
    we are going to see

27. [max yan …] max u-k'a't(-ih) u-yan-t-o'on …
    [who OBLIG?] who 3-want(-PM?) 3-help-TRAN-1pl
    who wants to help us,

28. ich-il tulakal a'-[,]-winik-oo'
    in-POS all DET-man-PL
    who among all of the men,

29. ah xi'-paal-oo'
    MASC male-child-PL
    the boys,

30. i ix ch'up u-paal-oo'-eh …
    and FEM girl 3Ppr-child-PL-TOP
    and the girls

31. (u)ch-ak u-k'äm-ik-oo' u-yan-t-o'on. …
    happen-IRREAL 3-want-PPM-PL 3-help-TRAN-1pl
    might want to help us.

32. T-a'-haab' man-ih-eh …
    in-DET-year pass-3sg-REL
    In the year that passed,

33. b'ay-lo' ti-ki-b'et-ah-eh
    like-DIST COM-1pl-do-DPM-REL
    it is thus that we did it

34. i hok'-o'on hach ma'lo'-il
    and leave-1pl very well-POS
    and we came out very well

35. tumen … yan-ah-ih pax …
    because COP-DIST-3sg music
    because there was music

36. i hach yaab' mak tal-ih,
    and very much person come-3sg
    and very many people came

37. i yan-ah-ih to'on ta'=k'in
    and COP-DIST-3sg 1plIOpr money
    and we had money

38. ti('ih) ki-lah-b'o'-t-ik-al [a'-,] a'-pax,
    SUB 1pl-all-pay-TRAN-PPM-SUB [DET-] DET-music
    to completely pay for the music,

39. tulakal a'-b'a'ax ti-ki-män-ah-eh. …
    all DET-thing COM-1pl-buy-DPM-REL
    everything that we bought.

40. I ma' hok'-ih ki-p'äx-ik mix b'a'al. …
    and NEG leave-3sg 1pl-owe-PPM NEG thing
    And we didn't come out owing anything.

41. Layt(i') a'-lo' u-k'a't-ih a'-mak-oo'-eh,
   3Ipr DET-DIST 3-want-PM? DET-person-PL-TOP
   It is that that the people want,

42. ke tulakal ka' hok'-ok hach ma'lo',
   SUB all SUB leave-IRREAL very well
   that it all should come out very well,

43. i ma' u-yan-tal, u-p'ax a'-kah-eh. ...
   and NEG 3-COP-INCHOAT 3Ppr-debt DET-town-TOP
   and the town won't have debt.

44. I b'a-lah,
   and TEMP-PROX
   And now,

45. mia ich a'-k'in-oo' he'-la'
   DUB in DET-day-PL OST-PROX
   I think that during these days

46. b'el ki-ka'a ki-chun-u' ...
   go 1pl-go 1pl-begin-SPM
   we are going to begin it,

47. tumen b'el u-ka'a ti ts'iib'-(b')-il, u-hu'um-il ...
   because go 3-go to write-PAS-INTRAN 3Ppr-book-POS
   because it is going to be written (in) the official book

48. yok' u-[,]-p'at-äl, u-k'ab'a'
   SUB 3-remain-INTRAN 3Ppr-name
   so the names remain

49. tulakal a'-[,]-mak-oo' k-u-b'el-oo' ti meyah-eh. ...
   all DET-person-PL INC-3-go-PL SUB work-REL
   of all of the people that are going to work.

50. B'ay-lo [ya yohe] ya ki-wohel
   like-DIST [already know?] already 1pl-know
   Thus, we already know

51. max-oo' tak-i'ih. ...
   who-PL DESID-SCOPE
   who they will be.

52. I ki-mol-ik ki-b'ah a'-k'in,
   and INC/1pl-collect-PPM 1plPpr-REFL DET-day
   And we meet (collect ourselves) the day

53. b'el ki-ka'a ki-chun-u' ki-meyah-eh.
   go 1pl-go 1pl-begin-SPM 1plPpr-work-REL
   that we are going to begin our work.

10. Making a Canoe

Told by Fernando Tesucún on May 29, 1980

1. Hok'-ih ten hum p'e meyah …
    leave-3sg 1sgIOpr one INAM job
    A job came to me

2. i b'in-een im-b'et-eh. …
    and go-1sg 1sg-do-SPM
    and I went to do it.

3. U-yum-il a'-meyah-eh …
    3Ppr-owner-POS DET-work-TOP
    The boss of the job

4. t-u-ya'al-ah ten-eh
    COM-3-say-DPM 1sgIOpr-TOP
    told me

5. ke ka' im-b'et-eh, hum p'e mo'nok chem,
    SUB SUB 1sg-make-SPM one INAM small canoe
    that I should make a small canoe

6. ti'ih u-tz'ik u-yuk'-ul tulakal u-tzimin-oo'. …
    SUB 3-give/PPM 3Ppr-drink-NOM all 3Ppr-horse-PL
    to give drink to all of his horses.

7. Tumen u-kuuch
    because 3Ppr-place
    Because their place

8. a'-tu'ux yan a'-ha'-eh,
    DET-where COP DET-water-REL
    where the water is,

9. hach tz'op-ot …
    very swampy-?
    is very swampy,

10. i ma' patal-u-yok-ol a'-b'a'al=che'-oo'
    and NEG ABIL-3-enter-INTRAN DET-animal-PL
    and the animals can't enter

11. ti uk'-ul tak t-u-chi' a'-ha'-eh,
    SUB drink-INTRAN up to at-3Ppr-edge DET-water-TOP
    to drink up to the edge of the water

12. tumen, hach, k-u-sut, puro luk'-il. …
    because much INC-3-return pure mud-POS
    because it turns into pure mud a lot.

13. I a'-ha'-eh,
    and DET-water-TOP
    And the water,

14. komo te' k-u-ch'i'-ik a'-[,]-mak-oo' u-yuk'-oo'-eh …
    as LOC INC-3-get-PPM DET-person-PL 3-drink-PL-REL
    since it's there that the people get it to drink it,

15. k-u-känän-t-ik-oo'
    INC-3-guard-TRAN-PPM-PL
    they guard it,

16. ma' u-k'a't-oo'
    NEG 3-want-PL
    they don't want

17. ka' luk'-ak. …
    SUB mud-IRREAL
    it to get muddy.

18. I a'-winik-eh t-u-ya'al-ah ten-eh
    and DET-man-TOP COM-3-say-DPM 1sgIOpr-TOP
    And the man told me

19. ke ka' xik-en,
    SUB SUB go/IRREAL-1sg
    that I should go

20. im-men-t-eh hum p'e chem ti'ih. …
    1sg-make-TRAN-SPM one INAM canoe 3IOpr
    to make a canoe for him.

21. Ii, ka' t-u-tz'ah ten hun tuul ah wach …
    and then COM-3-give/DPM 1sgIOpr one ANIM MASC Mexican
    And then he gave me a Mexican,

22. hun tuul ah Yukatan-il,
    one ANIM MASC PN-POS
    a Yucatecan,

23. u-yan-t-een,
    3-help-TRAN-1sg
    to help me

24. in-meyah-t-eh. …
    1sg-work-TRAN-SPM
    do the work.

25. I a'-yax k'in
    and DET-first day
    And the first day

26. ka', b'in-een in-chun-u' in-meyah-eh …
    when go-1sg 1sg-begin-SPM 1sgPpr-work-REL
    when I went to begin my work,

27. ka' k'och-ih a'-[,]-nohoch winik
    then arrive-3sg DET-big man
    then the big man arrived,

28. u-yum-il a'-meyah-eh
    3Ppr-owner-POS DET-work-TOP
    the boss of the work,

29. ka' t-u-ya'al-ah ten-eh:
    then COM-3-say-DPM 1sgIOpr-TOP
    and he told me:

30. "A'-che' he'-la'-eh,
    DET-tree OST-PROX-TOP
    "This tree,

31. layti' a'-ki' t-in-wich-eh
    3Ipr DET-good to-1sgPpr-eye-REL
    it is the one I like,

32. layti' in-k'a't-ih
    3Ipr 1sg-want-PM?
    it is (from) it that I want

33. k(a')-a-men-t-eh ten a'-chem-eh." …
    SUB-2-make-TRAN-SPM 1sgIOpr DET-canoe-TOP
    you to make me the canoe."

34. A'-che'-eh,
    DET-tree-TOP
    The tree

35. pul-a'an. …
    throw-PART
    was lying down.

36. Ten-eh ka', nak'-een yok' a'-che'-eh
    1sgIpr-TOP then climb-1sg over DET-tree-TOP
    Me, then I climbed on top of the tree,

37. kap-een in-wil-a'. ,
    begin-1sg 1sg-see-SPM
    I began to examine it.

38. T-im-p'is-ah … u-chawak-il,
    COM-1sg-measure-DPM 3Ppr-long-POS
    I measured its length

39. i t-im-p'is-ah u-polok-il. ...
and COM-1sg-measure-DPM 3Ppr-wide-POS
and I measured its width.

40. Ka' t-in-wa'al-ah ti'ih-e'
then COM-1sg-say-DPM 3IOpr-TOP
Then I told him

41. ke a'-che'-eh,
SUB DET-tree-TOP
that the tree

42. hach yutzil. ,
very pretty
is very pretty.

43. He'-u-hok'-ol hum p'e ma'lo' chem-i'ih-eh. ...
ASSUR-3-leave-INTRAN one INAM good canoe-PARTIT-TOP
A good canoe will come out of it.

44. Ka' kap-een [in-,] in-yul-u'. ...
then begin-1sg [1sg-] 1sg-cut-SPM
Then I began to cut it.

45. In-ten-eh mix hum pak in-meyah-t-eh
EMP-1sg-TOP NEG one time 1sg-work-TRAN-SPM
Me, not even once have I done

a'-meyah he'-lo'. ,
DET-work OST-DIST
that work.

46. Chen in-wil-m-ah
only 1sg-see-PERF-DPM
I have only seen

47. [b'ix u-] b'ix u-men-b-el. ...
[how 3-] how 3-do-PAS-INTRAN
how it is done.

48. Ii, ya, chen t-in-na'at
and already only from-1sgPpr-thought
And only from my thoughts

49. t-in-hok'-s-ah
COM-1sg-leave-CAUS-DPM
did I bring out

50. b'ix, k-im-b'el im-b'et-eh. ...
how INC-1sg-go 1sg-do-SPM
how I am going to do it. (i.e., not from practical experience)

51. Ka' t-in-ch'äk-ah ka' p'eel u-xet'-el che'-eh,
    then COM-1sg-cut-DPM two INAM 3Ppr-piece-POS wood-TOP
    Then I cut two pieces of wood,

52. ka' t-im-päk'-ah …
    then COM-1sg-plant-DPM
    then I planted them,

53. ka' t-in-[,]-tz'ah yalam,
    then COM-1sg-put/DPM below
    and I put them underneath

54. yok' u-kuch-ik u-ni' a'-che'-eh,
    SUB 3-carry-PPM 3Ppr-tip DET-tree-TOP
    to support the top of the tree

55. tumen [u-chi' a'-,] u-ni' a'-che'-eh,
    because [3Ppr-edge DET-] 3Ppr-tip DET-tree-TOP
    because the top of the tree

56. ma' tak'-al tak ti lu'um. …
    NEG stick-PART down to on earth
    isn't stuck down to earth.

57. A'-ka' ho'm-ih in-tz'ik [u-,]
    DET-when TERM-3sg 1sg-give/PPM [3Ppr-]
    When I finished putting

58. u-xo'om tak a'-noh che'-eh,
    3Ppr-pole up to DET-big tree-TOP
    the poles up to the big tree,

59. ka' kap-een in-yul-u' t-u-chun. …
    then begin-1sg 1sg-cut-SPM at-3Ppr-trunk
    then I began to cut it at the trunk.

60. In-ten-eh mix tz'eek kun-ah-een in-tuk-l-eh,
    EMP-1sgIpr-TOP NEG bit conjure?-DIST-1sg 1sg-think-?-SPM
    Me, not a bit did I dream to think

61. ke a'-che'-eh,
    SUB DET-tree-TOP
    that the tree,

62. yan hum p'eel [u-,] u-motz,
    COP one INAM [3Ppr-] 3Ppr-root
    it has a root

63. u-mäch-m-ah …
    3-hold-PERF-DPM
    that has held it,

64. t-u-chun. ...
    at-3Ppr-trunk
    at its base.

65. I koomo yalam yan-eh,
    and as below COP-TOP
    And as it's underneath,

66. [pech'-a'an,] pech'-a'an yan-il,
    [crush-PART] crush-PART COP-POS
    it's crushed,

67. ma' chik-a'an. ...
    NEG see-PART
    it isn't visible.

68. I, in-ten-eh t-in-wil-ik a'-che'-eh,
    and EMP-1sgIpr-TOP DUR-1sg-see-PPM DET-tree-TOP
    And me, I was seeing the tree

69. chil-a'an ti lu'um. ,
    lie-PART on earth
    laid on the ground.

70. Mix tz'eek t-in-tuk-l-ah,
    NEG bit COM-1sg-think-?-DPM
    Not a bit did I think

71. ke u-chun a'-che'-eh patal-u-wa'-tal t-u-ka'ye'. ...
    SUB 3-trunk DET-tree-TOP ABIL-3-stand-POSIT to-3Ppr-again
    that the trunk of the tree could stand up again.

72. Ka' kap-een in-yul-u'. ...
    then begin-1sg 1sg-sever-SPM
    Then I began to trim it.

73. I a'-ka' ti p'ik-ih [u-...] u-chun a'-che'
    and DET-when SUB snap-3sg [3Ppr-] 3Ppr-trunk DET-tree
    And when the trunk of the tree snapped

74. tu'ux t-in-yul-ah-eh ...
    where COM-1sg-cut-DPM-REL
    where I trimmed it,

75. i ten-eh wa'an-en
    and 1sgIpr-TOP stand/PART-1sg
    and I am standing

76. [t-u-,] t-u-[,]-chun tu'ux, yan a'-,
    [at-3Ppr-] at-3Ppr-trunk where COP DET-,
    on the trunk where there are the,

77. komo nukuch u-tel=chaak-il u-chun a'-che'-eh. …
    like big 3Ppr-buttress-POS 3Ppr-trunk DET-tree-TOP
    like buttresses of the trunk of the tree.

78. I a'-tu'ux xu'l-ih u-tel=chaak-il-eh
    and DET-where end-3sg 3Ppr-buttress-POS-TOP
    And where the buttresses ended,

79. te' t-in-yul-ah-i'ih. …
    LOC COM-1sg-sever-DPM-SCOPE
    there I trimmed it.

80. I ya tak-[u-,]-u-yul-ul-eh,
    and already DESID-[3-]-3-sever-INTRAN-TOP
    And it already wanted to break

81. ka', ti wa'-l-ah-een ma'lo',
    then SUB stand-POSIT-DIST-1sg well
    and I stood well

82. t-u-chun tu'ux yan u-tel=chaak-il a'-[,]-che'-eh. ,
    on-3Ppr-trunk where COP 3Ppr-buttresses-POS DET-tree-TOP
    on the trunk where the tree has its buttresses.

83. I a'-ka' pik'-ih-eh …
    and DET-when snap-3sg-TOP
    And when it snapped,

84. u-motz a'-che'-eh,
    3Ppr-root DET-tree-TOP
    the root of the tree

85. t-u-hil-t-ah et-e tulakal u-muk'. …
    COM-3-pull-TRAN-DPM with-POS all 3Ppr-strength
    pulled it with all of its strength.

86. I a'-che'-e,
    and DET-tree-TOP
    And the tree,

87. u-chun-e wa'-l-ah-ih. ,
    3Ppr-trunk-TOP stand-POSIT-DIST-3sg
    its trunk stood up.

88. I ten-eh,
    and 1sgIpr-TOP
    And me,

89. b'in-een,
    go-1sg
    I went,

90. t-u-pul-ah-een tak ka'nal. …
    COM-3-throw-DPM-1sg up to above
    it threw me up above.

91. Ma' t-in-wohel-t-ah [mix,]
    NEG COM-1sg-know-TRAN-DPM [NEG]
    I didn't know

92. mix b'ix ich [in-,] in-lub'-ul … lele'kal. …
    NEG how in [1sg-] 1sg-fall-INTRAN head first
    even how I fell, headfirst.

93. Chen men Dios nohoch-eh
    only because God great-TOP
    It's only because God is great

94. ma' ti kach-ih wal in-kal-eh,
    NEG SUB break-3sg perhaps 1sgPpr-neck-TOP
    that I didn't break my neck perhaps,

95. porke lub'-een lele'kal …
    because fall-1sg headfirst
    because I fell headfirst

96. ich-il tulakal u-se'es a'-che'-oo'
    in-POS all 3Ppr-chips DET-branch-PL
    among all the chips of the branches

97. tu'ux ho'm-ih in-xot'-ik-eh,
    where TERM-3sg 1sg-cut-PPM-REL
    where I finished cutting it,

98. te' lub'-een-i'ih. …
    LOC fall-1sg-SCOPE
    there I fell.

99. I a'-k'in-eh chokoh.
    and DET-sun-TOP hot
    And the sun is hot.

100. Ten-eh, ichki(l)-mak-en et-el in-k'ilka'. …
     1sgIpr-TOP bathe-person-1sg with-POS 1sgPpr-sweat
     Me, I am bathed with my sweat.

101. Chen a'-ka' ti lik'-een,
     only DET-when SUB get up-1sg
     Only when I got up

102. ka' man-ih u-k'as-il in-wool-eh
     when pass-3sg 3Ppr-bad-POS 1sgPpr-body-TOP
     and my body's weakness passed,

103. k-in-wil-ik-eh
     INC-3-see-PPM-TOP
     I see that

104. tulakal in-näk' ih in-tzem-eh,
     all 1sgPpr-stomach and 1sgPpr-chest-TOP
     all of my stomach and my chest

105. tun-chul-b'ah u-k'ik'-el,
     DUR/3-drip-INTRAN 3Ppr-blood-POS
     are dripping blood

106. tu'ux t-u-xot'-ah-een tak u-tzeel a'-che',
     where COM-3-cut-DPM-1sg up to 3Ppr-splinters DET-tree
     where it cut me on the splinters of the tree

107. tu'ux lub'-een-eh. …
     where fall-1sg-REL
     where I fell.

108. I ya ma' tak-ah-ih mas in-meyah,
     and already NEG DESID-DIST-3sg more 1sg-work
     And then I didn't want to work more,

109. ka' b'in-een ti chi-tal t-in-k'aan. …
     then go-1sg SUB lie-POSIT in-1sgPpr-hammock
     and I went to lie down in my hammock.

110. Aasta ka' man-ih [u-,] u-k'as-il in-wool-eh
     until when pass-3sg [3Ppr-] 3Ppr-bad-POS 1sgPpr-body-TOP
     When the weakness of my body passed

111. ya tun-yok-ol k'in. ,
     already DUR/3-enter-INTRAN sun
     the sun was already setting.

112. U-yum-il a-meyah-e'
     3Ppr-owner-POS DET-work-TOP
     The boss of the job,

113. ka' tal-ih-e'
     when come-3sg-TOP
     when he came,

114. t-u-patz'-t-ah-een. …
     COM-3-massage-TRAN-DPM-1sg
     he massaged me.

115. Ii … [k] b'ay-lo' ka', ok-ih k'in-eh
     and like-DIST when enter-3sg sun-TOP
     And thus when the sun set

116. ka' wen-een. ,
     then sleep-1sg
     then I slept.

117. Ya ma' segiir-n-ah-ih in-meyah,
     already NEG continue-DETRAN-DIST-3sg 1sgPpr-work
     Then my work didn't continue

118. aasta t-u-laak' u-k'in-il-eh,
     until on-3Ppr-other 3Ppr-day-POS-TOP
     until the next day

119. ka' kap-een in-meyah-t-eh. …
     when begin-1sg 1sg-work-TRAN-SPM
     when I began to work it.

120. I meyah-[…]-n-ah-een ox p'e k'in. ,
     and work-DETRAN-DIST-1sg three INAM day
     And I worked three days.

121. T-u-ox p'e k'in-eh
     on-3Ppr-three INAM day-TOP
     On the third day

122. t-in-ho'm-s-ah a'-mo'nok chem-eh,
     COM-1sg-finish-CAUS-DPM DET-little canoe-TOP
     I finished the little canoe,

123. ka' t-in-k'ub'-ah ti'ih. ,
     then COM-1sg-deliver-DPM 3IOpr
     then I delivered it to him.

124. Ha'l(i') a'-meyah he'-lo' t-im-b'et-ah-eh
     only DET-work OST-DIST COM-1sg-do-DPM-REL
     It's only that work that I did,

125. ka' tal-een t-in-wotoch. …
     then come-1sg to-1sgPpr-home
     then I came to my home.

126. Ii b'aay-loh,
     and like-DIST
     And thus

127. b'a-lah ya mas yan in-na'at. …
     TEMP-PROX already more COP 1sgPpr-thought
     now I already have more thoughts.

128. I mentäk-eh,
     and therefore-TOP
     And therefore,

129. k-in-k'ub'en-t-ik ti tulakal in-wet'ok-oo'
     INC-1sg-recommend-TRAN-PPM to all 1sgPpr-friend-PL
     I recommend to all of my companions

130. k-u-meyah-t-ik-oo' [a'-,] a'-meyah he'-loh,
     INC-3-work-TRAN-PPM-PL [DET-] DET-work OST-DIST
     that do that work

131. k(a')-u-känän-t-u-b'ah-oo'
     SUB-3-guard-TRAN-3Ppr-REFL-PL
     to guard themselves

132. tumen a'-che'-eh,
     because DET-tree-TOP
     because the tree,

133. ma' tun-k'a'ol-t-ik mak,
     NEG DUR/3-know-TRAN-PPM person
     one doesn't know

134. wa yan u-motz,
     COND COP 3Ppr-root
     if it has its root

135. tak'-al yalam,
     stick-PART below
     attached underneath

136. i kil-u-wa'-tal [?] u-chun a'-che' he'-lo'-eh,
     and when-3-stand-POSIT 3Ppr-trunk DET-tree OST-DIST-TOP
     and when the trunk of that tree stands up,

137. patal-u-kin-s-ik mak
     ABIL-3-die-CAUS-PPM person
     it could kill a person

138. tu'ux k-u-lub'-ul mak
     where INC-3-fall-INTRAN person
     where a person falls

139. lele'kal.
     headfirst
     headfirst.

11. Hunting with a Friend

Told by Fernando Tesucún on July 8, 1980

1. Akä'-ah-ih b'in-o'on ti tz'on. …
   night-DIST-3sg go-1pl SUB shoot
   Last night we went to hunt.

2. B'in-o'on tulakal t-a'-noh b'eh
    go-1pl all on-DET-big way
    We went all the way on the road

3. k-u-b'el tak Sik'u'-eh. ,
    INC-3-go up to PN-REL
    that goes up to La Trinidad.

4. Te'-lo' ti-ki-ch'a'-ah u-b'en-il tzimin. …
    LOC-DIST COM-1pl-take-DPM 3Ppr-path-POS mule
    There we took the mule path.

5. Ka' nak'-o'on … t-a'-yax kol-oo' …
    then climb-1pl to-DET-first milpa-PL
    Then we climbed to the first milpas

6. yan, t-u-chi' a'-noh b'eh-eh. …
    COP on-3Ppr-edge DET-big way-REL
    that are on the edge of the road.

7. A'-ka' k'och-o'on-eh,
    DET-when arrive-1pl-REL
    When we arrived,

8. k-in-wa'l-ik t-in-wet'ok-eh: ,
    INC-1sg-say-PPM to-1sgPpr-friend-TOP
    I say to my friend:

9. "Ko'ox ki-wutz-kin-t-eh ki-k'aak',
    HORT 1pl-good-CAUS-TRAN-SPM 1plPpr-fire
    "Let's fix our light

10. ti'a'al ka' ki-tich'=k'ak'-t-eh
    SUB SUB 1pl-illuminate-TRAN-SPM
    so that we can illuminate

11. a'-kol he'-la'-eh." …
    DET-milpa OST-PROX-TOP
    this milpa."

12. I layti' k-u-ya'(a)l-ik ten-eh:
    and 3Ipr INC-3-say-PPM 1sgIOpr-TOP
    And he says to me:

13. "Ma'lo'." …
    fine
    "Fine."

14. "Tz'-ah tulakal [a'-…] a'-bateriia ma'lo', t-a-fook-eh …
    give/IMP all [DET-] DET-battery good in-2Ppr-flashlight-TOP
    "Put all the good batteries in your flashlight

15. ii … yok' u-sas-i(l)-tal [u-,] u-yich a'-k'aak'-eh." …
    and SUB 3-bright-POS-INCHOAT [3Ppr-] 3Ppr-eye DET-light-TOP
    (and) so that the light's bulb is bright."

16. I layt(i') a'-lo'
    and 3Ipr DET-DIST
    And it's that (place)

17. näk-l-ah-o'on yok' hun p'e che' …
    sit-POSIT-DIST-1pl over one INAM log
    we sat on a log

18. in-wutz-kin-t-eh in-k'aak'-eh. …
    1sg-good-CAUS-TRAN-SPM 1sgPpr-light-TOP
    for me to fix my light.

19. Ka' ti-ki-wu'y-ah-eh,
    then COM-1pl-hear-DPM-REL
    Then we heard it,

20. wak'-ih, u-hum, hun p'e tz'on, ich a'-kol
    explode-3sg 3Ppr-sound one INAM gun in DET-milpa
    the sound of a gun exploded in the milpa

21. tu'ux, b'el ki-ka'a kuch-ih
    where go 1pl-go before-3sg
    where we were going before

22. ki-[,]-tich'=k'ak'-t-eh in-to'on-eh. …
    1pl-illuminate-TRAN-SPM EMP-1plIpr-REL
    to illuminate it ourselves.

23. Ih k-in-wa'al-ik ti'ih-eh: …
    and INC-1sg-say-PPM 3IOpr-TOP
    And I say to him:

24. "Ma' tan-ki-b'el ki-wil-a' mix b'a'al-i'ih,
    NEG DUR-1pl-go 1pl-see-SPM NEG thing-SCOPE
    "We aren't going to see anything

25. tumen yah … yan mak
    because already COP person
    because there are already people

26. tal-ih taan-il to'on. ….
    come-3sg front-POS 1plIOpr
    that came in front of us.

27. I b'a-lah,
    and TEMP-PROX
    And now

28. ko'ox, tak ka'nal. …
HORT up to top
let's go up to the top.

29. I t-a'-[,]-b'eh-eh,
and on-DET-way-TOP
And on the road

30. yan u-laak' kol
COP 3Ppr-other milpa
there is another milpa

31. in-k'a'ool. …
1sg-know
I know.

32. Uch-ak, patal-ki-kil-ik, b'a'al=che'-i'ih." …
happen-IRREAL ABIL-1pl-see-PPM animal-LOC
Perhaps we can see animals there."

33. I ka' nak'-o'on. …
and then climb-1pl
And then we climbed.

34. Ok-o'on t-a'-kol-eh
enter-1pl to-DET-milpa-TOP
We entered the milpa,

35. [ka' kap-o'on] ka' kap-een in-tich'=k'ak'-t-eh. …
[then begin-1pl] then begin-1sg 1sg-illuminate-TRAN-SPM
then I began to illuminate it.

36. Mix ba'al ti-ki-wil-ah. …
NEG thing COM-1pl-see-DPM
We saw nothing.

37. In-ten-eh yan in-b'en-il
EMP-1sgIpr-TOP COP 1sgPpr-path-POS
Me, I have my path

38. [in- in-,] in-heb-m-ah,
[1sg- 1sg-] 1sg-clear-PERF-DPM
that I have cleared

39. tu'ux k-in-[…]-hok'-ol …
where INC-1sg-leave-INTRAN
where I go out

40. tu'ux yan a'-[,]-muknal a'-[,]-kim-en-oo' uch=ben-oo',
where COP DET-grave DET-die-NOM-PL old-PL
where there are the graves of the ancient dead

41. tu'ux k-in-känän-t-ik-eh. …
    where INC-1sg-guard-TRAN-PPM-REL
    where I guard it.

42. Ka' k'och-o'on-eh …
    when arrive-1pl-TOP
    When we arrived,

43. komo han-il tulakal u-b'aak' a'-witz-oo'-eh,
    as clear-POS all 3Ppr-perimeter DET-hill-PL-TOP,
    as all of the perimeter of the mounds is clear,

44. ka' kap-een in-tich'=k'ak'-t-eh tulakal
    then begin-1sg 1sg-illuminate-TRAN-SPM all
    then I began to illuminate it all

45. a'-tu'ux han-il-eh,
    DET-where clear-POS-REL
    around where it is clear,

46. a'-ka' t-in-wil-ah-eh,
    DET-when COM-1sg-see-DPM-TOP
    when I saw it,

47. te', chil-a'an hun tuul keeh-i'ih. …
    LOC lie-PART one ANIM deer-SCOPE
    there was lying a deer.

48. Ii, in-ten-eh
    and EMP-1sgIpr-TOP
    And I,

49. t-in-t'an-eh wa b'alum. …
    in-1sgPpr-thought-TOP COND jaguar
    I thought it might be a jaguar.

50. Ma' t-in-wil-ik ma'lo',
    NEG DUR-1sg-see-PPM well
    I'm not seeing it well

51. komo chen u-yich
    since only 3Ppr-eye
    since it's only its eyes

52. a'-[,]-k-in-[,]-tich'=k'ak'-t-ik-eh. …
    DET-INC-1sg-illuminate-TRAN-PPM-REL
    that I am lighting.

53. I in-to'on-eh
    and EMP-1plIpr-TOP
    And as for us,

54. nak'-a'an-o'on t-u-ni' a'-witz-eh.
climb-PART-1pl at-3Ppr-top DET-hill-TOP
we were up at the top of the hill,

55. yok' a'-witz-eh. ...
over DET-hill-TOP
on top of the hill.

56. I ka' t-in-wa'al-ah t-in-wet'ok-eh:
and then COM-1sg-say-DPM to-1sgPpr-friend-TOP
And then I said to my companion:

57. "[Ma' a-b'el a-men] Ma' a-b'el ti t'an,
[Neg 2-go 2-do] NEG 2-go SUB speak
"Don't go speaking,

58. a'-lah keeh." ...
DET-PROX deer
this is a deer."

59. Ka' kap-een [in-...]
then begin-1sg [1sg-]
Then I began,

60. t-in-ch'a'-ah a'-tz'on-eh ...
COM-1sg-grab-DPM DET-gun-TOP
I grabbed the gun,

61. ka'[,] t-in-[,]-tz'on-ah. ...
then COM-1sg-shoot-DPM
then I shot it.

62. Ii a'-b'a'ax uch-ih to'on-eh,
and DET-thing happen-3sg 1plIOpr-REL
And the thing that happened to us

63. kee u-b'a'al in-tz'on-eh
SUB 3Ppr-bullet 1sgPpr-gun-TOP
is that the bullet of my gun

64. ma' wak'-ih. ...
NEG explode-3sg
didn't explode.

65. Ka' p'eel u-b'a'al [t-in-,] t-in-tz'ah ich-il,
two INAM 3Ppr-bullet [COM-1sg-] COM-1sg-put/DPM in-POS
Two bullets I put inside

66. i ma' wak'-ih t-u-ka' p'el-il. ...
and NEG explode-3sg in-3Ppr-two INAM-POS
and they didn't fire, the two.

67. I layt(i') a'-lo'
     and 3Ipr DET-DIST
     And it is this

68. [k-in-wa'al-ik] k-in-wa'al-ik ti'ih-eh:
     [INC-1sg-say-PPM] INC-1sg-say-PPM 3IOpr-REL
     I say to him:

69. "Man-es ten [a'-...] a'-riifle
     pass-CAUS/IMP 1sgIOpr [DET-] DET-rifle
     "Pass me the rifle

70. k-a-man-s-ik-eh,
     INC-2-pass-CAUS-PPM-REL
     that you are carrying

71. yok' in-wil-ik
     SUB 1sg-see-PPM
     for me to see

72. wa k-in-tz'on-ik." ,
     COND INC-1sg-shoot-PPM
     if I can shoot it."

73. T-u-man-s-ah ten. ...
     COM-3-pass-CAUS-DPM 1sgIOpr
     He passed it to me.

74. I a'-ka' t-u-man-s-ah ten-eh,
     and DET-when COM-3-pass-CAUS-DPM 1sgIOpr-TOP
     And when he passed it to me,

75. a'-keeh-eh wak'-ih u-siit'. ...
     DET-deer-TOP explode-3sg 3Ppr-jump
     the deer, it lept.

76. Ma' pat-ah-ih in-tz'on-ik,
     NEG ABIL-DIST-3sg 1sg-shoot-PPM
     I couldn't shoot it

77. i b'in-ih. ...
     and go-3sg
     and it went.

78. I to'on-eh
     and 1plIpr-TOP
     And we,

79. ka' tal-o'on. ,
     then come-1pl
     then we came (back).

80. Yaa … ti-ki-wil-ah
    already COM-1pl-see-DPM
    We already saw

81. ke ma' pat-ah-ih ki-käx-t-ik mix b'a'al. …
    SUB NEG ABIL-DIST-3sg 1pl-find-TRAN-PPM NEG thing
    that we couldn't find anything.

82. B'in-o'on kuch-ih [et-e …] et-e swerte
    go-1pl before-3sg [with-POS] with-POS luck
    We were going with luck

83. pero [ma' ti-ki- …] ma' ti-ki-woo(1)-t-ah
    but [NEG COM-1pl-] NEG COM-1pl-know-TRAN-DPM
    but we didn't know

84. ki-ta-s-ik,
    1pl-come-CAUS-PPM
    how to bring it in,

85. porke a'-b'a'al=che'-eh
    because DET-animal-TOP
    because the animal

86. b'in-i(h) to'on.
    go-3sg 1plIOpr
    went from us.

II. FOLKTALES AND LORE

12. A Man and a Jaguar

Told by Julian Tesucún on September 20, 1979

1. He'e-la' k-im-b'el in-tzikb'al-t-e(h) tech-eh,
    OST-PROX INC-1sg-go 1sg-tell-TRAN-SPM 2sgIOpr-REL
    This that I am going to tell you

2. u-tzikb'al-il hun tuul winik,
    3Ppr-talk-POS one ANIM man
    is the story of a man

3. yet-el hun tuul b'alum. …
    3Ppr/with-POS one ANIM jaguar
    and a jaguar.

4. Hach uch-i(h) tun b'in-eh,
    very happen-3sg then REPORT-TOP
    Long ago then, they say,

5. haal b'in hum p'e noh kah-eh,
    edge REPORT one INAM big town-TOP
    at the edge of a big town, they say,

6. käh-a'an b'in hun tuul winik,
    live-PART REPORT one ANIM man
    lived a man

7. yet-el hun tuul u-yätan. …
    3Ppr/with-POS one ANIM 3Ppr-wife
    with his wife.

8. Sas-ah-i(h) ka(') hum p'eel u-k'in-il-e'
    clear-DIST-3sg world one INAM 3Ppr-day-POS-TOP
    One day dawned

9. ka' t-u-ya'l-ah u-yätan ti'ih-eh:
    then COM-3-say-DPM 3Ppr-wife 3IOpr-TOP
    and his wife said to him:

10. "Ma'an ki-si'." …
    NEG/COP 1plPpr-firewood
    "We don't have firewood."

11. "Ma(')alo' …
    fine
    "Fine,

12. samal im-b'el in-tal-es si'." …
    tomorrow 1sg-go 1sg-come-CAUS/SPM firewood
    tomorrow I'm going to bring firewood."

13. Ka' sas-ah-ih ka'-eh,
    then clear-DIST-3sg world-TOP
    Then it dawned,

14. t-u-laak' k'in-il-eh
    on-3Ppr-other day-POS-TOP
    the next day,

15. ho'm-ih u-han-al-oo'. …
    TERM-3sg 3-eat-INTRAN-PL
    they finished eating.

16. Ka', t-u-mäch(-ah) u-b'aat …
    then COM-3-grab-DPM 3Ppr-ax
    Then he grabbed his ax,

17. t-u-mäch(-ah) u-hool,
    COM-3-grab(-DIST) 3Ppr-bag
    he grabbed his bag,

18. t-u-mäch(-ah) u-maskab',
    COM-3-grab(-DPM) 3Ppr-machete
    he grabbed his machete,

19. ka' b'in-ih. …
    then go-3sg
    then he went.

20. Ka' k'och-ih-eh,
    when arrive-3sg-TOP
    When he arrived,

21. b'ay hun awat b'in t-a(')-haal kah-eh,
    like one shout REPORT from-DET-edge town-TOP
    like at a shout's distance from the town, they say,

22. ka' ok-ih …
    then enter-3sg
    then he entered,

23. haal b'eh …
    edge road
    at the side of the road,

24. ka' t-u-käxän-t-ah hum p'e che'. …
    then COM-3-seek-TRAN-DPM one INAM tree
    and he looked for a tree.

25. Ka' t-u-ya'l-ah:
    then COM-3-say-DPM
    Then he said:

26. "'A'-la' ma'lo', tikin …
    DET-PROX good dry
    "This is good, dry,

27. hach t-u-p'is,
    very at-3Ppr-measure,
    a very good size,

28. hun tuul meek' u-chun." ,
    one ANIM armful 3Ppr-trunk
    its trunk is an armful."

29. Ka' hop'-i(h) u-ch'äk-ä'. …
    then begin-3sg 3-cut-SPM
    Then he began to cut it.

30. Ka' lub'(-ih) ah tikin che'-eh. …
    then fall(-3sg) MASC dry tree-TOP
    Then the dry tree fell.

31. Ka' t-u-p'is-ah hun yuul-(i')ih. …
    then COM-3-measure-DPM one piece-PARTIT
    Then he measured a piece of it.

32. Ka' hop'-(ih)-u-pa'-ik.
    then begin-(3sg)-3-split-PPM
    Then he began to split it.

33. Ka' t-u-ch'äk-ah
    then COM-3-cut-DPM
    Then he cut it,

34. t-u-pa'-ah.
    COM-3-split-DPM
    he split it.

35. Tan-u-pa'-ik u-si'-eh. …
    DUR-3-split-PPM 3Ppr-firewood-TOP
    He was splitting wood.

36. Natz'-il b'in-eh
    close-POS REPORT-TOP
    Nearby, they say,

37. tun-man hun tu nohoch b'alum …
    DUR/3-pass one ANIM big jaguar
    a big jaguar was passing,

38. (u-)käxän-t-eh u-han-al. …
    (3-)seek-TRAN-SPM 3Ppr-eat-NOM
    looking for its food.

39. Tz'o'k-i(h) u-man ka' p'eel k'in,
    TERM-3sg 3-pass two INAM day
    Two days had passed,

40. t-u-ox p'e k'in ma' han-ak. …
    on-3Ppr-three INAM day NEG eat-IRREAL
    it was into the third day that it hadn't eaten.

41. Ka' natz'-i(h) [a'-,] a'-nohoch b'alum-eh,
    then close-3sg [DET-] DET-big jaguar-TOP
    Then the big jaguar came close

42. kan a'-winik-eh. …
    with DET-man-TOP
    to the man.

43. Ka' hop'-i(h) u-cha'an-t-eh. …
    then begin-3sg 3-watch-TRAN-SPM
    Then it began to watch him.

44. Ka' t-u-ya'al-ah b'in-eh: ,
    Then COM-3-say-DPM REPORT-TOP
    Then it said, they say:

45. "B'a-lah si,
    TEMP-PROX yes
    "Now, yes,

46. b'a-lah in-ka'a ti han-al,
    TEMP-PROX 1sg-go SUB eat-INTRAN
    now I am going to eat,

47. tumen wi'ih-en." …
    because hungry-1sg
    because I am hungry."

48. Ka' ti(i), näk-l-ah-ih u-cha'an-t-eh. …
    then SUB sit-POSIT-DIST-3sg 3-watch-TRAN-SPM
    Then it sat to watch him.

49. Tun-letz'-t-ik u-taan u-k'ab',
    DUR/3-lick-TRAN-PPM 3Ppr-sole 3Ppr-arm
    It is licking the soles of its paws,

50. tun-letz'-t-ik u-me'ex,
    DUR/3-lick-TRAN-PPM 3Ppr-whiskers
    it is licking its whiskers,

51. tun-[pe]-pek-s-ik u-neh. …
    DUR-3-move-CAUS-PPM 3Ppr-tail
    it is moving its tail.

52. Ka' t-u-ya'al-a(h) a'-b'alum-eh: …
    then COM-3-say-DPM DET-jaguar-TOP
    Then the jaguar said:

53. "[k] in-ka'a in-t'än-ä'." ,
    1sg-go 1sg-speak-SPM
    "I am going to speak."

54. Ka' t-u-t'än-ah,
    then COM-3-speak-DPM
    Then it spoke,

55. u-k'a'ool-t-eh u-yil-a' b'a'ax-i'ih. …
    3-know-TRAN-SPM 3-see-SPM what-SCOPE
    to know him, to see what he was.

56. Ka' t-u-yil-ah,
    then COM-3-see-DPM
    And it saw him,

57. layt(i') a'-winik-eh. …
    3Ipr DET-man-TOP
    the man.

58. "In-tech nohoch winik?"
    EMP-2sgIpr great man
    "You are a great man?"

59. "In-ten." ,
    EMP-1sgIpr
    "I am."

60. "B'a'ax k-a-men-t-ik?"
    what INC-2-do-TRAN-PPM
    "What are you doing?"

61. "Tan-in-si'. …
    DUR-1sg-cut firewood
    "I am cutting firewood.

62. In-tech nohoch b'alum?"
    EMP-2sgIpr big jaguar
    You are a big jaguar?"

63. "In-ten." ,
    EMP-1sgIpr
    "I am."

64. "B'a'ax k-a-man a-käx-t-eh wa'yeh." ,
    what INC-2-pass 2-seek-TRAN-SPM here
    "What are you walking to look for here?"

65. "Tan-in-man in-käx-t-(e)h in-han-al. …
DUR-1sg-pass 1sg-seek-TRAN-SPM 1sgPpr-eat-NOM
"I am walking to look for my food.

66. Ma' han-ak-en. …
NEG eat-IRREAL-1sg
I haven't eaten.

67. Tz'o'k-u-man ka' p'eel k'in
TERM-3-pass two INAM day
Two days already passed,

68. t-u-ox p'e k'in k-u-b'el
in-3Ppr-three INAM day INC-3-go
it's going into the third day

69. ma' han-ak-en. …
NEG eat-IRREAL-1sg
I haven't eaten.

70. Ma' tan-ta-s-ik han-al?"
NEG DUR/2-come-CAUS-PPM eat-NOM
You aren't bringing food?"

71. "Ma'." …
NEG
"No."

72. "Pwes, [eeh,] yan-in-han-t-ik-ech …
well OBLIG-1sg-eat-TRAN-PPM-2sg
"Well, I have to eat you,

73. tumen wi'ih-en." …
because hungry-1sg
because I am hungry."

74. "Ma' a-b'el a-han-t-een" ,
NEG 2-go 2-eat-TRAN-1sg
"You aren't going to eat me,"

75. ki a'-winik ti'ih-eh. …
say/3sg DET-man 3IOpr-TOP
the man said to it.

76. "Ten-e(h) yan in-wakax, …
1sgIpr-TOP COP 1sgPpr-cattle
"Me, I have cattle,

77. natz' haal kah. ,
near edge town
near the edge of town.

78. K-in-si'-ik tech hun tuul-(i')ih. …
     INC-1sg-donate-PPM 2sgIOpr one ANIM-PARTIT
     I'll give you one of them.

79. Wa k-a-wan-t-ik-en im-pa'-a'
     COND INC-2-help-TRAN-PPM-1sg 1sg-split-SPM
     If you help me split

     in-si'-eh,
     1sgPpr-firewood-TOP
     my firewood,

80. ki-seeb'-b'el." …
     INC/1pl-quick-go
     we'll go soon."

81. "Ma'alo',"
     fine
     "Fine,"

82. ki a'-nohoch b'alum ti'ih-eh. …
     say/3sg DET-big jaguar 3IOpr-TOP
     the great jaguar said to him.

83. Ka' t-u-mäch-a(h) a'-winik-eh
     then COM-3-grab-DPM DET-man-TOP
     Then the man grabbed it

84. ka' t-u-men-t-ah hum p'eel ch'eeh. …
     then COM-3-make-TRAN-DPM one INAM wedge
     and he made a wedge.

85. Ka' t-u-[,]-pol-t(-ah) u-ni'. …
     then COM-3-work-TRAN-(DPM) 3Ppr-tip
     Then he worked its point.

86. Ka' t-u-tz'äp(-ah) u-b'aat t-a'-che'-eh. …
     then COM-3-plant(-DPM) 3Ppr-ax in-DET-tree-TOP
     Then he planted the ax in the log.

87. Ka' hek'(-ih) a'-che'-eh
     then open(-3sg) DET-tree-TOP
     Then the log opened

88. ka' t-u-[,]-b'ut'-ah a'-ch'eeh-eh. …
     then COM-3-insert-DPM DET-wedge-TOP
     and he inserted the wedge.

89. Ka' t-u-ya'al-ah [t-a'-winik-eh] (t-a'-b'alum-eh):
     then COM-3-say-DPM [to-DET-man-TOP] (to-DET-jaguar-TOP)
     Then he said to the jaguar:

90. "Chok'-o' a-k'ab'-ih-eh,
    put in-SPM/IMP 2Ppr-hand-LOC?-TOP
    "Put in your paws,

91. t-u-ka' p'el-il. ...
    at-3Ppr-two INAM-POS
    the two.

92. K-in-b'äh-ik a'-ch'eeh-eh
    INC-1sg-insert-PPM DET-wedge-TOP
    When I insert the wedge

93. k-u-he(k)'-paal a'-che'-eh,
    INC-3-open-INTRAN DET-log-TOP
    and the log opens,

94. k-a-hek'-ik in-tech." ...
    INC-2-open-PPM EMP-2sgIpr
    you break it open."

95. "Ma'alo' "
    fine
    "Fine,"

96. ki a'-nohoch b'alum-eh
    say/3sg DET-big jaguar-TOP
    said the big jaguar

97. ka' t-u-chok'-ah ka' taach u-k'ab'-(i')ih. ...
    then COM-3-put in-DPM two CLASS 3Ppr-hand-LOC?
    and it put in its two paws.

98. Ka' tal(-ih) a'-winik-eh
    then come(-3sg) DET-man-TOP
    Then the man came

99. ka' t-u-b'oh=huts'-t(-ah) [inaudible] (a'-)ch'eeh a'-che'-eh,
    then COM-3-hit=part-TRAN(-DPM) (DET-)wedge DET-tree-TOP
    and hit apart the wedge of the tree,

100. tzel-a'an. ,
     aside-PART
     on the side.

101. Ka' hotz'(-ih) a'-ch'eeh-eh,
     then leave(-3sg) DET-wedge-TOP
     Then the wedge came out,

102. ka' ti nat'(-ih) u-k'ab' a'-b'alum-eh. ...
     then SUB pinch(-3sg) 3Ppr-hand DET-jaguar-TOP
     and the jaguar's paws were pinched.

103. Ka' hop'-ih ti awat a'-b'alum-eh. …
      Then begin-3sg SUB roar DET-jaguar-TOP
      Then the jaguar began to roar.

104. T-u-ya'al-a(h) t-a'-winik-eh
      COM-3-say-DPM to-DET-man-TOP
      It said to the man

105. ka' hotz'-b'-ok u-k'ab' …
      SUB take out-PAS-IRREAL 3Ppr-hand
      that its paws should be freed,

106. nat'-al. …
      pinch-PART
      they were stuck.

107. Ka' t-u-ya'l(-ah) a'-winik ti'ih-eh: …
      then COM-3-say(-DPM) DET-man 3IOpr-TOP
      Then the man told him:

108. [eeh,] "Pak'-t-eh!" ki … [stumble]
              wait-TRAN-SPM/IMP say/3sg
      "Wait!" he said.

109. "Pak'-t-eh hum p'iit,
      wait-TRAN-SPM/IMP one bit
      "Wait a minute!"

110. Ka', t-u-[,]-hil-t(-ah) u-maskab'-eh
      then COM-3-pull-TRAN(-DPM) 3Ppr-machete-TOP
      Then he pulled out his machete,

111. ka' t-u-ch'äk-ah hun chaach u-yal che' …
      then COM-3-cut-DPM one handful 3Ppr-child? tree
      then he cut a handful of branches,

112. ka' hop'-i(h) u-täl-ik a'-nohoch b'alum-eh …
      then begin-3sg 3-beat-PPM DET-big jaguar-TOP
      and he began to beat the big jaguar,

113. [aasta ?] tak tu'ux t-u-nak-s(-ah) u-yool,
      [until] till where COM-3-tire-CAUS(-DPM) 3Ppr-body
      until he tired himself,

114. a'-winik-eh,
      DET-man-SPM
      the man,

115. u-täl-ä'.
      3-hit-SPM
      of beating it.

116. Ka' t-u-yil-ah-eh,
     then COM-3-see-DPM-TOP
     Then he saw it,

117. tun-hok'-ol u-k'ik'-el t-u-pach,
     DUR/3-leave-INTRAN 3Ppr-blood-POS from-3Ppr-back
     the blood is coming out of its back

118. tu'ux t-u-lah-toch-ah,
     where COM-3-all-hide?-DPM
     where he thoroughly hided it,

119. tu'ux t-u-täl-ah. ...
     where COM-3-beat-DPM
     where he beat it.

120. Ka' t-u-ya'al-ah ti'ih-eh:
     Then COM-3-say-DPM 3IOpr-TOP
     Then it said to him:

121. "Hotz'(-o') in-k'ab'!" ,
     take out(-SPM/IMP) 1sgPpr-hand
     "Free my paws!"

122. "Ma'alo', (in-)k(a'a)-in-hotz'-o' tech." ...
     fine (1sg-)go-1sg-take out-SPM 2sgIOpr
     "Fine, I'm going to take them out for you."

123. Ka' t-u-mäch(-ah) u-maskab' [a'-,] a'-winik-eh
     then COM-3-grab(-DPM) 3Ppr-machete [DET-] DET-man-TOP
     Then the man grabbed his machete

124. ka' hop'-i(h) u-[,]-lah-käx-t(-eh) u-mo'ok
     then begin-3sg 3-all-seek-TRAN-(SPM) 3Ppr-knot
     and he began to seek all of the knuckles (?)

125. u-yaal u-k'ab' a'-b'alum-eh,
     3Ppr-child 3Ppr-hand DET-jaguar-TOP
     of the fingers of the jaguar's paws,

126. ka' t-u-lah-xot'-ah u-yaal u-kab' a'-b'alum-eh
     then COM-3-all-cut-DPM 3Ppr-child 3Ppr-hand DET-jaguar-TOP
     and he cut off all of the fingers of the jaguar's paws

127. ka' p'at-i(h) u-yaal u-k'ab' a'-b'alum-eh,
     then remain-3sg 3Ppr-child 3Ppr-hand DET-jaguar-TOP
     and the fingers of the jaguar's paws remained,

128. nat'-al t-a'-che'. ...
     stick-PART in-DET-log
     stuck in the log.

129. Ka' p'at-ih chen u-noh [, noh] taan u-k'ab'. …
     then remain-3sg only 3Ppr-big [big] sole 3Ppr-hand
     Then only the big sole of its paw remained.

130. Ka' hok'-i(h) [stumble] a'-b'alum-eh
     then leave-3sg DET-jaguar-TOP
     Then the jaguar left,

131. ka' b'in-ih. …
     then go-3sg
     then it went.

132. Ka' t-u-kuch(-ah) u-si' a'-nohoch winik-eh
     then COM-3-load(-DPM) 3Ppr-firewood DET-great man-TOP
     Then the great man loaded his firewood

133. ka' b'in-i(h) t-u-yotoch. …
     then go-3sg to-3Ppr-home
     and he went home.

134. Mentäk-eh b'ay-lo' p'at-ik-il u-pach a'-b'alum-eh,
     therefore-TOP thus-DIST remain-?-? 3Ppr-back DET-jaguar-TOP
     Therefore, thus the jaguar's back remained,

135. we'we'el, säk i b'ox. …
     spotted white and black
     spotted white and black.

136. Layt(i') a'-tu'ux t-u-yoox-t(-ah) u-b'ah-eh,
     3Ipr DET-where COM-3-dry-TRAN(-DPM) 3Ppr-REFL-TOP
     It is where it dried itself

137. ka' lub'(-ih) u-yoox-il-eh
     then fall(-3sg) 3Ppr-dry-POS-TOP
     and when the scab (dry part) fell,

138. ka' p'at-ih säk. …
     then remain-3sg white
     then it stayed white.

139. B'ay-lo' ich u-p'at-äl piintoh-il a'-b'alum.
     like-DIST in 3-remain-INTRAN spotted-POS DET-jaguar
     Thus the jaguar remained spotted.

13. Two Brothers and a Beast

Told by Fernando Tesucún on October 1, 1979

1. Uch-ih …
   happen-3sg
   Long ago,

2. yan-ah-ih b'in ka' tu(ul) winik …
   COP-DIST-3sg REPORT two ANIM man
   there were, they say, two men

3. waye' t-a'-kah-eh. …
   here in-DET-town-TOP
   here in the town.

4. K'och-ih hun p'e k'in-eh
   arrive-3sg one INAM day-TOP
   A day came

5. ka' b'in-oo' ti tz'on. …
   when go-PL SUB shoot
   when they went to shoot.

6. B'in-oo', naach waye',
   go-PL far here
   They went far from here

7. ti hum p'e paay,
   to one INAM beach
   to a beach

8. u-k'ab'a', Hob'on Pich. …
   3Ppr-name hollow pich tree
   that's name is Jobon Pich.

9. U-k'ab'a' he'-lo'-eh …
   3Ppr-name OST-DIST-TOP
   That name

10. tz'a-b'-ih ti'ih hach uch-ih,
    give-PAS-3sg 3IOpr very happen-3sg
    was given to it very long ago

11. tumen, t-u[uu,]-chi' a'[,]-ha'-eh …
    because at-3Ppr-edge DET-water-TOP
    because at the edge of the water (lake)

12. yan b'in hum p'e noh che'. …
    COP REPORT one INAM big tree
    there was, they say, a big tree.

13. A'-che' he'-lo'-eh yan u-hol, hob'on. …
    DET-tree OST-DIST-TOP COP 3Ppr-hole hollow
    That tree has a hole, hollow.

14. I men yan u-hol-eh …
    and because COP 3Ppr-hole-TOP
    And it's because it had a hollow,

15. ka' tz'a-b'-ih u-kab'a'-t-eh Hob'on Pich. ...
    SUB give-PAS-3sg 3-name-TRAN-SPM hollow pich tree
    that it was named "Hollow *Pich*."

16. Tumen pich-eh,
    because pich-TOP
    Because *pich*,

17. layti' u-k'ab'a' a'-che'-eh. ...
    3Ipr 3Ppr-name DET-tree-TOP
    that is the name of the tree.

18. Ii ka' k'och-oo'-eh
    and when arrive-PL-TOP
    And when they arrived

19. ka' nak'-oo'. ...
    then climb-PL
    then they climbed.

20. T-u-xi'ma-t-ah-oo' hun luub'. ...
    COM-3-walk-TRAN-DPM-PL one league
    They walked one league.

21. Ka' k'och-oo'
    then arrive-PL
    Then they arrived

22. tu'ux k-u-b'el-oo' ti wen-el-eh,
    where INC-3-go-PL SUB sleep-INTRAN-REL
    where they were going to sleep,

23. ka' t-u-men-t-ah-oo' u-mo'nok otoch. ...
    then COM-3-make-TRAN-DPM-PL 3Ppr-small home
    then they made their little home.

24. I hun tuul ich a'-suku'un-oo'-eh
    and one ANIM of DET-older brother-PL-TOP
    And one of the brothers

25. k-u-ya'al-ik t-u-yitz'in-eh: ...
    INC-3-say-PPM to-3Ppr-little brother-TOP
    says to his little brother:

26. "T'äb-ä' a'-k'aak'-eh ...
    light-SPM/IMP DET-fire-TOP
    "Light the fire,

27. i ten-eh b'el in-ka'a in-ch'äk-ä' tz'eek si'. ...
    and 1sgIpr-TOP go 1sg-go 1sg-cut-SPM little firewood
    and I'm going to go cut a little firewood.

28. U-ho'm-ol ki-b'et-ik ki-wuk'-ul-eh,
    3-end-INTRAN 1pl-make-PPM 1plPpr-drink-NOM-TOP
    After we make our drink,

29. [ki-b'el kii...] ki-b'el ti xi'mal,
    [1pl-go 1pl?] 1pl-go SUB walk
    we're going to walk

30. ki-kil-a'
    1pl-see-SPM
    to see

31. a'-b'a'ax ki-wil-ik ...
    DET-what INC/1pl-see-PPM
    what we can see

32. ich a'-k'aax-eh." ...
    in DET-forest-TOP
    in the forest."

33. Ka' b'in-oo'. ...
    then go-PL
    Then they went.

34. Ka' ho'm-ih u-yuk'-ik-oo' u-yuk'-ul-eh, ...
    when TERM-3sg 3-drink-PPM-PL 3Ppr-drink-NOM-TOP
    When they finished drinking their drink,

35. ka' t-u-ch'a'-ah-oo' u-tz'on-oo'-eh
    then COM-3-take-DPM-PL 3Ppr-gun-PL-TOP
    then they took their guns

36. ka' b'in-oo'. ...
    then go-PL
    and they went.

37. Ma' yaab' u-xi'ma-t-oo',
    NEG much 3-walk-TRAN-PL
    They didn't walk much

38. ka' t-u-yu'b'-ah-oo'
    then COM-3-hear-DPM-PL
    when they heard

    u-hum u-lik'-il a'[,]-k'ämb'äl-eh. ...
    3Ppr-sound 3-rise-INTRAN DET-pheasant-TOP
    the sound of the pheasant taking flight.

39. Ka' kap-oo' ti tz'on. ...
    then begin-PL SUB shoot
    Then they began to shoot.

40. Ka' kap-oo' ti tz'on-eh ...
     then begin-PL SUB-shoot-TOP
     Then they began to shoot,

41. i layti'-oo'-eh hach ki' u-yool-oo',
     and 3Ipr-PL-TOP very good 3Ppr-spirit-PL
     and them, their spirits were very high

42. tumen, yaab' ch'iich' k-u-yil-ik-oo'. ,
     because many bird INC-3-see-PPM-PL
     because they saw a lot of birds.

43. He-b'ix u-tz'on-ik-oo'-eh,
     OST-how 3-shoot-PPM-PL-TOP
     Just as they shot them,

44. he-b'ix u-lub'-ul a'[,]-b'a'al=che'-oo',
     OST-how 3-fall-INTRAN DET-animal-PL
     thus the animals fell

45. t-u-yaam a'-witz-eh. ...
     in-3Ppr-clearing DET-hill-TOP
     in the clearing of the hill.

46. Ka' ho'm-ih u-tz'on-oo'-eh,
     when TERM-3sg 3-shoot-PL-TOP
     When they finished shooting,

47. ka' t-u-ya'al-ah [a'-,] a'-suku'un-tzil t-u-yitz'in-eh: ,
     then COM-3-say-DPM DET-older bro.-REV to-3Ppr-younger bro.-TOP
     then the older brother said to his younger brother:

48. "Ko'ox ki-mol-oo' a'-ki-ch'iich'-eh. ,
     HORT 1pl-gather-SPM/PL DET-1plPpr-bird-TOP
     "Let's gather our birds.

49. Ya, tan-u-yok-ol k'in. ...
     already DUR-3-enter-INTRAN sun
     The sun is already setting.

50. A'-k'in-eh ya tan-u-b'el ...
     DET-sun-TOP already DUR-3-go
     The sun is already going

51. i wa ma' tan-ki-aseb'il-kun-t-ik
     and COND NEG DUR-1pl-hurry-CAUS-TRAN-PPM
     and if we don't hurry

     ki-b'ah-eh,
     1plPpr-REFL-TOP
     ourselves,

52. he'-u-yok-ol to'on k'in ti b'eh-eh." ...
    ASSUR-3-enter-INTRAN 1pIIOpr sun on road-TOP
    it will set on us on the road."

53. Ka' b'in-oo'. ,
    then go-PL
    Then they went.

54. Layti' k-u-yem-el-oo' ...
    3Ipr INC-3-descend-INTRAN-PL
    They descend

55. u-mäch-ä'-oo' [a'-,]
    3-grab-SPM-PL
    to get

56. a'-yax ch'iich' t-u-tz'on-ah-oo'-eh,
    DET-first bird COM-3-shoot-DPM-PL-REL
    the first bird that they shot,

57. chen a'-ka' t-u-yu'b'-ah-oo'-eh,
    only DET-when COM-3-hear-DPM-PL-TOP
    only then they heard it,

58. u-hum u-[,]-koh a'-b'a'al=che'
    3Ppr-sound 3Ppr-tooth DET-animal
    the sound of the teeth of the animal

59. tu'ux tan-u-chach-t-ik a'-u-han-al-eh. ...
    where DUR-3-chew-TRAN-PPM DET-3Ppr-eat-NOM-REL
    where it was chewing its food.

60. Ka' wa'-l-ah-oo'-eh
    when stand-POSIT-DIST-PL-TOP
    When they stood,

61. ka' t-u-yil-ah-oo',
    then COM-3-see-DPM-PL
    then they saw

62. b'a'ax a'-b'a'al=che'
    what DET-animal
    what the animal was

63. k-u[u,]-hum u-han-al-eh. ...
    INC-3-sound 3-eat-INTRAN-REL
    that was making noise eating.

64. K-u-yil-ik-oo'-eh hun tuul noxi' ah koh. ...
    INC-3-see-PPM-PL-TOP one ANIM big MASC lion.
    They saw a big lion.

65. A'-b'a'al=che'-eh …
    DET-animal-TOP
    The animal,

66. tulakal u-yich,
    all 3Ppr-face
    all of its face

67. ma' chik-a'an et-el u-tzo'otz-el. …
    NEG see-PART with-POS 3Ppr-hair-POS
    was not visible with its fur.

68. I ka' t-u-mäch-ah-oo'-eh …
    and when COM-3-grab-DPM-PL-TOP
    And when they grabbed onto it (a tree)

69. ka' nak'-oo'
    then climb-PL
    then they climbed

70. porke a'-b'a'al=che'-eh
    because DET-animal-TOP
    because the animal

    tan-u-han-t-ik [a'-,] a'-ch'iich'-eh,
    DUR-3-eat-TRAN-PPM [DET-] DET-bird-TOP
    was eating the bird

71. i tak-[u-,]u-pul-ik u-b'ah yok' a'-winik-oo'-eh. ,
    and DESID-[3-]3-throw-PPM 3Ppr-REFL over DET-man-PL-TOP
    and wanted to throw itself on top of the men.

72. Layti'-oo'-eh,
    3Ipr-PL-TOP
    As for them,

73. ma'=ta'ax u-yil-ik-oo' a'-b'a'al=che' he'-lo'. ,
    never 3-see-PPM-PL DET-animal OST-DIST
    they had never seen that animal.

74. Ma' u-k'a'ool-oo'. ,
    NEG 3-know-PL
    They didn't know it.

75. Ka' nak'-oo' t-u-ni' hum p'e che'. …
    then climb-PL to-3Ppr-tip one INAM tree
    Then they climbed to the top of a tree.

76. I a'-b'a'al=che'-eh
    and DET-animal-TOP
    And the animal,

77. a'-ka' ho'm-ih u-lah-han-t-ik a'-ch'iich'
     DET-when TERM-3sg 3-all-eat-TRAN-PPM DET-bird
     when it finished eating all of the birds

78. t-u-tz'on-m-ah-oo' layti'-oo'-eh,
     COM-3-shoot-PERF-DPM-PL 3Ipr-PL-REL
     that they themselves had shot,

79. ka' kap-ih ti siit'. …
     then begin-3sg SUB jump
     then it began to jump.

80. U-k'a't-ih kuch-ih u-han-t-oo a'-[,]-ka' tuul winik-oo'-eh. …
     3-want-PM? before-3sg 3-eat-TRAN-PL DET-two ANIM man-PL-TOP
     It wanted to eat the two men.

81. Men ka'nal yan-il-oo'-eh
     because high COP-POS?-PL-TOP
     Because they were high up

82. ma' t-u-chuk-ah-oo'. ,
     NEG COM-3-reach-DPM-PL
     it didn't reach them.

83. I layti'-oo'-eh,
     and 3Ipr-PL-TOP
     And them,

84. kil-u-wak'-äl u-siit' a'-b'a'al=che',
     when 3-explode-INTRAN 3Ppr-leap DET-animal
     when the animal made its leap,

85. layti'-oo'-eh
     3Ipr-PL-TOP
     them,

86. k-u-tz'on-ik-oo' ti ik'. …
     INC-3-shoot-PPM-PL in air
     they shot in the air.

87. Ka' lub'(-ih) a'-b'a'al=che'-eh,
     then fall(-3sg) DET-animal-TOP
     Then the animal fell,

88. ya kim-en. ,
     already die-NOM
     already dead.

89. Asta ka' t-u-yil-ah-oo'
     until when COM-3-see-DPM-PL
     Only when they saw

90. ke ya kim-en a'-b'a'al=che'
    SUB already die-NOM DET-animal
    that the animal was already dead,

91. ka' lik'-oo',
    then get up-PL
    then they got up

92. ka' em-oo' t-a'-che'-eh. ...
    then descend-PL from-DET-tree-TOP
    and descended from the tree.

93. I hun tuul [a'-,] a'-itz'in-tzil-eh,
    and one ANIM [DET-] DET-younger brother-REVER-TOP
    And one, the younger brother

94. k-u-ya'al-ik t-u-suku'un-eh: ,
    INC-3-say-PPM to-3Ppr-older brother
    says to his older brother:

95. "Ko'ox ki-sol-t-eh. ,
    HORT 1pl-skin-TRAN-SPM
    "Let's skin it.

96. Ki-b'is-ik [u-,] u-k'ewel-al." ...
    INC/1pl-go/CAUS-PPM [3Ppr-] 3Ppr-hide-POS?
    We'll take its hide."

97. Ka' kap-ih u-p'e'es-t-oo'. ,
    then begin-3sg 3-flay-TRAN-PL
    Then they began to flay it.

98. Ka' t-u-luk'-s-ah-oo' u-k'ewel-il a'-b'a'al=che'-eh. ,
    then COM-3-remove-CAUS-DPM-PL 3Ppr-hide-POS DET-animal-TOP
    Then they removed the hide of the animal.

99. Ka' t-u-ya'l-ah b'in hun tuul t-u-yet'ok-eh: ,
    then COM-3-say-DPM REPORT one ANIM to-3Ppr-companion-TOP
    Then one said to his companion:

100. "Yutzil wab'in a'-k'ewel-eh! ,
    beautiful EMP DET-hide-TOP
    "The hide is so beautiful!

101. Ko'ox ki-wil-a'
    HORT 1pl-see-SPM
    Let's see

102. wa chuk-a'an t-in-wok'-ol." ,
    COND fit-PART to-1sgPpr-over-POS
    if it fits over me."

103. Ka' ti xäk-l-ah-ih [a'-,]
     then SUB crouch-POSIT-DIST-3sg [DET-]
     Then (the younger brother) crouched

     a'-[i,]itz'in-tzil-eh,
     DET-younger bro.-REV-TOP

104. ka' t-u-wäl-ah a'-k'ewel t-u-pach-eh. ,
     then COM-3-stretch-DPM DET-hide on-3Ppr-back-TOP
     and he stretched the hide on his back.

105. Chen a'-ka' t-u-yil-ah-eh …
     only DET-when COM-3-see-DPM-TOP
     Only when he saw that

106. tak'-ih a'-k'ewel-eh
     stick-3sg DET-hide-TOP
     the hide stuck,

107. ya ma' pat-ah-ih u-läk-ik. ,
     already NEG ABIL-DIST-3sg 3-pull off-PPM
     already he couldn't pull it off.

108. I ka' sut-n-ah-ih, ya ti b'a'al=che'-i(l) xan. …
     and then turn-DETRAN-DIST-3sg already to animal-POS also
     And he already turned into an animal too.

109. Ii a'-suku'un-tzil-eh k-u-yil-ik
     and DET-older bro.-REV-TOP INC-3-see-PPM
     And the older brother sees

     u-yitz'in-eh
     3Ppr-younger bro.-TOP
     his little brother,

110. ya hun tuul noxi' ah koh. …
     already one ANIM big MASC lion
     he's already a big lion.

111. I k-u-ya'al-ik b'in ti'ih-eh:
     and INC-3-say-PPM REPORT 3IOpr-TOP
     And he says to him:

112. "Ay suku'un-eh
     EXCLAM older brother-TOP
     "Oh older brother,

113. b'a-he'-la'-eh xen. ,
     TEMP-OST-PROX-TOP go/IMP
     now go!

114. Wa ma' tan-a-b'el-eh …
     COND NEG DUR-2-go-TOP
     If you don't go . . .

115.   In-ten-eh hach wi'ih-en. ,
       EMP-1sgIpr-TOP very hungry-1sg
       I am very hungry.

116.   Ya tan-a-wil-ik ke ten-eh,
       already DUR-2-see-PPM SUB 1sgIpr-TOP
       You are aready seeing that I . . .

117.   A'al-eh ti' ki-na'
       say-SPM/IMP to 1plPpr-mother
       Tell our mother

118.   ke ten-e ma' tan-im-b'el
       SUB 1sgIpr-TOP NEG DUR-1sg-go
       that I'm not going

119.   ti sut
       SUB return
       to return

120.   ti k'och-ol
       to arrive-INTRAN
       to arrive

121.   ti ki-wotoch,
       SUB 1plPpr-house
       to our house

122.   tumen ten-eh ya sut-n-ah-een b'a'al=che'-il. ,
       because 1sgIpr-TOP already turn-DETRAN-DIST-1sg animal-POS
       because I have already turned into an animal.

123.   I xen! ,
       and go/IMP
       And go!

124.   Ma' a-wa'-tal! ,
       NEG 2-stand-POSIT
       Don't stand!

125.   Wa ma', tak in-tech k-im-b'el in-han-t-eech
       COND NEG even EMP-2sgIpr INC-1sg-go 1sg-eat-TRAN-2sg
       If not, even you, I am going to eat you

126.   tumen ten-eh,
       because 1sgIpr-TOP
       because me,

127.   ya hach wi'ih-en
       already very hungry-1sg
       I already am very hungry,

128. ya ma' t-in-muk'yah-t-ik in-näk',
     already NEG INC-1sg-control-TRAN-PPM 1sgPpr-stomach
     already I can't control my stomach

129. yet-el in-wi'ih-il." ,
     3Ppr/with-POS 1sgPpr-hungry-POS
     with my hunger."

130. Ka' t-u-yil-ah otzil u-suku'un-eh
     then COM-3-see-DPM poor 3Ppr-older brother-TOP
     When his older brother saw the wretch,

131. tan-u-yok'-ol-eh.
     DUR-3-cry-INTRAN-TOP
     he was crying.

132. Ka' t-u-kuch-ah [u-,] a'-u'-nok'
     then COM-3-load-DPM [3Ppr-] DET-3Ppr-bag
     Then he loaded on his back his bag

133. t-a'-tu'ux k-u-wen-el
     from-DET-where INC-3-sleep-INTRAN
     from where he sleeps

134. i u-tz'on-eh
     and 3Ppr-gun-TOP
     and his gun,

135. ka' em-ih tun-yalka'.
     then descend-3sg DUR/3-run
     then he went down running.

136. Mix hun tu ch'iich' t-u-ta-s-ah-oo'. ,
     NEG one ANIM bird COM-3-come-CAUS-DPM-PL
     He didn't bring even one bird.

137. I ka' k'och-ih u-suku'un,
     and when arrive-3sg 3Ppr-brother
     And when the older brother arrived,

138. chi' a'-ha'-eh,
     edge DET-water-TOP
     at the edge of the water,

139. ah koh-eh tun-hum u-yakan
     MASC lion-TOP DUR/3-sound 3Ppr-roar
     the lion, his roar was sounding,

140. tun-tal-el t-u-pach
     DUR/3-come-INTRAN at-3Ppr-back
     he was coming behind him,

141. tun-tal u-chuk-u'. ,
      DUR/3-come 3-reach-SPM
      he was coming to overtake him.

142. T-u-t'ut'-l-ah u-pach. …
      COM-3-follow-?-DPM 3Ppr-back
      He followed behind.

143. I a'-ka' k'och-ih a'-b'a'al=che' tak t-u-chi
      and DET-when arrive-3sg DET-animal till to-3Ppr-edge
      And when the animal arrived up to the edge

      a'-ha'-eh,
      DET-water-TOP
      of the water,

144. a'-[suk'un-,]-suku'un-tzil-eh,
      DET-[older bro.]-older brother-REV-TOP
      the older brother

145. t-u-tutz'-ah u-chem-eh
      COM-3-put out-DPM 3Ppr-canoe-TOP
      put out his canoe,

146. ka' kap-ih ti b'a'te',
      then begin-3sg SUB paddle
      then he began to paddle,

147. tun-b'a'te'. ,
      DUR/3-paddle
      he was paddling.

148. Ka' tal-ih,
      then come-3sg
      Then he came,

149. i tun-tal chumuk ha'-eh. ,
      and DUR/3-come middle water-TOP
      and he was coming in the middle of the lake.

150. A'-b'a'al=che' tun-tal tulakal t-u-haal ha'
      DET-animal DUR/3-come all on-3Ppr-shore water
      The animal was coming all along the shore of the lake,

151. tun-hum u-yawat. ,
      DUR/3-sound 3Ppr-roar
      his roar was sounding.

152. I k-u-ya'al-ik t-u-suku'un-eh:
      and INC-3-say-PPM to-3Ppr-older brother-TOP
      And he says to his older brother:

153. "Pak'-t-een! ,
     wait-TRAN-1sg
     "Wait for me!

154. Pak'-t-een! ,
     wait-TRAN-1sg
     Wait for me!

155. Ma' a-b'el!,
     NEG 2-go
     Don't go!

156. Ko'on!
     come/IMP
     Come!

157. Hach wi'ih-en. ,
     very hungry-1sg
     I'm very hungry.

158. Tak-in-han-t-ik-ech" ,
     DESID-1sg-eat-TRAN-PPM-2sg
     I want to eat you,"

159. ki b'in t-u-suku'un-eh. ,
     say/3sg REPORT to-3Ppr-older brother-TOP
     they say he said to his older brother.

160. I u-suku'un-eh,
     and 3Ppr-older brother-TOP
     And the older brother,

161. hach chiich u-b'a'te'
     very hard 3-paddle
     he paddled very hard

162. asta ka' k'och-ih wa'ye'-eh. …
     until when arrive-3sg here-TOP
     until he arrived here.

163. I a'-[,]-ka' tu winik-oo' b'in he'-lo'-eh,
     and DET-two ANIM man-PL REPORT OST-DIST-TOP
     And they say those two men,

164. [u-,] u-k'ab'a'-oo'-eh ah Chan-oo'. ,
     [3Ppr-] 3Ppr-name-PL-TOP MASC PN-PL
     their names were the Chans.

165. I mentäk-eh,
     and therefore-TOP
     And therefore,

166. a'-b'a'al=che'-oo' he'-lo',
      DET-animal-PL OST-DIST
      those animals,

167. tak b'a-he'-la'-eh,
      till TEMP-OST-PROX-TOP
      until now

168. te' yan a'-noh witz [?] ,
      LOC COP DET-big hill
      there is that big hill,

169. Hobon Pich-eh,
      PN-TOP
      Jobon Pich,

170. ii k-u-yaal-b'-äl ti'ih-eh
      and INC-3-say-PAS-INTRAN 3IOpr-TOP
      and it is called

171. u-witz ah Chan-oo'. …
      3Ppr-hill MASC PN-PL
      the hill of the Chans.

172. Te' b'in p'at-oo'-i'ih
      LOC REPORT remain-PL-SCOPE
      There, they say, they remained,

173. te' xu'l-oo'-i'ih
      LOC end-PL-SCOPE
      there they ended,

174. te' kim-oo'-i'ih.
      LOC die-PL-SCOPE
      there they died.

14. The Rabbit and the Fox

Told by Fernando Tesucún on November 8, 1979

1. Yan-ah-ih b'in,
    COP-DIST-3sg REPORT
    There was, they say,

2. hun tuul nohoch ko'lel. …
    one ANIM great lady
    a great lady.

3. I yan-ah-ih ka' tuul u-paal. …
    and COP-DIST-3sg two ANIM 3Ppr-child
    And she had two children.

4. Hun tuul-eh,
    one ANIM-TOP
    One,

5. u-k'ab'a'-eh,
    3Ppr-name-TOP
    his name was

6. Ah T'u'ul. ...
    MASC rabbit
    Mr. Rabbit.

7. U-laak'-eh
    3Ppr-other-TOP
    The other,

8. u-k'ab'a'-bin-eh,
    3Ppr-name-REPORT-TOP
    they say his name was

9. Ah och. ...
    MASC fox
    Mr. Fox.

10. I a'-ka' tuul winik-oo' he'-la'-eh,
    and DET-two ANIM man-PL OST-PROX-TOP
    And these two men

11. ma' tun-b'is-ik u-b'ah-oo'. ...
    NEG DUR/3-go/CAUS-PPM 3Ppr-REFL-PL
    didn't get along with each other.

12. Ah T'u'ul-eh,
    MASC rabbit-TOP
    Mr. Rabbit,

13. layti' a'-winik-eh,
    3Ipr DET-man-TOP
    he is the man

14. hach yan u-na'at. ...
    much COP 3Ppr-idea
    that has a lot of ideas.

15. Ma' patal-[u-,]-u-lox-ik [u-,] u-suku'un-eh ...
    NEG ABIL-[3-]-3-hit-PPM [3Ppr-] 3Ppr-older brother-TOP
    He can't hit his older brother

16. tumen mas yan u-muk'. ...
    because more COP 3Ppr-strength
    because he has more strength.

17. A'-och-eh mas yan bin u-muk' ke Ah T'u'ul-eh. …
    DET-fox-TOP more COP REPORT 3Ppr-strength than MASC rabbit-TOP
    The fox has, they say, more strength than Mr. Rabbit.

18. Yan-ah-ih hum p'e k'in-eh …
    COP-DIST-3sg one INAM day-TOP
    There was one day

19. Ah T'u'ul-eh,
    MASC rabbit-TOP
    Mr. Rabbit

20. t-u-tz'ah u-b'ah u-tuk-l-eh …
    COM-3-give/DPM 3Ppr-REFL 3-think-?-SPM
    gave himself to think

21. u-yil-a'
    3-see-SPM
    to see

22. b'ix patal-u-mäch-ik a'-u-suku'un
    how ABIL-3-grab-PPM DET-3Ppr-older brother
    how he could grab his older brother

23. u-lox-oh-eh. …
    3-hit-SPM-TOP
    to hit him.

24. Ka' t-u-tuk-l-ah-eh …
    then COM-3-think-?-DPM-TOP
    Then he thought,

25. chen tun-b'et-ik hum p'e hol. …
    only DUR/3-make-PPM one INAM hole
    he was just going to make a hole.

26. Ka' t-u-ya'l-ah-eh:
    then COM-3-say-DPM-TOP
    Then he said:

27. "B'el in-k(a'a)-im-b'et-eh in-ch'e'em. …
    go 1sg-go-1sg-make-SPM 1sgPpr-cave
    "I am going to make my cave (den).

28. I a'-ch'e'em-eh,
    and DET-cave-TOP
    And the cave,

29. b'el in-k(a'a)-im-b'et-eh, kooch,
    go 1sg-go-1sg-make-SPM wide
    I am going to make it wide

30. a'-hol tu'ux k-u-b'el ti ok-ol-eh,
    DET-hole where INC-3-go SUB enter-INTRAN-REL
    at the mouth where he is going to enter,

31. i nuut' pach-il
    and narrow back-POS
    and narrow at the back

32. tu'ux k-im-b'el ti hok'-ol. …
    where INC-1sg-go SUB leave-INTRAN
    where I am going to leave.

33. In-ten-eh patal-in-wok-ol
    EMP-1sgIpr-TOP ABIL-1sg-enter-INTRAN
    I can enter

34. i patal-in-hok'-ol …
    and ABIL-1sg-leave-INTRAN
    and I can leave

35. tumen in-k'a'ool ma'lo'. …
    because 1sg-know well
    because I know it well.

36. I ka' tak a'-och-eh …
    and when come/IRREAL DET-fox-TOP
    And when the fox comes,

37. [te] in-ten-eh b'el in-ka'a in-ye'ye'=lox-t-eh,
    [?] EMP-1sgIpr-TOP go 1sg-go 1sg-threaten=hit-TRAN-SPM
    I am going to threaten to punch him

38. yok' u-tal [u-,] u-yalkä'-t-een. …
    SUB 3-come [3-] 3-run-TRAN-1sg
    so that he comes to chase me.

39. A'-ka' tak u-yalkä'-t-een-eh
    DET-when come/IRREAL 3-run-TRAN-1sg-TOP
    When he comes to chase me,

40. in-ten-eh [k-in-wok,] k-in-wok-ol
    EMP-1sgIpr-TOP [INC-1sgIpr-enter] INC-1sg-enter-INTRAN
    me, I enter

    t-a'-ch'e'em-eh
    in-DET-cave-TOP
    in the cave

41. i k-in-hok'-ol tan=xeel-il. …
    and INC-1sg-leave-INTRAN other side-POS
    and I leave at the other side.

42. I layti'-eh,
    and 3Ipr-TOP
    And he,

43. ma' u-k'a'ool a'-hol-eh. ,
    NEG 3-know DET-hole-TOP
    he isn't familiar with the hole.

44. A'-ka' tak-eh,
    DET-when come/IRREAL-TOP
    When he comes,

45. k-u-hup-ik u-pol-i'ih-eh,
    INC-3-insert-PPM 3Ppr-head-LOC-TOP
    he puts his head in there,

46. te' k-u-b'el ti k'a'l-äl-i'ih. …
    LOC INC-3-go SUB stick-INTRAN-SCOPE
    there he's going to get stuck.

47. I a'-ka' k'a'l-äk-eh
    and DET-when stick-IRREAL-TOP
    And when he is stuck,

48. in-ten-eh k-im-b'el ti tal pach-il-eh,
    EMP-1sgIpr-TOP INC-1sg-go SUB come back-POS-TOP
    I am going to come behind him,

49. k-im-mäch-ik tun-eh
    INC-1sg-grab-PPM then-TOP
    I grab him then,

50. k-in-kap-äl in-[,]-kokolche'-t-eh
    INC-1sg-begin-INTRAN 1sg-trample-TRAN-SPM
    I begin to trample him,

51. in-lox-o'. …
    1sg-punch-SPM
    to punch him.

52. U-ho'm-ol-eh k-im-b'el. ,
    3-end-INTRAN-TOP INC-1sg-go
    (When) it's done I go.

53. K-im-p'ät-ik te' pul-a'an-i'ih. ,
    INC-1sg-leave-PPM LOC throw-PART-SCOPE
    I leave him thrown there.

54. Ya ma'an u-yool,
    already NEG/COP 3Ppr-breath
    Then he doesn't have his breath

55. tu'ux t-in-sen-lox-ah." …
    where COM-1sg-INTENS-hit-DPM
    where I hit him so much."

56. I hum p'e k'in b'in-eh,
    and one INAM day REPORT-TOP
    And one day, they say,

57. k-u-ya'al-ik-eh: ,
    INC-3-say-PPM-TOP
    he says:

58. "B'el in-k(a'a)-in-wil-a',
    go 1sg-go-1sg-see-SPM
    "I am going to see

59. b'ix k-in-b'el in-mäch-ä' Ah T'u'ul-eh,"
    how INC-1sg-go 1sg-grab-SPM MASC Rabbit-TOP
    how I am going to grab Mr. Rabbit,"

60. ki b'in a'-och-eh. …
    say/3sg REPORT DET-fox-TOP
    they say the fox said.

61. Ii, te'-lo'-eh,
    and LOC-DIST-TOP
    And there,

62. ka' t-u-yil-a(h) b'in u-b'ah a'-och-eh
    then COM-3-see-DPM REPORT 3Ppr-REFL DET-fox-TOP
    then the fox met

63. et-e hun tuul nohoch winik u-k'ab'a' Ayin. …
    with-POS one ANIM great man 3Ppr-name alligator
    with a great man whose name was Alligator.

64. I k-u-ya'al-ik b'in a'-ayin ti'ih-eh: …
    and INC-3-say-PPM REPORT DET-alligator 3IOpr-TOP
    And they say the alligator tells him:

65. "A-k'a't(-ih) a-mäch-ä a-suku'un-eh,
    2-want(-PM?) 2-grab-SPM 2Ppr-older brother-TOP
    "You want to catch your brother,

66. pah-t-eh a-kim-il. …
    pretend-TRAN-SPM/IMP 2-die-INTRAN
    play dead.

67. T-u-chi' a'-noh ha' he'-lo' yan-eh …
    at-3Ppr-edge DET-big water OST-DIST COP-REL
    At the edge of that big lake there,

68. te' patal-a[a]-chi-tal-i'ih,
    LOC ABIL-2-lie-POSIT-SCOPE
    there you can lie down

69. a-pah-t-eh a-kim-il,
    2-pretend-TRAN-SPM 2-die-INTRAN
    to play dead,

70. ke tan-a-kim-il. …
    SUB DUR-2-die-INTRAN
    that you are dying.

71. A'-ka' tak layti'-eh
    DET-when come/IRREAL 3Ipr-TOP
    When he comes

72. k(a')-u-yil-a-'-eech
    SUB-3-see-SPM-2sg
    to see you,

73. ke tech-e tan-a-kim-il,
    SUB 2sgIpr-TOP DUR-2-die-INTRAN
    that you are dying,

74. pero nich'-i' a-koh
    but bare-SPM/IMP 2Ppr-tooth
    but bare your teeth

75. [yok' u-,] yok'ol-al u-yok-ol [t-u-,] t-u-ho'ol
    [for 3-] SUB-SUB 3-enter-INTRAN [in-3Ppr-] in-3Ppr-head
    so that it enters his head (he believes)

76. ke tech-eh ya tan-a-kim-il. …
    SUB 2sgIpr-TOP already DUR-2-die-INTRAN
    that you are already dying.

77. I a'-ka' natz'-äk t-a-wuknal-eh,
    and DET-when near-IRREAL to-2Ppr-with-TOP
    And when he's close to you,

78. k-a-mäch-ik. …
    INC-2-grab-PPM
    you grab him.

79. K-a-mäch-ik-eh
    when/INC-2-grab-PPM-TOP
    When you grab him,

80. k-a-lox-ik
    INC-2-punch-PPM
    you punch him,

81. k-a-kokolche-t-ik
     INC-2-trample-TRAN-PPM
     you trample him,

82. he-b'ix ich u-b'et-ik tech-eh. ,
     OST-how in 3-do-PPM 2sgIOpr-TOP
     just as he did to you.

83. Ha'li b'ay-lo' patal-u-b'o'-t-ik tech
     only like-DIST ABIL-3-pay-TRAN-PPM 2sgIOpr
     Only in that way can he pay you

84. a'-b'a'ax t-u-b'et-ah tech-eh." ...
     DET-what COM-3-do-DPM 2sgIOpr-REL
     for what he did to you."

85. A'-lo' [u-,] u-na'at Yun Ayin. ...
     DET-DIST [3Ppr-] 3Ppr-idea Sir Alligator
     That is the idea of Sir Alligator.

86. I ka' k'och-ih [a'-,] a'-och-eh,
     and when arrive-3sg [DET-] DET-fox-TOP
     And when the fox arrived,

87. ka' t-u-yil-ah a'-Yun T'u'ul-eh
     then COM-3-see-DPM DET-Sir Rabbit-TOP
     then he saw Sir Rabbit

88. te' chil-a'an-i'ih,
     LOC lie-PART-SCOPE
     lying there,

89. nich'-a'an u-koh,
     bare-PART 3Ppr-tooth
     his teeth bared,

90. pero k-u-ya'al-ik ti'(ih) a'-och-eh: ,
     but INC-3-say-PPM 3IOpr DET-fox-TOP
     but the fox says to him:

91. "Otzil in-suku'un-eh
     poor 1sgPpr-older brother-TOP
     "My poor older brother,

92. mia kim-ih. ...
     DUB die-3sg
     I think he died.

93. Pero in-ten-eh
     but EMP-1sgIpr-TOP
     But as for me,

94. k-u-yaal-b'-äl ten-eh
  INC-3-say-PAS-INTRAN 1sgIOpr-TOP
  it is said to me

95. ke a'-kim-en-oo'-eh …
  that DET-die-NOM-PL-TOP
  that the dead,

96. ma' [t-u-] nich'-a'an u-koh-oo'. ,
  NEG [COM-3] bare-PART 3Ppr-tooth-PL
  don't have their teeth bared.

97. I a'-la'-eh,
  and DET-PROX-TOP
  And this,

98. ma' in-wohel
  NEG 1sg-know
  I don't know

99. wa kim-en
  COND die-NOM
  if it's a corpse

100. wa tan-u-che'eh." …
  COND DUR-3-smile
  or if he's smiling."

101. Ka' natz'-i(h) b'in a'-och
  then near-3sg REPORT DET-fox
  Then, they say, the fox drew near

102. u-hach-'il-a'-eh. …
  3-much-see-SPM-TOP
  to see it well.

103. A'-ka' t-u[u]-yil-ah a'-och-eh …
  DET-when COM-3-see-DPM DET-fox-TOP
  Then the fox saw

104. ke a'-Yun T'u'ul-eh [k-u-pek-s-ik u-,]
  SUB DET-Sir Rabbit-TOP [INC-3-move-CAUS-PPM 3Ppr-]
  that Sir Rabbit,

105. k-u-tz'äl-b'ah u-xikin. …
  INC-3-tremble-INTRAN 3Ppr-ear
  his ear trembled.

106. "Haah!" ki b'in a'-och-eh,
  EXCLAM say/3sg REPORT DET-fox-TOP
  "Aha!" they say the fox said,

107. "Tech-eh chen tan-a-[men-,]-pah-t-ik
      2sgIpr-TOP only DUR-2-[do]-pretend-TRAN-PPM
      "You, you are only playing

      a-kim-en-il,
      2Ppr-die-NOM-POS
      dead,

108. pero in-ten-e(h) ma' tan-mäch-ik-en. …
      but EMP-1sgIpr-TOP NEG DUR/2-grab-PPM-1sg
      but me, you are not grabbing me.

109. Ii a-k(a'a) a-mäch-ä',
      and 2-go 2-grab-SPM
      And you are going to grab,

110. kien sa' max-i'ih,
      who know who-SCOPE
      who knows who it is

111. a'-k-a-b'el a-mäch-ä'-eh,
      DET-INC-2-go 2-grab-SPM-REL
      that you are going to grab,

112. in-ten-eh ma' tan-mäch-ik-en." …
      EMP-1sg-TOP NEG DUR/2-grab-PPM-1sg
      me, you are not grabbing."

113. Ii, ka' t-u-mäch-ah [a'-…] a'-och-eh,
      and then COM-3-grab-DPM [DET-] DET-fox-TOP
      And then the fox grabbed him,

114. ka' k'äs natz'-ih-eh
      when little near-3sg-TOP
      when he got a little closer

115. ka' t-u-pak'=tuut-ah u-yich Ah T'u'ul-eh
      then COM-3-spit-DPM 3Ppr-eye MASC Rabbit-TOP
      then he spat in the eyes of Mr. Rabbit

116. ka' hok'-ih ti alka'-eh
      then leave-3sg SUB run-TOP
      and he left running

117. ka' b'in-ih. …
      then go-3sg
      and he went.

118. Y ya ma' [t-u-ka'-sut-ah]
      and then NEG [COM-3-REPET-return-DPM]
      And then he didn't

(ka'-)sut-n-ah-ih
(REPET-)return-DETRAN-DIST-3sg
return again

119. u-yil-a' u-suku'un-eh.
3-see-SPM 3Ppr-older brother-TOP
to see his older brother.

15. The Lord of the Deer

Told by Fernando Tesucún on July 15, 1980

1. Uch-ih b'in-eh
happen-3sg REPORT-TOP
Long ago, they say

2. yan-ah-ih hun tuul winik,
COP-DIST-3sg one ANIM man
there was a man

3. käh-a'an wa'ye' …
live-PART here
living here

4. i hach u-yohel=tz'on. …
and much 3-know=shoot
and he knew a lot about shooting.

5. Tulakal k'in k-u-hok'-ol,
every day INC-3-go out-INTRAN
Every day he goes out

6. ti xi'mal,
SUB walk
to walk

7. ich a'-kol-oo'-eh,
inside DET-milpa-PL-REL
among the milpas,

8. k-u-tz'on-ik keeh. …
INC-3-shoot-PPM deer
he shoots deer.

9. I b'aay-loh
and like-DIST
And thus,

10. i b'aay-loh,
and like-DIST
and thus,

11. kap-ih ti tz'on,
    begin-3sg SUB shoot
    he began to shoot

12. i ti tz'on. ...
    and SUB shoot
    and to shoot.

13. I layti',
    and 3Ipr
    And him,

14. k-u-kon-ik yaab' b'äk'
    INC-3-sell-PPM much meat
    he sells a lot of meat

15. porke [chen a'-,] chen a'-lo' u-meyah-eh
    because [only DET-] only DET-DIST 3Ppr-work-TOP
    because only that is his work,

16. chen a'-lo' [k-u] tu'ux k-u-kux-tal-eh. ...
    only DET-DIST [INC-3] where INC-3-live-POSIT-REL
    only that was where he makes a living.

17. Pero yan-ah-ih b'in hun p'e k'in ...
    but COP-DIST-3sg REPORT one INAM day
    But there was, they say, one day

18. layti'-eh,
    3Ipr-TOP
    he,

19. t-u-yil-ah ah noh b'a'al=che',
    COM-3-see-DPM MASC big animal
    he saw the big animal

20. wa'an chumuk kol-eh,
    stand/PART mid milpa-REL
    standing in the middle of the milpa,

21. ka' t-u-tz'on-ah. ...
    then COM-3-shoot-DPM
    and he shot it.

22. I a'-ka' [t-u-tz',] wak'-ih u-tz'on-eh ...
    and DET-when [COM-3-] fire-3sg 3Ppr-gun-TOP
    And when his gun fired,

23. a'-keeh-eh,
    DET-deer-TOP
    the deer

24. wak'-ih u-siit'. …
    explode-3sg 3Ppr-jump
    made a leap.

25. Ma' lub'-ih. …
    not fall-3sg
    It didn't fall.

26. A'-b'a'ax t-u-b'et-ah a'-keeh-eh
    DET-what COM-3-do-DPM DET-deer-REL
    What the deer did

27. ka' tal-ih,
    then come-3sg
    was then it came

28. tun-siit',
    DUR/3-jump
    jumping

29. yok' a'-winik-eh. …
    over DET-man-TOP
    over the man.

30. I a'-winik-eh
    and DET-man-TOP
    And the man,

31. t-u-ka'-tz'on-ah. …
    COM-3-REPET-shoot-DPM
    he shot it again.

32. I a'-ka' ti' … wak'-ih u-tz'on-eh,
    and DET-when SUB explode-3sg 3Ppr-gun-TOP
    And when his gun fired,

33. a'-b'a'al=che'-eh
    DET-animal-TOP
    the animal,

34. ka' hok'-ih u-yalka'-eh
    then leave-3sg 3-run-TOP
    then it left running

35. ka' b'in-ih,
    then go-3sg
    and it went,

36. ok-ih ich k'aax-eh,
    enter-3sg in forest-TOP
    it entered into the forest,

37. b'el t-u-b'et-ah. …
    exit COM-3-make-DPM
    it made an exit.

38. Ma' kim-ih. …
    NEG die-3sg
    It didn't die.

39. Ii, ah tz'on-eh
    and MASC-shoot-TOP
    And the hunter,

40. ka' wa'-l-ah-ih u-yil-a' …
    then stand-POSIT-DIST-3sg 3-see-SPM
    then stood to see

41. a'-tu'ux b'in(-ih) a'-b'a'al=che'-eh. …
    DET-where go(-3sg) DET-animal-REL
    where the animal went.

42. Ka', b'in-ih t-u-pach. …
    then go-3sg at-3Ppr-back
    Then he went behind it.

43. A'-b'a'al-che'-eh
    DET-animal-TOP
    The animal

44. t-u-pul-ah yaab' k'ik'. …
    COM-3-throw-DPM much blood
    lost a lot of blood.

45. I tan-u-b'el
    and DUR-3-go
    And he is going,

46. k-u-yil-ik
    INC-3-see-PPM
    he sees

47. tu'ux k-u-b'el a'-k'ik'-eh,
    where INC-3-go DET-blood-REL
    where the blood goes,

48. te' b'in-ih-i'ih. …
    LOC go-3sg-SCOPE
    there he goes.

49. I b'in-ih,
    and go-3sg
    And he went,

50. b'in-ih tulakal
    go-3sg all
    he went all over,

51. [tu...tun-t'ut'-,] tun-t'ut'-l-ik
    [DUR/3-follow] DUR/3-follow-?-PPM
    he was following

52. a'-tu'ux b'in(-ih) a'-b'a'al=che'-eh. ...
    DET-where go(-3sg) DET-animal-REL
    where the animal went.

53. A'-ka' t-u-yil-ah-eh,
    DET-when COM-3-see-DPM-TOP
    When he saw it,

54. k'och-ih t-u-chun hun kuul witz ...
    arrive-3sg at-3Ppr-base one CLASS hill
    he arrived at the base of a hill,

55. i t-u-chun a'-witz-eh,
    and at-3Ppr-base DET-hill-TOP
    and at the base of the hill

56. yan hun p'eel noh aktun,
    COP one INAM big cave
    was a big cave,

57. b'ay u-hol hun kuul nah-eh. ...
    like 3Ppr-entrance one CLASS house-TOP
    like the door of a house.

58. K-u-yil-ik-eh ...
    INC-3-see-PPM-REL
    He sees

59. ke a'-k'ik'-eh
    SUB DET-blood-TOP
    that the blood

60. ok-ih ich a'-aktun-eh. ...
    enter-3sg in DET-cave-TOP
    entered inside the cave.

61. I ka' wa'-l-ah-ih b'in-eh
    and then stand-POSIT-DIST-3sg REPORT-TOP
    And then he stood, they say,

62. k-u-ya'al-ik-eh: ,
    INC-3-say-PPM-REL
    he says:

63. "A'-aktun he'-la'-eh
     DET-cave OST-PROX-TOP
     "As for this cave,

64. wa'ye' ok(-ih) a'-b'a'al=che'-eh. …
     here enter(-3sg) DET-animal-TOP
     here the animal entered.

65. In-ten in-wok-ol in-wil-a'-eh. …
     EMP-1sgIpr 1sg-enter-INTRAN 1sg-see-SPM-TOP
     Me, I'm going in to see it.

66. A'-aktun-eh
     DET-cave-TOP
     The cave,

67. sas-il [u-,] u-hol,
     bright-POS [3Ppr-] 3Ppr-entrance
     its entrance is bright,

68. chik-a'an kooch ich-il." …
     see-PART wide in-POS
     it appears wide inside."

69. Ka' t-u-mäch-ah-eh,
     then COM-3-grab-DPM-TOP
     Then he grabbed it,

70. t-u-[,]-mäch-ah u-tz'on-eh
     COM-3-grab-DPM 3Ppr-gun-TOP
     he grabbed his gun,

71. ka' ok-ih ich a'-aktun-eh. ,
     then enter-3sg in DET-cave-TOP
     then he entered into the cave.

72. B'in-ih,
     go-3sg
     He went

73. i b'in-ih,
     and go-3sg
     and he went,

74. tun-t'ut'-l-ik a'-k'ik'-eh. …
     DUR/3-follow-?-PPM DET-blood-TOP
     following the blood.

75. A-ka' k'och-ih-eh …
     DET-when arrive-3sg-TOP
     When he arrived,

76. k-u-yil-ik b'in-eh,
     INC-3-see-PPM REPORT-TOP
     he sees, they say,

77. te' wa'an, hun tuul nohoch winik-i'ih. ...
     LOC stand/PART one ANIM great man-SCOPE
     there is standing an old man.

78. A'-ka', k'och-ih-eh,
     DET-when arrive-3sg-TOP
     When he arrived,

79. k-u-yil-ik-eh
     INC-3-see-PPM-TOP
     he sees it,

80. b'aay,
     like
     like,

81. b'ay hun p'e noh kah-tal-il
     like one INAM big live-POSIT-NOM
     like a big ranch

82. a'-tu'ux yan-il [a'-,] a'-chämach-eh. ...
     DET-where COP-POS [DET-] DET-old man-REL
     where the old man was.

83. I layti'-eh
     and 3Ipr-TOP
     And as for him,

84. wa'an [a'-,] a'-chämach-eh
     stand/PART [DET-] DET-old man-TOP
     the old man is standing

85. tun-tz'ik u-han-al u-b'a'al=che'-oo'. ...
     DUR/3-give/PPM 3Ppr-eat-NOM 3Ppr-animal-PL
     giving the animals food.

86. I te' t-u-yil-ah yaab' keeh,
     and LOC COM-3-see-DPM many deer
     And there he saw a lot of deer

87. k-u-man u-b'aak'-t-oo' a'-winik-eh,
     INC-3-pass 3-surround-TRAN-PL DET-man-REL
     that pass surrounding the man,

88. i [stumble] a'-winik-eh
     and DET-man-TOP
     and the man

89. k-u-tz'ik u-han-al. …
    INC-3-give/PPM 3Ppr-food-NOM
    gives their food.

90. I k-u-yil-ik-eh
    and INC-3-see-PPM-TOP
    And he sees that

91. te' wa'an a'-noh keeh …
    LOC stand/PART DET-big deer
    there is standing the big deer

92. [t-u-tz'on-,] t-u-tz'on-ah xan-eh. ,
    [COM-3-shoot-] COM-3-shoot-DPM also-REL
    that he shot too.

93. Te' yan-i'ih
    LOC COP-SCOPE
    There it is,

94. tun-chul u-k'ik'-el. …
    DUR/3-drip 3Ppr-blood-POS
    its blood is dripping.

95. I k-u-ya'al-ik b'in
    and INC-3-say-PPM REPORT
    And (the old man) says, they say,

96. a'-[,]-nohoch winik ti'ih-eh: …
    DET-great man 3IOpr-TOP
    to him:

97. "Kon ke tech ah tz'on-ech-eh,
    with that 2sgIpr MASC shoot-2sg-TOP
    "Since you are the hunter,

98. in-tech a'-[,]-winik-ech
    EMP-2sgIpr DET-man-2sg
    you are the man

99. k-a-sen=kech-tz'on-ik a'-im-b'a'al=che'-oo'-eh. …
    INC-2-much-shoot-PPM DET-1sgPpr-animal-PL-REL
    that so often shoots my animals.

100. B'a-lah, tan-wil-ik b'oon b'a'al-che',
     TEMP-PROX DUR/2-see-PPM how many animal
     Now you see how many animals

101. ho'm-ih [a-,] a-k'oh-a'an-kun-t-es-ik ten. ,
     TERM-3sg [2-] 2-sick-PART-CAUS-TRAN-CAUS-PPM 1sgIOpr
     you have made sick for me.

102. Tulakal a'-b'a'al=che'-oo' he'-la'
     all DET-animal-PL OST-PROX
     All of these animals

103. k-a-wil-ik-oo'-eh …
     INC-2-see-PPM-PL-REL
     that you see,

104. a-lah-tz'on-m-ah,
     2-totally-shoot-PERF-DPM
     you have shot them all,

105. i ten-eh,
     and 1sgIpr-TOP
     and as for me,

106. yan-ah-ih [ii,] in-lah-tz'äk-ik. …
     OBLIG-DIST-3sg 1sg-totally-cure-PPM
     I had to cure them all.

107. I b'a-lah …
     and TEMP-PROX
     And it is (only) now

108. asta ka' k'och-ih t-u-k'in …
     until SUB arrive-3sg to-3Ppr-day
     that the day has come

109. in-k'a'ool-t-ik-ech" ,
     1sg-know-TRAN-PPM-2sg
     I meet you,"

110. ki b'in a'-nohoch winik ti'ih-eh. …
     say/3sg REPORT DET-old man 3IOpr-TOP
     they say the old man said to him.

111. I a'-winik-eh
     and DET-man-TOP
     And the man,

112. ma' yan-ah-ih u-t'an,
     NEG COP-DIST-3sg 3Ppr-speech
     he didn't have words,

113. ma' pat-ah-ih u-ya'al-ik mix b'a'al ti'ih
     NEG ABIL-DIST-3sg 3-say-PPM NEG thing 3IOpr
     he couldn't say anything to him

114. tumen u-yohel-e
     because 3-know-TOP
     because he knows

115. ke layti' u-si'p-il t-u-hah-il
SUB 3Ipr 3Ppr-crime-POS to-3Ppr-true-POS
that it is his crime truly,

116. [a'-,] a'-tun-yaal-b'-ä(l) ti'ih-eh. …
[DET-] DET-DUR/3-say-PAS-INTRAN 3IOpr-REL
what was being said to him.

117. I entonses
and then
And then

118. a'-nohoch winik-eh,
DET-great man-TOP
the old man

119. k-u-ya'al-ik b'in ti'ih-eh: …
INC-3-say-PPM REPORT 3IOpr-TOP
says to him, they say:

120. "B'a-lah, k-in-k'ub'en-t-ik tech …
TEMP-PROX INC-1sg-recommend-TRAN-PPM 2sgIOpr
"Now I recommend to you

121. ke t-u-laak' k'in-eh …
SUB on-3Ppr-other day-TOP
that on another day,

122. ka' a-tz'on-o' a'-b'a'al=che'-eh …
when 2-shoot-SPM DET-animal-TOP
when you shoot the animal,

123. tz'on-o' ma'lo' …
shoot-SPM/IMP well
shoot it well,

124. ma' a-maan-tz'on-t-ik. …
NEG 2-badly-shoot-TRAN-PPM
don't shoot it badly.

125. Wa mah,
COND NEG
If not,

126. waye' k-in-b'el in-pak'-t-eech t-u-ka'ye'-eh,
here INC-1sg-go 1sg-await-TRAN-2sg to-3Ppr-again-REL
it's here I'm going to await you again,

127. ke waye' yan-a-ka'-k'och-ol." …
SUB here OBLIG-2-REPET-arrive-INTRAN
it's here you have to arrive again."

128. Entonses a'-winik-eh,
     then DET-man-TOP
     Then the man,

129. ka' t-u-ch'a'-ah saak-il. …
     then COM-3-take-DPM fear-POS
     then he took fright.

130. I ka' b'in t-u-ya'l-ah a'-nohoch winik ti'ih-eh:
     and then REPORT COM-3-say-DPM DET-old man 3IOpr-TOP
     And then, they say, the old man said to him:

131. "B'a-la ko'ox,
     TEMP-PROX HORT
     "Now let's go,

132. b'el in-ka'a in-hok'-es-eech,
     go 1sg-go 1sg-leave-CAUS-2sg
     I'm going to take you out

133. ka' xik-ech t-a-wotoch. …
     SUB go/IRREAL-2sg to-2Ppr-house
     for you to go to your house.

134. Pero yan-a-mutz'-ik a-wich,"
     but OBLIG-2-close-PPM 2Ppr-eye
     But you have to close your eyes,"

135. ki b'in ti'ih. …
     say/3sg REPORT 3IOpr
     they say he said to him.

136. I a'-winik-eh,
     and DET-man-TOP
     And the man,

137. ah tz'on-eh
     MASC shoot-TOP
     the hunter,

138. ka' t-u-mutz'-ah u-yich. …
     then COM-3-shut-DPM 3Ppr-eye
     then he shut his eyes.

139. "Asta in-wa'al-ik tech
     until 1sg-say-PPM 2sgIOpr
     "(Not) until I tell you

140. ke k-a-heb'-e' a-wich-eh
     SUB SUB-2-open-SPM 2Ppr-eye-TOP
     that you should open your eyes

141. k-a-heb'-ik,"
INC-2-open-PPM
do you open them,"

142. ki b'in [a'-,] a'-chämach ti'ih-eh. ,
say/3sg REPORT [DET-] DET-old man 3IOpr-TOP
they say the old man said to him.

143. I layti'
and 3Ipr
And he,

144. ka' t-u-mutz'-ah u-yich. ,
then COM-3-close-DPM 3Ppr-eye
then he closed his eyes.

145. Ka' t-u-ya'l-ah a'-chämach ti'ih-eh: ,
then COM-3-say-DPM DET-old man 3IOpr-TOP
Then the old man said to him:

146. "B'a-lah heb'-e' a-wich." ...
TEMP-PROX open-SPM/IMP 2Ppr-eye
"Now open your eyes."

147. A-ka' t-u-heb'-ah u-yich b'in
DET-when COM-3-open-DPM 3Ppr-eye REPORT
When he opened his eyes, they say,

148. [a'-] a'-winik,
[DET-] DET-man
the man,

149. ah tz'on-eh,
MASC-shoot-TOP
the hunter,

150. k-u-yil-ik-eh ...
INC-3-see-PPM-TOP
he sees that

151. t-u-chun a'-witz-eh
at-3Ppr-base DET-hill-TOP
at the base of the hill,

152. te' wa'an-i'ih,
LOC stand/PART-SCOPE
there he is standing

153. a'-tu'ux ok-ih-eh. ...
DET-where enter-3sg-REL
where he entered.

154. Pero a'-ka' hok'-ih-eh,
      but DET-when leave-3sg-TOP
      But when he left,

155. ya [ma' t-u-ka'-,] ma' sut-n-ah-ih
      then [NEG COM-3-REPET-] NEG return-DETRAN-DIST-3sg
      then he didn't return

      u-yil-a',
      3-see-SPM
      to see

156. u-hol a'-aktun-eh,
      3Ppr-mouth DET-cave-TOP
      the mouth of the cave,

157. ya ma'an aktun. …
      already NEG/COP cave
      already there was no cave.

158. I ka' tal-ih, layti',
      and then come-3sg 3Ipr
      And then he came,

159. wa'-l-ah-ih u-yil-a' a'-witz'-eh,
      stand-POSIT-DIST-3sg 3-see-SPM DET-hill-TOP
      he stood to see the hill

160. i k'ah-ih ti'ih
      and remember-3sg 3IOpr
      and he remembered

161. ke, t-u-chun a'-witz-eh,
      SUB at-3Ppr-base DET-hill-TOP
      that at the base of the hill

162. t-u-yil-ah a'-aktun-eh
      COM-3-see-DPM DET-cave-TOP
      he saw the cave

163. i ich a'-aktun he'-loh
      and in DET-cave OST-DIST
      and inside that cave,

164. te' ok-ih-i'ih. …
      LOC enter-3sg-SCOPE
      there he entered.

165. Pero layti'-eh
      but 3Ipr-TOP
      But as for him,

166. k'ub'en-b'-ih ti'ih men a'-chämach-eh,
recommend-PAS-3sg 3IOpr by DET-old man-TOP
it was recommended to him by the old man

167. ke ma' u-b'el u-tzikb'al-t-eh mix b'a'al. ...
SUB NEG 3-go 3-say-TRAN-SPM NEG thing
that he not go saying anything.

168. Ka' tal-ih,
then come-3sg
Then he came,

169. ka' k'och-ih t-u-yotoch-eh. ...
then arrive-3sg at-3Ppr-home-TOP
then he arrived at his home.

170. U-yätan i tulakal u-me(h)en paal-oo'-eh,
3Ppr-wife and all 3Ppr-small child-PL-TOP
His wife and all of his small children,

171. a'-ka' t-u-yil-ah-oo'
DET-when COM-3-see-DPM-PL
when they saw

172. ke tun-tal a'-winik, t-u-yotoch-eh,
SUB DUR/3-come DET-man to-3Ppr-home-TOP
that the man was coming to his home,

173. ka' kap-oo' ti ok'-ol,
then begin-PL SUB cry-INTRAN
then they began to cry

174. et-el u-ki'-il [u-yu'ub',] u-yu'ub'-ih-oo'-eh. ...
with-POS 3Ppr-good-POS [3-feel] 3-feel-?-PL-REL
with the happiness they felt.

175. Kap-oo' ti ok'-ol
begin-PL SUB cry-INTRAN
They began to cry,

176. ka' tal-oo' a'-[,]-p'aal-oo'-eh
then come-PL DET-child-PL-TOP
then the children came,

177. k'och-oo' u-mek'-t-oo' u-tat-eh ...
arrive-PL 3-hug-TRAN-PL 3Ppr-father-TOP
they arrived to hug their father

178. i u-yätan-eh ...
and 3Ppr-wife-TOP
and his wife,

179. tak layti' xan. …
     till 3Ipr too
     even her too.

180. I layti'-eh
     and 3Ipr-TOP
     And he,

181. hak'-a'an u-yool,
     surprise-PART 3Ppr-spirit
     surprised,

182. [k-u-ya'al-ik,] k-u-ya'al-ik t-u-paal-oo'
     [INC-3-say-PPM] INC-3-say-PPM to-3Ppr-child-PL
     says to his children

183. i t-u-yätan-eh:
     and to-3Ppr-wife-TOP
     and to his wife:

184. "B'a'ax u-ka'a tan-wok'-ol-e'ex?" …
     what 3-go DUR/2-cry-INTRAN-2pl
     "Why are you all crying?"

185. I k-u-ya'al-ik u-yätan ti'ih-eh:
     and INC-3-say-PPM 3Ppr-wife 3IOpr-TOP
     And his wife says to him:

186. "B'ix ma' ki-wok'-ol
     how NEG 1pl-cry-INTRAN
     "Why wouldn't we be crying

187. si tech-eh,
     if 2sgIpr-TOP
     if you,

188. sat-al-ech? …
     lose-PART-2sg
     you are lost?

189. Ya yan, ox p'e mes,
     already COP three INAM month
     It's already three months

190. xik-ech, ti tz'on
     go/IRREAL-2sg SUB shoot
     (since) you went to shoot

191. i ma' tak-ech.
     and NEG come/IRREAL-2sg
     and you haven't come (back).

192. Asta b'a-he'-lah
      until TEMP-OST-PROX
      (Not) until now

193. tan-ki-kil-ik, a-wich-eh. ,
      DUR-1pl-see-PPM 2Ppr-face-TOP
      are we seeing your face.

194. In-to'on-eh ti ki-t'an-eh
      EMP-1plIpr-TOP in 1plPpr-thought/speech-TOP
      Us, we were wondering

195. wa yah ho'm-ih a-kim-il." …
      COND already TERM-3sg 2-die-INTRAN
      if you had already finished dying."

196. "B'ix a-wohel-e'ex
      how 2-know-2pl
      "How do you know

197. [kaa,] ka' kim-ik-en
      [SUB] SUB die-IRREAL-1sg
      that I would die

198. si ten-eh
      if 1sgIpr-TOP
      if I

199. b'a-he'-la' k'och-een kan a'-no(h)och winik-eh?" ,
      TEMP-OST-PROX arrive-1sg with DET-old man-TOP
      arrived now from the old man?"

200. Layti'-eh,
      3Ipr-TOP
      As for him,

201. t-u-t'an-eh
      in-3Ppr-thought-TOP
      he was thinking

202. wa layt(i')[a'-,] a'-k'in he'-lo',
      COND 3Ipr [DET-] DET-day OST-DIST
      it was that day

203. t-u-tz'on-ah a'-keeh-eh
      COM-3-shoot-DPM DET-deer-REL
      that he shot the deer,

204. layt(i') a'-miismo k'in he'-lo'
      3Ipr DET-same day OST-DIST
      it was that same day

205. sut-k'-ah-ih-eh. ,
      return-CELER?-DIST-3sg-REL
      that he returned.

206. I ke si layti',
      and that if 3Ipr
      And that if he

207. xan-ah-ih, ox p'e mes …
      delay-DIST-3sg three INAM month
      dallied three months,

208. [sat-al ?,] sat-ih, ox p'e mes …
      [lose-PART] lose-3sg three INAM month
      he was lost three months,

209. ich u-yok-ol ich a'-ch'e'em-eh
      in 3-enter-INTRAN inside DET-cave-TOP
      when he entered inside the cave,

210. xan-ah-ih.
      delay-DIST-3sg
      he lingered.

211. I layti',
      and 3Ipr
      And he,

212. a'-ka' hok'-ih-eh,
      DET-when leave-3sg-TOP
      when he left,

213. t-u-t'an-eh
      in-3Ppr-thought-TOP
      it was in his mind

214. wa layt(i') a'-mismo k'in he'-lo'
      COND 3Ipr DET-same day OST-DIST
      that it might be that same day

215. k'och-ih t-u-yotoch-eh. ,
      arrive-3sg to-3Ppr-home-REL
      that he arrived to his home.

216. B'aay-lo' b'in uch-ih
      like-DIST REPORT happen-3sg
      Thus, they say, it happened

217. a'-winik hach (u-)yohel=tz'on-eh. ,
      DET man much (3-)know=shoot-REL
      to the man that really knows hunting.

218. A'-loh k-u-tzikb'al-t-ik to'on,
DET-DIST INC-3-say-TRAN-PPM 1plIOpr
That, (our grandmother) told us

219. ki-noolah uch-ih …
1plPpr-grandmother happen-3sg
long ago

220. mehen-o'on toh. … (tape change)
small-1pl still
when we were still little.

221. I layt(i') a'-lo'
and 3Ipr DET-DIST
And it is that,

222. k'äh-a'an ten-eh. ,
remember-PART 1sgIOpr-REL
which I remember.

223. Tak b'a-he'-la'-eh
until TEMP-OST-PROX-TOP
Until now

224. ma' tub'-uk ten. ,
NEG forget-IRREAL 1sgIOpr
it hasn't been forgotten by me.

225. I layt(i') a'-lo'
and 3Ipr DET-DIST
And it is that

226. k-in-tzikb'al-t-ik tech-eh …
INC-1sg-say-TRAN-PPM 2sgIOpr-REL
which I say to you

227. yok' a-wu'y-ik-e'ex
SUB that 2-hear-PPM-2pl
so that you all hear

228. b'ix u-tz'o'ok-ol a'-winik,
how 3-end-INTRAN DET-man
how the man ended

229. ah hach-yohel=tz'on=keeh-eh.
MASC-much-3/know=shoot=deer-REL
that was a real deer hunter.

16. Deer Lore

Told by Fernando Tesucún on July 18, 1979

Part I

1. T-u-tzikb'al-t-ah ten hun tuul in-wet-meyah …
   COM-3-tell-TRAN-DPM 1sgIOpr one ANIM 1sgPpr-with-work
   One of my co-workers told me,

2. in-wet'ok …
   1sgPpr-companion
   my companion,

3. ke yan b'in … u-yum-il [a'-…] a'-b'a'al=che'-oo'-eh. …
   SUB COP REPORT 3Ppr-owner-POS [DET-] DET-animal-PL-TOP
   that they say that the animals have their owner (lord).

4. Ii … k-u-ya'al-ik ten-eh …
   and INC-3-say-PPM 1sgIOpr-TOP
   And he asks me

5. ke wa ma' in-wohel
   SUB COND NEG 1sg-know
   if I don't know

6. b'ix [u-,] u-men-b'-el u-sektreetoh-il …
   como [3-] 3-make-PAS-INTRAN 3Ppr-secret-POS
   how their charm is made

7. ti'a'(al) ka' pat-ak u-tz'on-ik mak, a'-keeh-oo'-eh. …
   SUB SUB ABIL-IRREAL 3-shoot-PPM person DET-deer-PL-TOP
   so that one would be able to shoot the deer.

8. I ten-eh,
   and 1sgIpr-TOP
   And me,

9. t-in-wa'l-ah ti'ih-eh,
   COM-1sg-say-DPM 3IOpr-TOP
   I said to him

10. ke ma' in-wohel …
    SUB NEG 1sg-know
    that I don't know;

11. ke ten-eh,
    SUB 1sgIpr-TOP
    that me,

12. k-in-hok'-ol ti tz'on
    INC-1sg-leave-INTRAN SUB shoot
    I go out to shoot,

13. pero … chen a'-k'in …
but only DET-day
but only on the day

14. ke Dios k-u-tz'ik ten a'-b'a'al=che'
SUB God INC-3-give/PPM 1sgIOpr DET-animal
that God gives me the animal

t-in-b'en-il-eh,
in-1sgPpr-path-POS-REL
on my path

15. k-in-tz'on-ik …
INC-1sg-shoot-PPM
do I shoot it.

16. i a'-k'in ma'-eh pwes,
and DET-day NEG-TOP well
and the day that he doesn't, well,

17. ma' t-in-tz'on-ik mix b'a'al. …
NEG INC-1sg-shoot-PPM NEG thing
I don't shoot anything.

18. Layti'-e
3Ipr-TOP
Him,

19. ka' t-u-ya'al-ah ten-eh:
then COM-3-say-DPM 1sgIOpr-TOP
then he told me:

20. "Es ke tech-e
it's that 2sgIpr-TOP
"It's that you

21. ma' a-wohel,
NEG 2-know
don't know

22. b'ix u-men-b'-el. …
how 3-make-PAS-INTRAN
how it is made.

23. A'-k'in ka' a-tz'on-o' hun tu keeh-eh" ki ten …
DET-day SUB 2-shoot-SPM one ANIM deer-REL say/3sg 1sgIOpr
The day that you shoot a deer," he told me,

24. "ma' a-b'el a-han-t-eh u-yok …
NEG 2-go 2-eat-TRAN-SPM 3Ppr-foot
"don't go eating its feet,

25. u-yok tu'ux yan u-may-eh. …
    3Ppr-foot where COP 3Ppr-hoof-REL
    its feet where it has its hooves.

26. In-tech-e mäch-ä' …
    EMP-2sgIpr-TOP grab-SPM/IMP
    You take them,

27. i k'äx-ä' [u-,] u-may-eh. …
    and tie-SPM/IMP [3Ppr-] 3Ppr-hoof-TOP
    and tie its hooves.

28. K-a-ch'uy-kin-t-ik yok' k'aak',
    INC-2-hang-CAUS-TRAN-PPM over fire
    You hang them over the fire

29. yok'ol-al [u-,] u-tikin-tal. …
    SUB-SUB [3-] 3-dry-INCHOAT
    so that they dry.

30. I todos tikin-ak-eh …
    and all dry-IRREAL-TOP
    And when they all are dry,

31. te' k-a-b'el [a-,] a-ch'aa-i('ih)
    LOC INC-2-go [2-] 2-take/SPM-SCOPE
    there you are going to take them

32. t(i'ih)-a-ch'uy-kin-t-ik-al a-b'a'ax-tak,
    SUB-2-hang-CAUS-TRAN-PPM-SUB 2Ppr-thing-PL
    for hanging your things

33. ich a-kosiinah-eh. …
    in 2Ppr-kitchen-TOP
    in your kitchen.

34. I b'ay-lo'." ,
    and like-DIST
    And thus,"

35. t-u-ya'al-ah ten-eh,
    COM-3-say-DPM 1sgIOpr-TOP
    he said to me,

36. "i a-wil-ik-eh,
    and 2-see-PPM-TOP
    "and you will see,

37. a'-k'in ka' hok'-ok-ech ti tz'on-eh,
    DET-day SUB leave-IRREAL-2sg SUB shoot-REL
    the day that you go out to shoot,

38. b'el a-k(a'a) a-wil-a' keeh …
    go 2-go 2-see-SPM deer
    you are going to see deer,

39. i b'el a-ka'ah a-tz'on-o'." …
    and go 2-go 2-shoot-SPM
    and you are going to shoot them."

40. In-ten-e t-u-hah-il-e
    EMP-1sgIpr-TOP in-3Ppr-true-POS-TOP
    I, in truth,

41. komo ma' in-wohel-eh …
    as NEG 1sg-know-TOP
    as I didn't know,

42. pwes (t)-in-mäch-ah …
    well (COM)-1sg-take-DPM
    well, I took them,

43. ka' t-in-ch'uy-kin-t-ah. …
    then COM-1sg-hang-CAUS-TRAN-DPM
    then I hung them.

44. B'a-he'-lah …
    TEMP-OST-PROX
    Now,

45. ho'm-ih im-b'et-ik a'-[,]-sekreeto
    TERM-3sg 1sg-do-PPM DET-charm
    I finished making the charm

46. t-u-ya'al-ah ten-eh. …
    COM-3-say-DPM 1sgIOpr-REL
    that he told to me.

47. I te' in-ch'uy-kin-m-ah [yok' u-,]
    and LOC 1sg-hang-CAUS-PERF-DPM [over 3Ppr-]
    And there I have hung them

48. yok' u-k'aak' in-wätan,
    over 3Ppr-fire 1sgPpr-wife
    over the fire of my wife,

49. u-may-tak a'-keeh-eh. …
    3Ppr-hoof-PL DET-deer-TOP
    the hooves of the deer.

50. Tumen … [u-may a'-,] ich u-may b'in a'-keeh-eh,
    because [3Ppr-hoof DET-] in 3Ppr-hoof REPORT DET-deer-TOP
    Because they say inside the hoof of the deer,

51. yan b'in ix me(h)en nok'ol. …
     COP REPORT FEM small worm
     there are, they say, little worms.

52. Ix nok'ol he'-loh …
     FEM worm OST-DIST
     That worm,

53. layti' k-u-ya'al-ik [t-a'…] t-a'-b'a'al=che'-eh …
     3Ipr INC-3-say-PPM [to-DET] to-DET-animal-TOP
     it tells the animal

54. kil-u-tal a'-winik,
     when-3-come DET-man
     when the man comes

55. tun-man u-käxän-t-eh et u-tz'on-eh. …
     DUR/3-pass 3-seek-TRAN-SPM with 3Ppr-gun-REL
     that walks seeking it with his gun.

56. Ix nok'ol he'-loh,
     FEM worm OST-DIST
     That worm,

57. layti' [k-u-,] k-u-kap-äl u-han-t-eh b'in,
     3Ipr [INC-3-] INC-3-begin-INTRAN 3-eat-TRAN-SPM REPORT
     it begins to eat, they say,

58. u-chii', [u-,] u-mum-il u-yok a'-[,]-keeh-eh. ,
     3-bite/SPM [3Ppr-] 3Ppr-tender-POS 3Ppr-foot DET-deer-TOP
     to bite the tender part of the foot of the deer.

59. Entonses a'-keeh-e ya (u-)yohel,
     then DET-deer-TOP already (3-)know
     Then the deer already knows

60. ke winik, [k-u-man,] tun-man u-käxän-t-eh,
     SUB man [INC-3-pass] DUR/3-pass 3-seek-TRAN-SPM
     that a man is walking seeking it

61. i k-u-b'el. …
     and INC-3-go
     and it goes.

62. I mentäk-eh,
     and therefore-TOP
     And therefore,

63. k'äx-a'an u-yok a'-keeh,
     tie-PART 3Ppr-foot DET-deer
     the foot of the deer on being tied

64. yok' a'-k'aak'-eh,
    over DET-fire-TOP
    over the fire,

65. ix nok'ol he'-lo
    FEM worm OST-DIST
    that worm,

66. layti' b'in k-u-päy-ik u-yet'ok. ...
    3Ipr REPORT INC-3-call-PPM 3Ppr-friend
    they say it calls its friends.

67. I mentäk-eh
    and therefore-TOP
    And therefore,

68. k(il)-u-hok'-ol mak ti tz'on-eh ...
    when-3-leave-INTRAN person SUB shoot-TOP
    when one goes out to hunt,

69. k-u-ta-s-ik mak a'-b'a'al=che'-e
    INC-3-come-CAUS-PPM person DET-animal-TOP
    one brings in the animal

70. porke, k-u-yil-ik mak. ...
    because INC-3-see-PPM person
    because one sees it.[1]

Part II

71. Ii ... a'-winik, in-wet'ok he'-loh,
    and DET-man 1sgPpr-companion OST-DIST
    And the man, that companion of mine,

72. t-u-tzikb'al-t-ah ten xan ...
    COM-3-tell-TRAN-DPM 1sgIOpr also
    also told me

73. ke ... a'-b'a'al=che'-oo'-e yan u-yum-il. ...
    SUB DET-animal-PL-TOP COP 3Ppr-owner-POS
    that the animals have their owner (lord).

74. I yan-ah-ih b'in [hun tuu(l) . . .] hun tuu(l) winik-eh ...
    and COP-DIST-3sg REPORT [one ANIM] one ANIM man-TOP
    And there was, they say, a man

75. kap-ih ti sen=kech-tz'on. ...
    begin-3sg SUB INTENS-shoot
    that began to shoot a lot.

[1] When I asked about the charm in 1988, Fernando Tesucún reported that it worked well and helped him shoot many deer.

76. Ii, t-u-kin-s-ah yaab' b'a'al=che'. …
    and COM-3-die-CAUS-DPM many animal
    And he killed many animals.

77. [Despwes, despwes kee,]
    after after SUB

78. Ka' ho'm-ih u-sen=kech-tz'on-ik a'-b'a'al=che'-oo'-eh,
    then TERM-3sg 3-INTENS-shoot-PPM DET-animal-PL-TOP
    Then he finished shooting the animals so well,

79. ka' kap-ih [ti,] ti man-tz'on. …
    then begin-3sg [SUB] SUB mis-shoot
    and he began to mis-shoot.

80. Y ya ma' tan-u-kin-s-ik a'-b'a'al=che'-oo'-e
    and already NEG DUR-3-die-CAUS-PPM DET-animal-PL-TOP
    And then he wasn't killing the animals,

81. chen u-man-tz'on-ik. …
    only 3-mis-shoot-PPM
    he only wounded them.

82. Ii a'-b'a'al=che'-oo'-eh k-u-b'el. …
    and DET-animal-PL-TOP INC-3-go
    And the animals go. (i.e., they do not die)

83. I a'-winik-eh …
    and DET-man-TOP
    And the man,

84. hum p'e k'in b'in-eh,
    one INAM day REPORT-TOP
    one day, they say,

85. t-u-käxän-t-ah a'-[,]-noh keeh-eh
    COM-3-find-TRAN-DPM DET-big deer-TOP
    found the big deer

86. wa'an ich u-kol,
    stand/PART in 3Ppr-milpa
    standing inside his milpa

87. ka' t-u-tz'on-ah. …
    then COM-3-shoot-DPM
    and he shot it.

88. Ii, k(il)-u-wak'-äl u-tz'on-eh,
    and when-3-explode-INTRAN 3Ppr-gun-TOP
    And, when his gun fires,

89. a'-b'a'al=che' k-u-tal yok'-ol a'-winik-eh. …
    DET-animal INC-3-come 3Ppr/over-POS DET-man-TOP
    the animal comes over the man.

90. I layti' tun-b'el kukul=pach, kukul=pach. ...
    and 3Ipr DUR/3-go backwards backwards
    And he was going backwards, backwards.

91. I [a'-ka' ti . . .] a'-ka' t-u-yil-ah
    and [DET-when SUB] DET-when COM-3-see-DPM
    And when he saw

92. ke a'-b'a'al=che' ma' tun-kim-il-eh,
    SUB DET-animal NEG DUR/3-die-INTRAN-TOP
    that the animal wasn't dying,

93. ka' t-u-ka'-b'ut'-ah u-tz'on-eh
    then COM-3-REPET-load-DPM 3Ppr-gun-TOP
    then he reloaded his gun

94. ka' t-u-ka'-tz'on-ah. ...
    then COM-3-REPET-shoot-DPM
    and shot again.

95. T-u-tz'on-ah [ox p'ee . . .] ox pak. ...
    COM-3-shoot-DPM [three INAM] three time
    He shot three times.

96. I a'-t-u-ox-pak-eh,
    and DET-at-3Ppr-time-TOP
    And at the third time,

97. a'-[,]-keeh-eh ...
    DET-deer-TOP
    the deer,

98. ka' siit'-n-ah-ih-eh
    then jump-DETRAN-DIST-3sg-TOP
    then it jumped

99. ka' hok'-ih ti alka'. ...
    then leave-3sg SUB run
    and left running.

100. I a'-winik-e'
     and DET-man-TOP
     And the man

101. ka', tzay-i t-u-pach,
     then stick-3sg at-3Ppr-back
     then stuck behind it,

102. kap-i u-t'ut'-l-eh
     begin-3sg 3-track-?-SPM
     he began to track

103.   a'-tu'ux b'in(-ih) a'-keeh-eh. …
        DET-where go(-3sg) DET-deer-REL
        where the animal went.

104.   [A-ka' t-u-yil-ah …]
        [DET-when COM-3-see-DPM]

105.   A'-ka' t-u-yil-a(h) a'-winik … a'-keeh
        DET-when COM-3-see-DPM DET-man DET-deer
        When the man saw the deer,

106.   tu'ux t-u-yil-ah
        where COM-3-see-DPM
        where he saw

107.   ke lub'-ih-eh,
        SUB fall-3sg-REL
        that it fell,

108.   ka' b'in-ih u-yil-a'. ,
        then go-3sg 3-see-SPM
        then he went to see it.

109.   A'-ka' k'och-ih-eh,
        DET-when arrive-3sg-TOP
        When he arrived,

110.   k-u-yil-ik-eh,
        INC-3-see-PPM-TOP
        he sees that

111.   ya ma'an keeh-(i')ih,
        already NEG/COP deer-LOC
        then there is no deer there,

112.   hun tuul winik
        one ANIM man
        it is a man

113.   a'-wa'an-i'ih-eh. …
        DET-stand/PART-LOC-REL
        that is standing there.

114.   I ka' t-u-ya'l-(ah) a'-winik ti'ih-eh: ,
        and then COM-3-say-(DPM) DET-man 3IOpr-TOP
        And then the man said to him:

115.   "In-tech-eh
        EMP-2sgIpr-TOP
        "You,

116.   b'a'ax k-a-käx-t-ik wa'yeh?" …
        what INC-2-seek-TRAN-PPM here
        what are you seeking here?"

117. I [a' …] a'-[,]-winik-eh ma' pat-ah-ih u-t'an,
     and [DET-] DET-man-TOP NEG ABIL-DIST-3sg 3-speak
     And the man wasn't able to speak,

118. ka' tal-ih-eh ch'uch',
     when come-3sg-TOP mute
     when he came he was mute,

119. (k-u-)yub'-ik-eh [ma',]
     (INC-3-)feel-PPM-TOP [NEG]
     he felt

120. ya si'is=pome'en u-yak'
     already numb 3Ppr-tongue
     his tongue was numb,

121. ma' patal-[u-, u-,]-u-t'an. …
     NEG ABIL-[3- 3-]-3-speak
     he couldn't talk.

122. Ka' t-u-ya'l(-ah) a'-winik ti'ih-eh: ,
     then COM-3-say(-DPM) DET-man 3IOpr-TOP
     Then the man said to him:

123. "Xen! …
     go/IMP
     "Go!

124. Ma' t-in-b'is-ik-ech b'a-he'-la'-eh …
     NEG DUR-1sg-go/CAUS-PPM-2sg TEMP-OST-PROX-TOP
     I am not taking you now

125. [tumen …] tumen, tan-a-man [et-el a'-]
     [because] because DUR-2-pass [with-POS DET-]
     because you are walking

126. et-el a'-mo'nok paal he'-lo'-eh. ,
     with-POS DET-small child OST-DIST-TOP
     with that little child.

127. I yo'l-al a'-paal he'-lo',
     and SUB-SUB DET-child OST-DIST
     And for that child

128. k-u-man t-a-wet-el-eh,
     INC-3-pass to-2Ppr-with-POS-TOP
     that walks with you,

129. mentäk-eh ma' t-im-b'is-ik-ech. ,
     therefore-TOP NEG DUR-1sg-go/CAUS-PPM-2sg
     for that I am not carrying you off.

130. Wa tal-eech t-a-hun-al-eh,
     COND come-2sg to-2Ppr-one-POS?-TOP
     If you came alone,

131. ya ma' tan-ka'-sut t-a-wotoch-eh" ,
     already NEG DUR-REPET-return to-2Ppr-home-TOP
     you wouldn't be returning to your home again,"

132. [ki b'in a'-winik ti'ih a . . .]
     [say/3sg REPORT DET-man 3IOpr DET?]

133. ki b'in [a'-,] a'-winik wa'an,
     say/3sg REPORT [DET-] DET-man stand/PART
     said, they say, the standing man

134. t-u-yil-ah ah, tz'on-eh. ...
     COM-3-see-DPM MASC shoot-REL
     that saw the hunter.

135. I a'-winik-eh,
     and DET-man-TOP
     And the man,

136. ka' tal-ih-eh ...
     then come-3sg-TOP
     then he came,

137. [de] a'-ka' ti(i) ho'm-ih u-t'an et-el [a'-,]
     [?] DET-when SUB finish-3sg 3-speak with-POS [DET-]
     when he finished speaking with

138. u-yum-il a'-keeh-eh,
     3Ppr-owner-POS DET-deer-TOP
     the lord of the deer,

139. ka' ti(i), kap-ih ti chokwil,
     then SUB begin-3sg SUB fever
     then he began to have fevers

140. i ke'el-il. ...
     and cold-INTRAN?
     and chills.

141. I a'-winik-eh,
     and DET-man-TOP
     And the man,

142. t-u-ya'al-ah ti'ih-eh,
     COM-3-say-DPM 3IOpr-TOP
     he said to him,

143. ah tz'on-eh: ,
     MASC shoot-TOP
     the hunter:

144. "Ma' a-bel a-tzikbal-t-eh mix b'a'al [t-a-w,] t-a-wätan. ...
      NEG 2-go 2-tell-TRAN-SPM NEG thing [to-2Ppr-] to-2Ppr-wife
      "Don't go telling anything to your wife.

145. Chen in-tech a-wohel
      only EMP-2sgIpr 2-know
      Only you know

146. a'-b'a'ax he'-la' uch-i(h) tech-eh. ,
      DET-thing OST-PROX happen-3sg 2sgIOpr-REL
      this thing that happened to you.

147. I ma' a-b'el [ti ka'-,] a-man-tz'on-t-eh keeh ...
      and NEG 2-go [to REPET-] 2-mis-shoot-TRAN-SPM deer
      And don't go wounding deer

148. porke waye' k-i(m-b'e)l im-pak'-t-eech-eh,
      because here INC-1sg-go 1sg-await-TRAN-2sg-TOP
      because here I am going to await you

149. ya ma' tan-b'e(l) ti sut t-a-wotoch t-u-ka'ye' " ,
      already NEG DUR/2-go SUB return to-2Ppr-home to-3Ppr-again
      and then you aren't going to return to your home again,"

150. ki b'in a'-winik ti'ih-eh. ...
      say/3sg REPORT DET-man 3IOpr-TOP
      they say the man said to him.

151. Pero ah tz'on-eh ...
      but MASC shoot-TOP
      But the hunter,

152. ich [uuu-,] u-sat-al-il u-yool et a'-chokwil,
      in [3Ppr-] 3Ppr-lose-PART-POS 3Ppr-mind with DET-fever
      in his loss of sense with the fever

153. k-u-tz'ik ti'ih-eh ...
      INC-3-give/PPM 3IOpr-REL
      that he gave him,

154. ka' kap(-ih) u-tzikb'a(l)-t-eh t-u-yätan,
      then begin(-3sg) 3-tell-TRAN-SPM to-3Ppr-wife
      then he began to tell it to his wife,

155. a'-b'a'ax t-u-yil-ah-eh ...
      DET-thing COM-3-see-DPM-REL
      the thing that he saw,

156. [ich k'a,] ich kol-eh. ...
      [in] in milpa-TOP
      in the milpa.

157. Ii chen ho'm-ih b'in u-tzikb'a(l)-t-ik t-u-yätan
and only finish-3sg REPORT 3-tell-TRAN-PPM to-3Ppr-wife
And they say he just finished telling his wife

158. a'-b'a'ax uch-i(h) ti'ih-eh,
DET-thing happen-3sg 3IOpr-REL
what happened to him,

159. ka' kim-ih. ...
then die-3sg
and he died.

160. A'-lo(h) [in-,] hun tuul in-wet-meyah-il
DET-DIST [1sgPpr-] one ANIM 1sgPpr-with-work-POS
That, one of my co-workers

161. t-u-tzikb'a(l)-t-ah ten.
COM-3-tell-TRAN-DPM 1sgIOpr
told me.

17. A Faithful Husband

Told by Fernando Tesucún on July 2, 1988

1. Yan-ah-ih b'in, uch-ih,
COP-DIST-3sg REPORT happen-3sg
There was, they say, long ago,

2. hun tuul winik,
one ANIM man
a man

3. i hun tuul ix ch'up. ...
and one ANIM FEM woman
and a woman.

4. Tz'o'k-a'an u-b'el-oo'. ...
end-PART 3Ppr-road-PL
They were married.

5. A'-winik-e(h), u-yicham ix ch'up-eh. ...
DET-man-TOP 3Ppr-husband FEM woman-TOP
The man was the husband of the woman.

6. Yan-ah-ih hum p'e k'in ...
COP-DIST-3sg one INAM day
One day

7. a'-winik-eh,
DET-man-TOP
the man,

8. k-u-tzikb'al et-el u-yätan. …
   INC-3-talk with-POS 3Ppr-wife
   he was talking with his wife.

9. Ii, t-u-ya'al-ah ti'ih-eh: …
   and COM-3-say-DPM 3IOpr-TOP
   And he said to her:

10. "Il-ah …
    see-SPM/IMP
    "Look,

11. a'-k'in ka' kim-ik-[en-](ech-)eh …
    DET-day SUB die-IRREAL-[1sg-](2sg-)REL
    the day that you die,

12. b'el in-ka'a ti muk-b'-ul ket t-a-wet-el …
    go 1sg-go SUB bury-PAS-INTRAN together to-2Ppr-with-POS
    I am going to be buried together with you

13. yok' a-wil-ik …
    SUB 2-see-PPM
    so that you see

14. ke ten-eh t-u-hah-il hach in-k'a't-eech. …
    SUB 1sgIpr-TOP in-3Ppr-true-POS much 1sg-love-2sg
    that I truly love you very much.

15. Wa tech k-a-kim-il taan-il-eh …
    COND 2sgIpr INC-2-die-INTRAN front-POS-TOP
    If you die first,

16. [yan-a-], in-ten k-im-b'el,
    [OBLIG-2] EMP-1sgIpr INC-1sg-go
    I am going

17. ti muk-b'-ul ket t-a-wet-el. …
    SUB bury-PAS-INTRAN together to-2Ppr-with-POS
    to be buried together with you.

18. Pero wa ten k-in-kim-il taan-il-eh,
    but COND 1sgIpr INC-1sg-die-INTRAN front-POS-TOP
    But if I die first,

19. in-tech yan-a-[,]-muk-b'-ul [ti] t-in-wet-el. …
    EMP-2sgIpr OBLIG-2-bury-PAS-INTRAN [to] to-1sg-with-POS
    you have to be buried with me."

20. Ka' t-u-ya'l-ah-oo'-eh: ,
    then COM-3-say-DPM-PL-TOP
    Then they said:

21. "Ma'lo',
    good
    "Good,

22. hach ma'lo'." …
    very good
    very good."

23. T-u-mäch-ah u-k'ab'-oo' …
    COM-3-grasp-DPM 3Ppr-hand-PL
    They shook hands (sealing the deal)

24. tu'ux k-u-ya'l-ik-oo'-eh
    where INC-3-say-PPM-PL-TOP
    where they said

25. ke b'ay-lo' k-u-b'el u-b'et-oo'-eh. …
    SUB like-DIST INC-3-go 3-do-PL-REL
    that thus they are going to do it.

26. A'-winik-eh …
    DET-man-TOP
    The man,

27. kux-l-ah-oo',
    live-POSIT-DIST-PL
    they lived,

28. i k-u-tzikb'al-oo' tulakal k'in,
    and INC-3-talk-PL every day
    and they talked every day,

29. et-el u-yätan. …
    with-POS 3Ppr-wife
    (he) with his wife.

30. Ka' k'oh-a'an-ah-ih u-yätan …
    then sick-PART-DIST-3sg 3Ppr-wife
    Then his wife got sick,

31. ka' kim-ih. …
    then die-3sg
    and she died.

32. I a'-winik-eh …
    and DET-man-TOP
    And the man,

33. p'at-ih t-u-hun-al. …
    remain-3sg to-3Ppr-one-POS?
    he remained alone.

34. Ka' t-u-k'a't-ah-eh,
    then COM-3-ask-DPM-TOP
    Then he asked

35. [ke,] ka' muk-b'-uk ket et-el u-yätan. ...
    [SUB] SUB bury-PAS-IRREAL together with-POS 3Ppr-wife
    that he be buried together with his wife.

36. Mäch-b'-ih-eh,
    take-PAS-3sg-TOP
    He was taken,

37. ka' ok-s-äb'-ih xan,
    then enter-CAUS-PAS-3sg also
    then he was entered also

38. ich a'-muknal tu'ux,
    in DET-tomb where
    in the tomb where

39. b'in-ih u-yätan-eh. ...
    go-3sg 3Ppr-wife-REL
    his wife went.

40. K'in k-u-man,
    day INC-3-pass
    Days pass,

41. k'in k-u-tal. ,
    day INC-3-come
    days come.

42. K'in k-u-man,
    day INC-3-pass
    Days pass,

43. k'in k-u-tal. ,
    day INC-3-come
    days come.

44. I a'-winik-eh,
    and DET-man-TOP
    And the man,

45. te' yan ich a'-muknal ket et u-yätan-eh. ...
    LOC COP inside DET-tomb together with 3Ppr-wife-TOP
    there he is inside the tomb together with his wife.

46. Laytih ...
    3Ipr
    He,

47. k-u-yil-ik [s,] tulakal k'in,
     INC-3-see-PPM every day
     he sees, every day

48. k-u-yil-ik u-yich u-yätan,
     INC-3-see-PPM 3Ppr-face 3Ppr-wife
     he sees (cherishes) the face of his wife

49. ich a'-muknal-eh. …
     inside DET-tomb-TOP
     inside the tomb.

50. Ii, ka' k'och-ih u-k'in-il-eh,
     and then arrive-3sg 3Ppr-day-POS-TOP
     And then the day came

51. ka' t-u-yil-ah-eh,
     when COM-3-see-DPM-TOP
     when he saw it,

52. hun tuul ah ch'o'. …
     one ANIM MASC mouse
     a mouse.

53. Hok'-ih … ich a'-muknal-eh,
     appear-3sg inside DET-tomb-TOP
     It appeared inside the tomb,

54. k'och-ih yäknal,
     arrive-3sg 3Ppr/with
     it arrived with him

55. i k-u-ta-s-ik …
     and INC-3-come-CAUS-PPM
     and it brings

56. hum p'eel u-mo'nok k'ab' top'. …
     one INAM 3Ppr-small hand flower
     a small bough of flowers.

57. T-u-chi' ah ch'o',
     in-3Ppr-mouth MASC mouse
     In the mouth of the mouse

58. k-u-ta-s-ik a'-top'-eh. …
     INC-3-come-CAUSE-PPM DET-flower-TOP
     it brings the flower.

59. I a'-winik-eh,
     and DET-man-TOP
     And the man

60. kun-ah-ih u-yil-a'. …
    remain-DIST-3sg 3-see-SPM
    stayed to see it.

61. Ka' tal-ih t-u-na'at-eh: …
    then come-3sg in-3Ppr-thought-TOP
    And it came into his thoughts:

62. "A'-mo'nok b'a'al=che' he'-la'-eh,
    DET-small animal OST-PROX-TOP
    "This little animal,

63. tu'ux t-u-ta-s-ah a'-top' he'-la'
    where COM-3-come-CAUS-DPM DET-flower OST-PROX
    from where does it bring this flower

64. k-u-ta-s-ik t-u-chi'-eh?" …
    INC-3-come-CAUS-PPM in-3Ppr-mouth-REL
    that it brings in its mouth?"

65. Ka' t-u-mäch-ah. …
    then COM-3-grab-DPM
    Then he grabbed it.

66. Chen t-u-mäch-ah a'-top'-eh,
    only COM-3-grab-DPM DET-flower-TOP
    He only grabbed the flower,

67. i ah ch'o'-eh b'in-ih. …
    and MASC mouse-TOP go-3sg
    and the mouse went.

68. A'-winik-eh …
    DET-man-TOP
    The man,

69. tal-ih t-u-na'at …
    come-3sg in-3Ppr-thought
    it came into his thoughts

70. u-man-es a'-top t-u-yich u-yätan-eh,
    3-pass-CAUS/SPM DET-flower on-3Ppr-face 3Ppr-wife-TOP
    to pass the flower over the face of his wife,

71. tulakal [t-u-,] t-u-b'äk'-el. …
    all [on-3Ppr-] on-3Ppr-flesh-POS
    all over her body.

72. K-u-mäch-ik-eh
    INC-3-grasp-PPM-TOP
    He grasps it (the flower),

73. k-u-man-s-ik t-u-pol tak
    INC-3-pass-CAUS-PPM to-3Ppr-head till
    he passes it from her head

    t-u-ni' u-yal u-yok. …
    to-3Ppr-tip 3Ppr-child 3Ppr-foot
    to the tips of her toes.

74. A'-lo' man-ih … waak haab' …
    DET-DIST pass-3sg seven year
    That happened for seven years,

75. muk-a'an-oo', ich a'-[,]-muknal-eh. …
    bury-PART-PL inside DET-tomb-TOP
    they were buried in the tomb.

76. Ka' t-u-ya'l-ah [a'-wi,] a'-winik-eh: …
    then COM-3-say-DPM [DET-] DET-man-TOP
    Then the man said:

77. "B'el in-ka'a [in-,] in-man-es,
    go 1sg-go [1sg-] 1sg-pass-CAUS/SPM
    "I am going to pass

78. tulakal k'in, a'-top' yok' in-wätan-eh." …
    every day DET-flower over 1sgPpr-wife-TOP
    the flower over my wife every day."

79. I b'aay-lo' t-u-b'et-ah-eh. …
    and thus-DIST COM-3-do-DPM-TOP
    And thus he did it.

80. Chen a'-ka' t-u-yil-ah-eh …
    only DET-when COM-3-see-DPM-TOP
    Only when he saw it,

81. kap-ih u-pek-es u-b'ah u-yätan-eh. …
    begin-3sg 3-move-CAUS/SPM 3Ppr-REFL 3Ppr-wife-TOP
    his wife began to move herself.

82. Kap-ih u-pek-es u-b'ah. ,
    begin-3sg 3-move-CAUS/SPM 3Ppr-REFL
    She began to move herself.

83. I layti'-eh,
    and 3Ipr-TOP
    And he,

84. t-u-man-s-ik a'-top'-eh
    DUR-3-pass-CAUS-PPM DET-flower-TOP
    he is passing the flower,

85. t-u-man-s-ik a'-top' yok'-ol u-yätan-eh. …
   DUR-3-pass-CAUS-PPM DET-flower 3Ppr/over-POS 3Ppr-wife-TOP
   he is passing the flower over his wife.

86. Asta ka' t-u-yil-ah-eh,
   until when COM-3-see-DPM-TOP
   Until when he noticed,

87. näk-l-ah-ih. …
   sit-POSIT-DIST-3sg
   she sat up.

88. Näk-l-ah-ih u-yätan-eh. …
   sit-POSIT-DIST-3sg 3Ppr-wife-TOP
   His wife sat up.

89. Ka' kap-oo' ti tzikb'al: ,
   then begin-PL SUB talk
   And they began to talk:

90. "I tech-eh,
   and 2sgIpr-TOP
   "And you,

91. tu'ux yan-en wa'yeh?" ,
   where COP-1sg here
   where am I here?"

92. ki b'in u-yätan ti'ih [a'-, (ti')ih] a'-winik-eh. …
   say/3sg REPORT 3Ppr-wife to [DET- to] DET-man-TOP
   they say the wife said to the man.

93. I k-u-ya'al-ik a'-winik ti'ih-eh: ,
   and INC-3-say-PPM DET-man 3IOpr-TOP
   And the man says to her:

94. "Si tech-eh kim-en-ech,
   if 2sgIpr-TOP die-NOM-2sg
   "If you are dead,

95. wa'ye muk-a'an ki-b'ah. …
   here bury-PART 1plPpr-REFL
   here we ourselves are buried.

96. Ma' tun-k'aal tech ke,
   NEG DUR/3-remember 2sgIOpr SUB
   Aren't you remembering

97. [a'-,] kux-a'an-ech-eh,
   [DET-] live-PART-2sg-TOP
   when you were alive

98. tzikb'al-n-ah-o'on
     talk-DETRAN-DIST-1pl
     we talked

99. i ti-ki-wa'l-ah-eh,
     and COM-1pl-say-DPM-TOP
     and we said (promised)

100. ke wa tech, k-a-kim-il taan-il-eh,
     SUB COND 2sgIpr INC-2-die-INTRAN front-POS-TOP
     that if you die first

101. in-ten k-im-b'el ti tal
     EMP-1sgIpr INC-1sg-go SUB come
     I am going to come

102. ti muk-b'-ul ket t-a-wet-el. …
     SUB bury-PAS-INTRAN together to-2Ppr-with-POS
     to be buried together with you.

103. Pero komo tech kim-eech taan-il-eh,
     but as 2sgIpr die-2sg front-POS-TOP
     But as you died first,

104. mentäk-eh wa'ye yan-en, t-a-wäknal
     therefore-TOP here COP-1sg to-2Ppr-with
     therefore I am here with you,

105. tan-in-känän-t-ik-ech. …
     DUR-1sg-guard-TRAN-PPM-2sg
     guarding you.

106. Pero b'a-lah ya kux-l-ah-eech. …
     but TEMP-PROX already live-POSIT-DIST-2sg
     But now you already revived.

107. I b'a-lah, ko'ox ki-wil-a'
     and TEMP-PROX HORT 1pl-see-SPM
     And now let's see

108. [b'ix,] b'ix [ki-,] patal-ki-hok'-ol wa'yeh. …
     [how] how [1pl-] ABIL-1pl-leave-INTRAN here
     how we can leave here."

109. Ka' kap-oo' b'in [u-,] u-kak-t-oo' a'-muknal-eh,
     then begin-PL REPORT [3-] 3-dig-TRAN-PL DET-tomb-TOP
     Then they began, they say, to dig out the tomb,

110. u-men-t-oo' hol …
     3-make-TRAN-PL hole
     to make a hole,

111. asta ka' hok'-oo'. ...
until then leave-PL
until they left.

112. I a'-ka' hok'-oo'-eh,
and DET-when leave-PL-TOP
And when they left,

113. a'-ix ch'up-eh ...
DET-FEM woman-TOP
as for the woman,

114. k-u-xi'ma-t-ik-oo' tz'eek-eh
INC-3-walk-TRAN-PPM-PL little-TOP
they walk a little,

115. k-u-näk-tal-oo'. ,
INC-3-sit-POSIT-PL
they sit.

116. Ka'n-a'an ix ch'up-eh b'ay käl-a'an-eh,
tire-PART FEM woman-TOP like drunk-PART-TOP
The woman is tired, like she is drunk,

117. tumen ... uch-ih tun ...
because happen-3sg then
because it was a long time then

118. muk-a'an [ich a'-,] ich a'-muknal-eh. ...
bury-PART [inside DET-] inside DET-tomb-TOP
she was buried inside the tomb.

119. Tantoh xi'mal-eh
so much walk-TOP
(After) a lot of walking

120. ka' k'och-oo' t-u-chi' hum p'e k'ab'naab'. ...
then arrive-PL at-3Ppr-edge one INAM sea
then they arrived at the shore of a sea.

121. Ka' näk-l-ah-oo',
then sit-POSIT-DIST-PL
Then they sat

122. ti he'l-el. ...
SUB rest-INTRAN
to rest.

123. I ix ch'up-eh ...
and FEM woman-TOP
And the woman,

124. käl-a'an, k-u-yub'-ik u-b'ah,
   drunk-PART INC-3-feel-PPM 3Ppr-REFL
   she felt drunk,

125. ka' chi-l-ah-ih. ,
   then lie-POSIT-DIST-3sg
   and she lay down.

126. A'-winik-eh
   DET-man-TOP
   The man

127. näk-l-ah-ih yok' hun kuul tunich. …
   sit-POSIT-DIST-3sg over one CLASS stone
   sat down on a rock.

128. Ii, a'-winik-eh …
   and DET-man-TOP
   And the man,

129. ka' näk-l-ah-ih,
   when sit-POSIT-DIST-3sg
   when he sat down,

130. ix ch'up-eh, [stumble]
   FEM woman-TOP
   the woman,

131. chi-l-ah-ih ix ch'up-eh,
   lie-POSIT-DIST-3sg FEM woman-TOP
   the woman lay down,

132. i a'-winik-eh t-u-tz'ah u-pol …
   and DET-man-TOP COM-3-put/DPM 3Ppr-head
   and the man put his head

133. yok' u-muk' u-yok u-yätan-eh. …
   over 3Ppr-strength 3Ppr-leg 3Ppr-wife-TOP
   on his wife's thigh.

134. Ii, te'-loh,
   and LOC-DIST
   And there,

135. ka' tal-ih hum p'e noh chem. …
   then come-3sg one INAM big canoe
   then came a large canoe.

136. Ka' hok'-ih a'-[,]-winik-oo'-eh,
   when leave-3sg DET-man-PL-TOP
   When the men came out,

137. k-u-yil-ik-oo' ix ch'up-eh,
      INC-3-see-PPM-PL FEM woman-TOP
      they see the woman,

138. hach yutzil,
      very pretty
      she is very pretty;

139. ki'-ah-ih t-u-yich-oo'. ,
      good-DIST-3sg to-3Ppr-eye-PL
      they like her.

140. K-u-ya'l-ik-oo' ti' ix ch'up-eh:
      INC-3-say-PPM-PL to FEM woman-TOP
      They say to the woman:

141. "Ko'ox. ,
      HORT
      "Let's go.

142. B'a'ax u-ka'a ma' tan-b'e(l) ti ki-wet-el?" ...
      what 3-go NEG DUR/2-go to 1plPpr-with-POS
      Why don't you come with us?"

143. I ix ch'up-eh ...
      and FEM woman-TOP
      And the woman,

144. ka' t-u-ya'l-ah t-a'-winik-oo'-eh:
      then COM-3-say-DPM to-DET-man-PL-TOP
      then she said to the men:

145. "Ma' patal-im-b'el
      NEG ABIL-1sg-go
      "I can't go

146. [porke,] tumen in-wicham-eh tan-u-wen-el. ...
      [because] because 1sgPpr-husband-TOP DUR-3-sleep-INTRAN
      because my husband is sleeping.

147. I komo yok' [in-,] u-muk' in-wok-eh
      and as over [1sgPpr-] 3Ppr-strength 1sgPpr-leg-TOP
      And as on my thigh,

148. te' yan u-ho'ol-i'ih. ...
      LOC COP 3Ppr-head-SCOPE
      there is his head."

149. I a'-winik-eh,
      and DET-man-TOP
      And the man,

150.   ka' t-u-ya'al-ah [t-a'-,] a'-winik,
       then COM-3-say-DPM [to-DET-] DET-man
       then said the man

151.   k-u-tal t-a'-[,]noh chem-eh,
       INC-3-come from-DET-big canoe-REL
       that comes from the big canoe,

152.   ka' t-u-ya'al-ah ti' ix ch'up-eh: …
       then COM-3-say-DPM to FEM woman-TOP
       then he said to the woman:

153.   "Wa a-k'a't-ih-eh
       COND 2-want-PM?-TOP
       "If you want,

154.   k-in-ta-s-ik tech hun kuul tunich. ,
       INC-1sg-come-CAUS-PPM 2sgIOpr one CLASS stone
       I'll bring you a stone.

155.   K-a-ts'ik yalam u-[,]-pol a-wicham-eh,
       INC-2-put/PPM below 3Ppr-head 2Ppr-husband-TOP
       You put it underneath your husband's head

156.   i k-a-b'el ti ki-wet-el." …
       and INC-2-go to 1pl-with-POS
       and you go with us."

157.   Ix ch'up-eh,
       FEM woman-TOP
       The woman,

158.   t-u-k'äm-ah. …
       COM-3-want-DPM
       she wanted to.

159.   Ka' tal(-ih) a'-winik-eh …
       then come(-3sg) DET-man-TOP
       Then the man came,

160.   t-u-tz'ah a'-tunich yalam [u-,]
       COM-3-put/DPM DET-stone below [3Ppr-]
       he put the stone beneath

161.   u-pol a'-u-yicham ix ch'up-eh. …
       3Ppr-head DET-3Ppr-husband FEM woman-TOP
       the head of the woman's husband.

162.   I ka' ok-ih ix ch'up ich a'-noh chem-eh
       and then enter-3sg FEM woman inside DET-big canoe-TOP
       And then the woman entered into the big canoe

163. ka' b'in-oo'. ,
     then go-PL
     and they went.

164. Putz'-ih ix ch'up-eh
     flee-3sg FEM woman-TOP
     The woman fled,

165. t-u-p'ät-ah u-yicham,
     COM-3-leave-DPM 3Ppr-husband
     she left her husband

166. tun-wen-el t-u-chi' a'-k'ab'naab'-eh. …
     DUR/3-sleep-INTRAN on-3Ppr-edge DET-sea-TOP
     sleeping on the shore of the sea.

167. Ka' b'in-oo',
     then go-PL
     Then they went,

168. b'in-oo'. ,
     go-PL
     they went.

169. K'in k-u-man
     day INC-3-pass
     Days pass,

170. k'in k-u-tal,
     day INC-3-come
     days come,

171. (as)ta ka' k'och-oo',
     until then arrive-PL
     until they arrived

172. ti hum p'e noh kah. …
     to one INAM big town
     at a city.

173. A'-ka' k'och-oo' ti hum p'e noh kah-eh,
     DET-when arrive-PL to one INAM big town-TOP
     When they arrived at a city,

174. t-u-käx-t-ah-oo' hun ku(ul) mo'nok nah
     COM-3-seek-TRAN-DPM-PL one CLASS small house
     they looked for a little house

175. tu'ux, k-u-b'el-oo' ti kux-tal. …
     where INC-3-go-PL SUB live-POSIT
     where they were going to live.

176. Te'-lo',
     LOC-DIST
     There,

177. ka' k'och-ih u-yohel-t-oo'-eh ...
     then arrive-3sg 3-know-TRAN-PL-TOP
     then they came to know

178. [ke a'-r̃ey,] ke hun tuul r̃ey,
     [SUB DET-king] SUB one ANIM king
     that a king

179. yan hun tuul u-paal ix ch'up-il,
     COP one ANIM 3Ppr-child FEM girl-POS
     had a child, a girl,

180. kim-en. ...
     die-NOM
     dead.

181. I k-u-ya'al-ik a'-r̃ey-eh,
     and INC-3-say-PPM DET-king-TOP
     And the king says

182. ke a'-winik k(a')-u-kux-[,]-tal-[,]-kun-t-eh
     SUB DET-man SUB-3-live-POSIT-CAUS-TRAN-SPM
     that the man that revives

     [u-,] u-paal-eh,
     [3Ppr-] 3Ppr-child-REL
     his daughter,

183. k-u-tz'ik ti'ih
     INC-3-give/PPM 3IOpr
     he gives her to him

184. ka' tz'o'ok-ok u-b'el yet-el. ...
     SUB end-IRREAL 3Ppr-road 3Ppr/with-POS
     for her to marry him.

185. A'-winik he'-la'-eh ...
     DET-man OST-PROX-TOP
     This man (who has followed his errant wife),

186. t-u-lik'-s-ah a'-mo'nok top',
     COM-3-guard-CAUS-DPM DET-small flower
     guarded the small flower,

187. u-k'ab' a'-top',
     3Ppr-hand DET-flower
     the bough of flowers

188. tu'ux t-u-[,]-kux-kin-t-ah u-yätan-eh. ,
     where COM-3-live-CAUS-TRAN-DPM 3Ppr-wife-REL
     where he revived his wife.

189. K-u-man-s-ik. ...
     INC-3-pass-CAUS-PPM
     He carries it.

190. U-lik'-s-äm-ah. ,
     3-guard-CAUS-PERF-DPM
     He has guarded it.

191. I a'-ka' t-u-yuub'-ah [a'-, a'-,]
     and DET-when COM-3-hear-DPM [DET- DET-]
     And when he heard

192. ke tun-yaal-b'-äl
     SUB DUR/3-say-PAS-INTRAN
     that it's being said

193. ke u-paal a'-r̄ey kim-en,
     that 3Ppr-child DET-king die-NOM
     that the child of the king was dead,

194. i a'-max k(a')-u-kux-kin-t-eh-eh ...
     and DET-who SUB 3-live-CAUS-TRAN-SPM-REL
     and whoever revives her,

195. k-u-tz'a-b'-äl u-yätan-t-eh,
     INC-3-give-PAS-INTRAN 3-wife-TRAN-SPM
     she is given to be his wife,

196. ka' t-u-mäch-ah [a'-,] u-k'ab' u-top'-eh
     then COM-3-grab-DPM [DET-] 3Ppr-hand 3Ppr-flower-TOP
     then he took his branch of flowers

197. ka' bin-ih. ...
     then go-3sg
     and he went.

198. Ka' k'och-ih kan a'-r̄ey-eh,
     When arrive-3sg with DET-king-TOP
     When he arrived with the king,

199. k-u-yil-ik-eh,
     INC-3-see-PPM-TOP
     he sees,

200. t-u-hah-il te' häw-a'an [a'-,] a'-kim-en-eh,
     in-3Ppr-true-POS LOC lie-PART [DET-] DET-die-NOM-TOP
     it is true, there was lying the corpse

201. [ich] ich u-yotoch a'- r̄ey-eh. ,
      [inside] inside 3Ppr-home DET-king-TOP
      inside the king's home.

202. Ka' ok-ih. …
      then enter-3sg
      Then he entered.

203. Ka' kap-ih u-man-es,
      then begin-3sg 3-pass-CAUS
      Then he began to pass

204. a'-top' yok' a'-[,]-ix ch'up kim-en-eh. …
      DET-flower over DET-FEM woman die-NOM-TOP
      the flower over the woman who is dead.

205. Ka' t-u-yil-ah-oo'-eh,
      then COM-3-see-DPM-PL-TOP
      Then they saw

206. ya ix ch'up-eh tan-u-pek-s-ik u-b'ah. …
      already FEM woman-TOP DUR-3-move-CAUS-PPM 3Ppr-REFL
      the woman is already moving herself.

207. Kux-l-ah-ih. …
      live-POSIT-DIST-3sg
      She revived.

208. A'-ka' t-u-yil-ah a'-r̄ey
      DET-when COM-3-see-DPM DET-king
      When the king saw

209. ke kux-l-ah-ih u-paal-eh,
      SUB live-POSIT-DIST-3sg 3Ppr-child-TOP
      that his child revived,

210. ka' t-u-t'än-ah a'-winik-eh,
      then COM-3-tell-DPM DET-man-TOP
      then he told the man

211. ke: "B'al-ah," ki ti'ih …
      SUB TEMP-PROX say/3sg 3IOpr
      that: "Now," he said to him,

212. "in-tech-eh t-a-kux-kin-t-ah im-paal,
      EMP-2sgIpr-TOP COM-2-live-CAUS-TRAN-DPM 1sgPpr-child
      "you revived my child

213. i b'a-lah in-tech, k-u-b'el u-yicham-t-eh. …
      and TEMP-PROX EMP-2sgIpr INC-3-go 3-husband-TRAN-SPM
      and now you are going to be her husband.

214. [yan-a-,] Yan-u-tz'o'k-ol a-b'el yet-el" ,
      [OBLIG-2-] OBLIG-3-end-INTRAN 2Ppr-road 3Ppr/with-POS
      You will marry her,"

215. ki b'in a'-r̃ey ti'ih-eh. ,
      say/3sg REPORT DET-king 3IOpr-TOP
      they say the king said to him.

216. Ka' t-u-ya'al-ah a'-winik-eh
      then COM-3-say-DPM DET-man-TOP
      Then the man said

217. ke ma'lo'. ...
      SUB fine
      that was fine.

218. Ka' tz'o'k(-ih) u-b'el-oo'. ,
      then end(-3sg) 3Ppr-road-PL
      Then they were married.

219. A'-r̃ey-eh t-u-tz'o'k-[?]-s-ah u-b'el-oo'. ...
      DET-king-TOP COM-3-end-CAUS-DPM 3Ppr-road-PL
      The king married them.

220. I ya a'-winik-eh u-yicham, u-paal a'-r̃ey-eh. ...
      and already DET-man-TOP 3Ppr-husband 3Ppr-child DET-king-TOP
      And then the man is the husband of the child of the king.

221. I ka' t-u-ya'al-ah a'-winik-eh:
      and then COM-3-say-DPM DET-man-TOP
      And then the man said:

222. "B'a-he'-lah,
      TEMP-OST-PROX
      "Now,

223. in-ka'a in-wa'l-eh t-a'-r̃ey-eh,
      1sg-go 1sg-say-SPM to-DET-king-TOP
      I'm going to say to the king

224. ke k(a')-u-täka'-t-eh tuulakal a'-[,]-poolis-oo',
      SUB SUB-3-order-TRAN-SPM all DET-police-PL
      that he should send all of the police

225. yan yäknal-eh,
      COP 3Ppr/with-REL
      that are with him

226. u-käx-t-oo' ix ch'up-eh,
      3-seek-TRAN-PL FEM-woman-TOP
      to seek the woman,

227. in-wätan kuch-ih-eh.",
     1sgPpr-wife before-3sg-TOP
     my former wife."

228. Ka' t-u-tz'ah u-k'ab'a' u-yätan t-a'-[,]-poolis-oo'-eh. ,
     then COM-3-give/DPM 3Ppr-name 3Ppr-wife to-DET-police-PL-TOP
     Then he gave his wife's name to the police.

229. Ka' lah-weh(-oo') a'-poolis-oo' ich a'-noh kah-eh,
     then all-spread(-PL) DET-police-PL in DET-big town-TOP
     Then the police all spread out in the city

230. u-käxän-t-oo' ix ch'up,
     3-seek-TRAN-PL FEM woman
     to seek the woman

231. putz'-ih ti'ih,
     flee-3sg 3IOpr
     that fled from him,

232. ke [t-u-kux-,] t-u-kux-kun-t-ah taan-il-eh. …
     SUB [COM-3-live-] COM-3-live-CAUS-TRAN-DPM front-POS-REL
     that he revived first.

233. I a'-ka' käxäm-b'-ih ix ch'up-eh …
     and DET-when find-PAS-3sg FEM woman-TOP
     And when the woman was found,

234. a'-winik-eh,
     DET-man-TOP
     the man,

235. u-yicham-eh,
     3Ppr-husband-TOP
     her husband,

236. t-u-tz'a-ah hum p'e noh … kum, ti k'aak' …
     COM-3-put-DPM one INAM big pot on fire
     put a big pot on the fire,

237. tul et-e(l) aseeteh. …
     full with-POS oil
     full with oil.

238. [a] Tan-u-lok a'-aseeteh
     [?] DUR-3-boil DET-oil
     The oil was boiling

239. ka' ta-s-äb'(-ih) ix ch'up-eh,
     when come-CAUS-PAS(-3sg) FEM woman-TOP
     when the woman was brought

240. ka' hup-b'-ih ich-il. …
     then put-PAS-3sg inside-POS
     and she was put inside.

241. [Te' stumble] Te' kim-ih ix ch'up-i'ih-eh. …
     [LOC] LOC die-3sg FEM woman-SCOPE-TOP
     There the woman died.

242. Ii, te' ho'm-ih a'-[,]-u-t'an-il,
     and LOC end-3sg DET-3Ppr-talk-POS
     And there ended the story

243. a'-ix ch'up putz'-ih
     DET-FEM woman flee-3sg
     of the woman who fled,

244. t-u-p'ät-ah [u-,] u-yicham,
     COM-3-leave-DPM [3Ppr-] 3Ppr-husband
     that left her husband

245. tun-wen-el chi' a'-k'ab'naab'-eh.
     DUR/3-sleep-INTRAN edge DET-sea-REL
     sleeping on the seashore.

18. Wild Beasts

Told by Fernando Tesucún on July 3, 1988

1. Uch-ih, tan-in-ch'iil …
   happen-3sg DUR-1sg-grow
   Before, when I was growing up,

2. ki[n]-tz'ik ki-b'ah,
   INC/1pl-give/PPM 1plPpr-REFL
   we gave ourselves

3. ti tzikb'al et-el im-b'al-oo'. …
   SUB talk with-POS 1sgPpr-brother-in-law-PL
   to talk with my brothers-in-law.

4. Yan ka' tuul im-b'al. …
   COP two ANIM 1sgPpr-brother-in-law
   I have two brothers-in-law.

5. I [layti',] layti'-oo'-eh k-u-tzikb'al-t-ik ten …
   and [3Ipr] 3Ipr-PL-TOP INC-3-tell-TRAN-PPM 1sgIOpr
   And they were telling me

6. kee u-tat-oo', k-u-tzikb'al-t-ik … ti'ih-oo' …
   SUB 3Ppr-father-PL INC-3-tell-TRAN-PPM 3IOpr-PL
   that their father was telling them

7. kee t-a'-witz-oo' yan, t-u-haal a'-ha' …
    SUB in-DET-hill-PL COP on-3Ppr-shore DET-water
    that in the hills that are on the shore of the lake,

8. Hobon Pich …
    PN
    Jobon *Pich*

9. i Ah Wo' …
    and PN
    and Ah Wo'

10. u-k'ab'a' a'-[,]-ka' kuul witz …
    3Ppr-name DET-two CLASS hill
    are the names of the two hills,

11. [t-a'-wi] t-u-näk' a'-witz-oo'-eh …
    [in-DET-] at-3Ppr-belly DET-hill-PL-TOP
    at the foot of the hills

12. yan, nukuch ch'e'em …
    COP big cave
    there are big caves

13. b'ay u-hol, nah-eh. …
    like 3Ppr-door house-TOP
    like the doors of houses.

14. I layti' [k-u-tzikb'al,] t-u-tzikb'al-t-ah-ten-oo' …
    and 3Ipr [INC-3-say] COM-3-say-TRAN-DPM-1sgIOpr-PL
    And they told me

15. ke ich a'-ch'e'em-oo' he'-lo'-eh …
    SUB inside DET-cave-PL OST-DIST-TOP
    that inside of those caves

16. te' käh-l-ah-ih …
    LOC live-POSIT-DIST-3sg
    there lived

17. nukuch a'-b'a'al=che',
    big DET-animal
    great animals

18. ke u-k'ab'a' ah b'oo'. …
    SUB 3Ppr-name MASC lion-like beast
    that are called *Ah Boo'*.

19. Ii a'-b'a'al=che'-oo' he'-lo'-eh …
    and DET-animal-PL OST-DIST-TOP
    And those animals

20. nukuch …
    big
    are big,

21. i k-u-han-t-ik-oo' mak. …
    and INC-3-eat-TRAN-PPM-PL person
    and they eat people.

22. I yan-ah-ih b'in hun tuul nohoch winik …
    and COP-DIST-3sg REPORT one ANIM big man
    And they say there was a great man,

23. ke u-yohel …
    SUB 3-know
    that knows (sorcery),

24. ah waay. …
    MASC sorcerer
    a sorcerer.

25. Yohel[l] tz'äk=yah. …
    3/know cure=pain
    He knows healing.

26. Ii … tulakal a'-mak-oo'-eh saak-oo'. …
    and all DET-person-PL-TOP fear-PL
    And all of the people are afraid.

27. K-u-ya'al-ik-oo'-eh kee,
    INC-3-say-PPM-PL-TOP SUB
    They say that

28. u-ka'a ti k'och-ol wal u-k'in …
    3-go SUB arrive-INTRAN perhaps 3Ppr-day
    perhaps the day will come

29. u-hok'-ol a'-[,]-b'oo'-oo'-eh,
    3-leave-INTRAN DET-beast-PL-REL
    that the beasts will come out

30. i b'el u-ka'ah,
    and go 3-go
    and they're going

31. u-han-t-eh yaab' mak. …
    3-eat-TRAN-SPM many person
    to eat a lot of people.

32. Ka' t-u-ya'al-ah [a'-,] a'-nohoch winik-eh,
    then COM-3-say-DPM [DET-] DET-big man-TOP
    Then said the great man,

33. ah waay-eh …
    MASC sorcerer-TOP
    the sorcerer,

34. ke ma' u-saak-tal mix mak,
    SUB NEG 3-fear-INCHOAT NEG person
    that no one should be afraid,

35. ke layti' k-u-b'el [u-…]
    SUB 3Ipr INC-3-go [3-]
    that he is going

36. [uu-,] u-k'äx-ä',
    [3-] 3-tie-SPM
    to tie

37. a'-b'a'al = che'-oo' ich a'-[,]-aktun-oo'-eh,
    DET-animal-PL in DET-cave-PL-TOP
    the animals inside the caves

38. yok' ma' u-hok'-ol. …
    SUB NEG 3-leave-INTRAN
    so they don't come out.

39. Ii hum p'e k'in-eh …
    and one INAM day-TOP
    And one day,

40. hum p'e k'in vieernes,
    one INAM day Friday
    one Friday, (Thursdays and Fridays are days of sorcerers)

41. b'in-ih b'in …
    go-3sg REPORT
    they say he went

42. u-b'et-eh u-meyah,
    3-do-SPM 3Ppr-work
    to do his work

43. t-u-hol tak a'-aktun-oo'-eh. …
    in-3Ppr-mouth up to DET-cave-PL-TOP
    in the mouth of the caves.

44. T-u-män-ah hum p'e lak tu'umb'en. …
    COM-3-buy-DPM one INAM plate new
    He bought a new clay plate.

45. Ka' t-u[u]-tul-ah et-e(l) ha'. …
    then COM-3-fill-DPM with-POS water
    Then he filled it with water.

46. Ka' t-u-b'i s-ah …
    then COM-3-go/CAUS-DPM
    Then he took it

47. u-p'ät-ä' t-u-hol a'-aktun-eh. …
    3-leave-SPM in-3Ppr-mouth DET-cave-TOP
    to leave it in the mouth of the cave.

48. Ii t-u-käx-t-ah … ox saap, k'uch. …
    and COM-3-seek-TRAN-DPM three armlength thread
    And he sought three arm's lengths of thread.

49. A'-k'uch he'-lo'-eh
    DET-thread OST-DIST-TOP
    That thread

50. layti' a'-k-u-b'et-ik a'-chämach-oo' uch-ih
    3Ipr DET-INC-3-make-PPM DET-elder-PL happen-3sg
    is the one that the old people before made

    et-el tämän. …
    with-POS cotton
    with cotton.

51. K-u-b'il-ik-oo' et-el pecheech. …
    INC-3-spin-PPM-PL with-POS spindle
    They spin it with a spindle.

52. Ii, t-u-mäch-ah a'-k'uch-eh,
    and COM-3-get-DPM DET-thread-TOP
    And he got the thread,

53. ka' t-u-b'i s-ah,
    then COM-3-go/CAUS-DPM
    then he took it,

54. ka' t-u-k'äx-ah. …
    then COM-3-tie-DPM
    then he tied it.

55. T-u-b'et-ah hum p'e krus …
    COM-3-make-DPM one INAM cross
    He made a cross

56. et-el a'-k'uch-eh. …
    with-POS DET-thread-TOP
    with the thread.

57. I komo layti'-eh ah waay b'in …
    and as 3Ipr-TOP MASC sorcerer REPORT
    And as he is a sorcerer, they say,

58. t-u[u]-b'et-ah u-[,]-orasion-il. …
     COM-3-make-DPM 3Ppr-prayer-POS
     he made his prayer.

59. B'ay-lo' a'-b'a'al=che'-e',
     like-DIST DET-animal-TOP
     Thus the animal,

60. kil-u-yub'-ik
     when-3-feel-PPM
     when it was feeling

61. ke wi'ih,
     SUB hungry
     that it was hungry,

62. tak-u-han-al-eh …
     DESID-3-eat-INTRAN-TOP
     it wants to eat,

63. k-u-kap-äl ti akan. …
     INC-3-begin-INTRAN SUB roar
     it begins to roar.

64. Ii, u-k'a't-ih hok'-ol t-a'-aktun-eh. …
     and 3-want-PM? leave-INTRAN from-DET-cave-TOP
     And it wants to leave the cave.

65. K-u-hok'-ol-eh
     INC-3-leave-INTRAN-TOP
     When it leaves,

66. k-u-tal. …
     INC-3-come
     it comes.

67. K-u-k'och-ol t-u-hol a'-aktun-eh
     INC-3-arrive-INTRAN at-3Ppr-door DET-cave-TOP
     It arrives at the mouth of the cave,

68. k-u-yil-ik-eh,
     INC-3-see-PPM-TOP
     it sees

69. äk-a'an a'-noh ha',
     pool-PART DET-big water
     a lake is formed

70. t-u-hol a'-aktun-eh. …
     in-3Ppr-door DET-cave-TOP
     at the mouth of the cave.

71. Ii [tak-u-...] tak-u-k'och-ol,
    and [DESID-3-] DESID-3-arrive-INTRAN
    And it wants to arrive,

72. u-hok'-ol ich a'-ha'-eh. ...
    3-leave-INTRAN inside DET-water-TOP
    to get out of the water.

73. K-u-tak'-äl et-el a'-[,]-k'uch tz'ah-a'an
    INC-3-stick-INTRAN with-POS DET-thread put-PART
    It sticks (is stuck) with the thread placed

    men a'-chämach-eh,
    by DET-old man-TOP
    by the old man,

74. i a'-k'uch he'-lo',
    and DET-thread OST-DIST
    and that thread,

75. k-u-sut ...
    INC-3-change
    it changes into

76. alaambreh-il et u-k'i'ix-el. ...
    wire-POS with 3Ppr-barb-POS
    wire with barbs.

77. I te'e-loh,
    and LOC-DIST
    And there,

78. k-u-yil-ik ma' patal-u-hok'-ol-eh
    INC-3-see-PPM NEG ABIL-3-leave-INTRAN-TOP
    it sees it can't get out,

79. k-u-ka'-sut, ich u-aktun. ...
    INC-3-REPET-return inside 3Ppr-cave
    it returns again, inside his cave.

80. Tun-yakan,
    DUR/3-roar
    It is roaring

81. kil-u-ka'-ok-ol b'in. ...
    when-3-REPET-enter-INTRAN REPORT
    when it again enters, they say.

82. I b'aay-loh,
    and like-DIST
    And thus,

83. b'aay-loh,
    like-DIST
    thus,

84. asta ka' man-i(h) yaab' haab' …
    until when pass-3sg many year
    until many years passed,

85. asta' ka' k'och-ih u-k'in-il-eh,
    until when arrive-3sg 3Ppr-day-POS-TOP
    until the day arrived

86. ka' kim-oo' a'-b'a'al=che'-oo'-eh. ,
    when die-PL DET-animal-PL-TOP
    when the animals died.

87. Ya mix, b'ik'in ka'-[,]-il-b'-ih t-u-ka'ye'.
    already NEG when REPET-see-PAS-3sg in-3Ppr-again
    Then they were never seen again.

III. EXPOSITORY DISCOURSE: LOCAL CUSTOMS AND WORK

19. Feeding the Winds

Told by Fernando Tesucún on June 25, 1988

1. In-ka'ah in-tzikb'al-t-eh …
   1sg-go 1sg-tell-TRAN-SPM
   I am going to tell

2. ti'ih … don Karlos Andres … Hoflink-eh …
   to PN-TOP
   don Carlos Andres Hofling

3. b'ix u-meyah-oo' a'-nukuch winik-oo' … uch-ih. …
   how 3-work-PL DET-great man-PL happen-3sg
   how the great men worked, before.

4. A'-nukuch winik-oo', k-u-tz'ik u-b'ah-oo' ti' meyah …
   DET-great man-PL INC-3-give/PPM 3Ppr-REFL-PL SUB work
   The great men put themselves to work

5. (u-)pul-oo', nukuch k'aax,
   (3-)fell-PL big forest
   to fell great forests

6. ti('ih) u-päk'-ik-al-oo' ixi'im. …
   SUB 3-plant-PPM-SUB-PL corn
   for planting corn.

7. Layti'-oo'-eh [hach,] hach yaab' u-na'at-oo' …
   3Ipr-PL-TOP [very] very much 3Ppr-idea-PL
   They have a lot of ideas (wisdom)

8. tumen, k-u-tzikb'al-t-ik-oo'-eh ke …
   because INC-3-say-TRAN-PPM-PL-TOP SUB
   because they said that

9. yan-u-men-t-ik-oo' tulakal
   OBLIG-3-do-TRAN-PPM-PL all
   they have to do all

10. a'-[,]-b'a'ax k-u-k'ub'en-b'-el-oo' ti'ih,
    DET-thing INC-3-recommend-PAS-INTRAN-PL 3IOpr
    the things recommended to them

11. men u-tat-oo', hach uch-ih. …
    by 3Ppr-father-PL very happen-3sg
    by their fathers long ago.

12. Ya, kil-u-ho'om-ol u-meyah-oo'-eh …
    already when-3-end-INTRAN 3Ppr-work-PL-TOP
    When their work ends,

13. k-u-k'och-ol u-k'in,
     INC-3-arrive-INTRAN 3Ppr-day
     the day arrives

14. ke b'el-u-ka'ah [u-,] u-took-t-oo' [a'-,] u-meyah-oo'
     SUB go-3-go [3-] 3-burn-TRAN-PL [DET-] 3Ppr-work-PL
     that they are going to burn their work

15. yok' (u-)päk'-ik[k]-al-oo' ma'lo' a'-ixi'im-eh. ...
     SUB (3-)plant-PPM-SUB-PL well DET-corn-TOP
     in order to plant the corn well.

16. K-u-men-t-ik-oo' ... u-han-al. ...
     INC-3-make-TRAN-PPM-PL 3Ppr-eat-NOM
     They make its food.

17. K-u-tz'ik-oo' u-yuk'-ul-il. ...
     INC-3-give/PPM-PL 3Ppr-drink-NOM-POS
     They give its drink.

18. Chumuk t-a'-[,]-nukuch ... che'-oo'
     mid of-DET-big tree-PL
     In the middle of the big trees

19. [k-u-pul-,] (u-)pul-m-ah-oo'-eh,
     [INC-3-fell-] (3-)fell-PERF-DPM-PL-REL
     that they have felled,

20. te' ... k-u-kin-s-ik-oo' ah kax,
     LOC INC-3-die-CAUS-PPM-PL MASC chicken
     there they kill a chicken,

21. wa ma', wa ma' ah kax-i'ih-eh kutz. ...
     COND NEG COND NEG MASC chicken-SCOPE-TOP turkey
     if not, if not a chicken, a turkey.

22. I k-u-men-t-ik-oo' hum p'e kum, k'eyem. ...
     and INC-3-make-TRAN-PPM-PL one INAM pot atole
     and they make a pot of atole.

23. La'-lo' a'-k'eyem-eh u-'uk'-ul-il,
     DET-DIST DET-atole-TOP 3Ppr-drink-NOM-POS
     That atole is its (the milpa's) drink,

24. tu'ux k-u-b'el u-men-t-oo' [a'-,]
     where INC-3-go 3-make-TRAN-PL [DET-]
     where they are going to make it (the place)

25. u-tz'ah-oo' a'-han-al chumuk t-a'-kol-eh. ...
     3-give/SPM-PL DET-eat-NOM mid of-DET-milpa-TOP
     to put the food in the middle of the milpa.

26. K-u-ho'm-ol u-took-t-ik-oo'
    INC-3-finish-INTRAN 3-burn-TRAN-PPM-PL
    After they burn

    [a'-] a'-u-meyah-oo'-eh,
    [DET-] DET-3Ppr-work-PL-TOP
    their work

27. k-u-ch'i'-ik-oo' a'-han-al-eh ...
    INC-3-grab-PPM-PL DET-eat-NOM-TOP
    they grab the food,

28. k-u-pul-ik-oo', tulakal t-u-[,]-haal a'-kol-eh. ...
    INC-3-throw-PPM-PL all at-3Ppr-edge DET-milpa-TOP
    they throw it all at the edges of the milpa.

29. K-u-t'än-ik-oo', u-yum-il [a'-,] a'-ik'-oo'-eh. ...
    INC-3-call-PPM-PL 3Ppr-owner-POS [DET-] DET-wind-PL-TOP
    They call the lords of the winds.

30. A'-ik'-oo'-eh,
    DET-wind-PL-TOP
    The winds,

31. yan u-k'ab'a'-oo'. ...
    COP 3Ppr-name-PL
    they have their names.

32. [U-hum] A'-[,]-tu'ux k-u-hok'-ol a'-k'in-eh
    [3Ppr-one?] DET-where INC-3-leave-INTRAN DET-sun-REL
    The one where the sun comes out

33. u-k'ab'a' ah lak'in,
    3Ppr-name MASC east
    is called *Ah Lak'in* (east),

34. tu'ux k-u-b'el a'-k'in-eh
    where INC-3-go DET-sun-REL
    where the sun goes

35. u-k'ab'a' ah chik'in ...
    3Ppr-name MASC west
    is called *Ah Chik'in* (west),

36. i tu'ux k-u-[,]-tal [ah . . .] ah nohol ...
    and where INC-3-come [MASC] MASC south
    and where it comes (is called) *Ah Nohol* (south),

37. ii, u-laak'-eh u-k'ab'a' ah xäman. ...
    and 3Ppr-other-TOP 3Ppr-name MASC north
    and the other is called *Ah Xäman* (north).

38. K-u-ho'm-ol u-t'an-ik-oo' t-u-k'ab'ah-eh,
    INC-3-finish-INTRAN 3-call-PPM-PL to-3Ppr-name-TOP
    After calling them by their names,

39. k-u-tz'ik-oo',
    INC-3-give/PPM-PL
    they give it,

40. k-u-mäch-ik-oo' a'-[,]-han-al
    INC-3-grab-PPM-PL DET-eat-NOM
    they take the food

41. yan t-a'-kum-eh,
    COP in-DET-pot-REL
    that is in the pot,

42. k-u-weh-ik-oo' chen ti ik',
    INC-3-toss-PPM-PL just to wind
    they toss it only to the wind,

43. k-u-pul-ik-oo'. ,
    INC-3-throw-PPM-PL
    they throw it.

44. A'-k'eyem-eh,
    DET-atole-TOP
    The atole,

45. k-u-pul-ik-oo' xan ti ik'. ...
    INC-3-throw-PPM-PL also to wind
    they also throw to the wind.

46. [yok' u-k'ub'en-t,]
    [SUB 3-recommend-TRAN]

47. K-u-k'ub'en-t-ik-oo' t-a'-ik'-eh,
    INC-3-recommend-TRAN-PPM-PL to-DET-wind-TOP
    They entrust it to the wind

48. yok' ma' [u-,] u-lub'-ul u-näl-oo'. ...
    SUB NEG [3-] 3-fall-INTRAN 3Ppr-corn ear-PL
    so that the corn ears don't fall (from the wind).

49. [stumble] K-u-k'och-ol [u-,] u-k'in-il
             INC-3-arrive-INTRAN [3Ppr-] 3Ppr-day-POS
             The day comes

50. ke ya yan ix kuxu=näl ich a'-kol-eh ...
    SUB already COP FEM live=corn ear in DET-milpa-REL
    that there are already tender ears in the milpa,

51. i layti'-oo'-eh [ma' tan-u,] hach ki'mak u-yool-oo'
    and 3Ipr-PL-TOP [NEG DUR-3] very happy 3Ppr-spirit-PL
    and they are very happy

52. tumen a'-ik'-eh,
     because DET-wind-TOP
     because the wind,

53. k-u-man tulakal t-u-haal a'-kol-oo'-eh
     INC-3-pass all at-3Ppr-edge DET-milpa-PL-TOP
     it passes all along the edges of the milpas

54. i tulakal a'-kol-oo' yan natz', t-u-b'ah-il-oo'-eh,
     and all DET-milpa-PL COP close to-3Ppr-REFL-POS-PL-REL
     and all of the milpas that are close to one another,

55. k-u-lah-b'el-oo' ti lu'um,
     INC-3-all-go-PL to earth
     they all went to earth,

56. i a'-kol, k-u-tz'a-b'-äl
     and DET-milpa INC-3-give-PAS-INTRAN
     and the milpa that is given

     [u-,] u-yuk'-ul-il-eh,
     [3Ppr-] 3Ppr-drink-NOM-POS-REL
     its drink,

57. a'-lo' ma' tan-u-lub'-ul
     DET-DIST NEG DUR-3-fall-INTRAN
     that one isn't falling,

58. mix hun teek k-u-b'el ti lu'um-i'(ih).
     NEG one CLASS INC-3-go to earth-LOC
     not one stalk goes to earth there.

59. Tuulakal, [k-u-l,] k-u-hoch-b'-ol [u-,] u-näl-il,
     all [INC-3-?] INC-3-harvest-PAS-INTRAN [3Ppr-] 3Ppr-ear-POS
     All of the ears are harvested,

60. i k-u-lik'-s-äb'-äl, men u-yum-il. ,
     and INC-3-guard-CAUS-PAS-INTRAN by 3Ppr-owner-POS
     and it's guarded by the lords (of the winds).

61. I a'-nukuch winik-oo'-eh
     and DET-great man-PL-TOP
     And the great men

62. [hach,] hach [u-,] ki'mak u-yool-oo',
     [very] very [3Ppr-] happy 3Ppr-spirit-PL
     are very happy

63. kil-u-yil-ik-oo' ke,
     when 3-see-PPM-PL SUB
     when they see that

64. hach ma'lo' [u-,] u-meyah-oo' t-u-lik'-s-äm-ah-oo'. ...
    very good [3Ppr-] 3Ppr-work-PL COM-3-guard-CAUS-PERF-DPM-PL
    they (the men) have guarded their work very well.

65. A'-lo' k-in-tzikb'al-t-ik [por] tumen,
    DET-DIST INC-1sg-tell-TRAN-PPM because
    That I tell because

66. in-noola k-u-tzikb'al-t-ik to'on hach uch-ih. ,
    1sgPpr-grandmother INC-3-tell-TRAN-PPM 1plIOpr very happen-3sg
    my grandmother told it to us long ago.

67. I b'al-ah,
    and TEMP-PROX
    And now,

68. tan-in-ka'-tzikb'al-t-ik ti'ih a'-nohoch winik he'-la'
    DUR-1sg-REPET-tell-TRAN-PPM to DET-big man OST-PROX
    I am telling it again to this gentleman

69. u-k'a't(-ih) u-yohel-t-eh.
    3-want(-PM?) 3-know-TRAN-SPM
    that wants to know it.

20. The Work of the Milpa

Told by Fernando Tesucún on July 23, 1988

1. In-k'ab'a' ...
   1sgPpr-name
   My name is

2. Feliks Fernando Tesukun. ,
   PN
   Felix Fernando Tesucún.

3. Käh-a'an-en wa'ye',
   live-PART-1sg here
   I live here

4. t-u-kah-ih San Beniito. ...
   in-3Ppr-town-POS PN
   in the town of San Benito.

5. B'el in-ka'a in-tzikb'a(l)-t-eh ...
   go 1sg-go 1sg-tell-TRAN-SPM
   I am going to tell

6. b'ix u-meyah-b'-äl, kol. ...
   how 3-work-PAS-INTRAN milpa
   how a milpa is worked.

7. Hun tu nohoch winik
   one ANIM great man
   A gentleman,

8. u-kaal, Estaados Uniidos,
   3Ppr-land PN
   his country is the United States,

9. i u-k'a't-ih u-yohel-t-eh,
   and 3-want-PM? 3-know-TRAN-SPM
   and he wants to know

10. b'ix u-meyah-b'-äl ...
    how 3-work-PAS-INTRAN
    how (a milpa) is worked

11. kol, wa'ye' ti Peten-eh. ...
    milpa here in PN-TOP
    here in the Petén.

12. Pwes u-meyah-il a'-kol-eh ...
    well 3Ppr-work-POS DET-milpa-TOP
    Well, the work of the milpa

13. k-u-chu'um-paal ...
    INC-3-begin-INTRAN
    begins

14. t-u-mes-i(l) disieembre. ...
    in-3Ppr-month-POS December
    in the month of December.

15. K-u-chu'um-paal u-meyah-t-ik mak. ...
    INC-3-begin-INTRAN 3-work-TRAN-PPM person
    One begins to work it.

16. Ya t-u-tz'o'k u-mes-i(l) disieembre ...
    already at-3Ppr-end 3Ppr-month-POS December
    Already at the end of the month of December,

17. k-u-chu'um-paal u-ch'aach'-t-ik mak a'-k'aax-eh. ...
    INC-3-begin-INTRAN 3-clear-TRAN-PPM person DET-forest-TOP
    one begins to clear the forest brush.

18. A'-yax meyah yan-u-b'et-ik mak-eh,
    DET-first work OBLIG-3-do-PPM person-REL
    The first job that one must do,

19. u-käx-t-ik ...
    3-seek-TRAN-PPM
    is to look for

20. tu'ux yan a'-[,]-lu'um ma'lo',
    where COP DET-land good
    where there is good land

21. tu'ux patal-u-tz'ik yaab' ixi'im. ...
    where ABIL-3-give/PPM much maize
    where it can produce a lot of maize.

22. Tumen ma' he'-tu'ux-ak patal-u-päk'-ik mak a'-ixi'im-eh,
    because NEG OST-where-? ABIL-3-plant-PPM person DET-corn-TOP
    Because not just any place can one plant maize,

23. yan-u-k'a'ool-t-ik mak,
    OBLIG-3-know-TRAN-PPM person
    one must know

24. a'-lu'um tu'ux patal-u-päk'-ik mak-eh. ...
    DET-land where ABIL-3-plant-PPM person-REL
    the land where one can plant it.

25. A'-tu'ux k-u-chik-paal a'-lu'um ma'lo'-eh ...
    DET-where INC-3-appear-INTRAN DET-land good-REL
    Where the good land appears (is found),

26. k-u-p'is-ik mak ...
    INC-3-measure-PPM person
    one measures

27. b'oon, mansaana ...
    how many manzana
    how many manzanas

28. u-k'a't-ih mak u-b'et-eh. ...
    3-want-PM? person 3-make-SPM
    one wants to make.

29. [k-u-,] K-u-kap-äl mak u-ch'aach'-t-eh. ...
    [INC-3-] INC-3-begin-INTRAN person 3-clear-TRAN-SPM
    One begins to clear it (of brush).

30. Iih, k-u-ho'm-ol u-ch'aach'-t-ik mak
    and INC-3-finish-INTRAN 3-clear-TRAN-PPM person
    And when one finishes clearing

    a'-k'aax-eh ...
    DET-forest-TOP
    the forest brush,

31. k-u-kap-äl mak ti pul=che'. ...
    INC-3-begin-INTRAN person SUB fell=tree
    one begins to fell trees.

32. Pwees, komo [mak...] mak-eh otzil ...
    well as [person] person-TOP poor
    Well, as one is poor,

33. yan-u[u-,]-meyah mak ... et-e(l) b'aat. ...
    OBLIG-3-work person with-POS ax
    one has to work with an ax.

34. Yan-u-pul-ik mak,
    OBLIG-3-fell-PPM person
    One has to fell

35. tulakal a'-nukuch che'-oo',
    all DET-big tree-PL
    all of the big trees

36. k-u-hok'-ol ich-il-eh,
    INC-3-leave-INTRAN in-POS-REL
    that come out inside (where it's cleared),

37. a'-tu'ux k-u-b'el mak ti meyah-eh. ...
    DET-where INC-3-go person SUB work-REL
    where one is going to work.

38. Y k-u-ho'm-ol u-lah-pul-paal tulakal a'-che'-eh ...
    and INC-3-finish-INTRAN 3-all-fall-INTRAN all DET-tree-TOP
    And when all of the trees are finished falling,

39. ya k-u-p'ät-ik mak,
    already INC-3-leave-PPM person
    then one leaves it

40. ka' tikin-ak. ...
    SUB dry-IRREAL
    to dry.

41. K-u-man u-mes-ii, tulakal u-mes-ih eneero,
    INC-3-pass 3Ppr-month-POS all 3Ppr-month-POS January
    The month passes, all of the month of January,

42. tan-u-meyah-t-ik mak. ...
    DUR-3-work-TRAN-PPM person
    one is working (felling) it.

43. Febreero ...
    February
    February,

44. ya, k-u-k'och-ol u[uu]-mes-ih maarsoh-eh,
    already INC-3-arrive-INTRAN 3Ppr-month-POS March-TOP
    already when the month of March enters,

45. yaa, a'-meyah-eh ya tan-u-tikin-tal. …
    already DET-work-TOP already DUR-3-dry-INCHOAT
    already the work, already it is drying.

46. Ya t-u-ts'o'k u-mes-ih abril,
    already at-3Ppr-end 3Ppr-month-POS April,
    Already at the end of the month of April,

47. ya k-u[u]-mäch-ik mak-eh. …
    already INC-3-grab-PPM person-TOP
    already a person grabs it. (i.e., seizes the opportunity)

48. K-u[u]-täk'-ik k'aak' ti'ih …
    INC-3-light-PPM fire 3IOpr
    He lights fire to it

49. yok'ol lah-el-el. …
    SUB all-burn-INTRAN
    so that it all burns.

50. I ya lah-[…]-el-al tulakal u[u-,]-che'-il-eh …
    and already all-burn-PART all 3Ppr-tree-POS-TOP
    And when all of its trees are completely burned,

51. ya k-u-chu'um-paal u-mes-ih maayo. …
    already INC-3-begin-INTRAN 3Ppr-month-POS May
    the month of May has already begun.

52. Ya k-u-lub'-ul a'-yax ha'-oo'
    already INC-3-fall-INTRAN DET-first water-PL
    Already the first rains are falling,

53. ah chaak-ih=ha'-oo'-eh. …
    MASC thunder-POS=water-PL-TOP
    the thunderstorms.

54. K-u-kap-oo' mak ti pak'. …
    INC-3-begin-PL person SUB plant
    The people begin to plant.

55. K-u-päk'-ik mak ixi'im. …
    INC-3-plant-PPM person corn
    One plants corn.

56. K-u-[pak'-,]-päk'-ik mak b'u'ul …
    INC-3-[plant-]-plant-PPM person bean
    One plants beans,

57. k'uum … sandiia … melon,
    squash watermelon melon
    squash, watermelon, melons,

58. tulakal a'-[,]-b'a'ax [...eeh] k-u-han-b'-äl-eh ...
     all DET-thing INC-3-eat-PAS-INTRAN-REL
     all the things that are eaten,

59. patal-u-päk'-ik mak,
     ABIL-3-plant-PPM person
     one can plant

60. ich a'-kol-eh. ... [6 second pause]
     in DET-milpa-TOP
     in the milpa.

61. Kil-u-hok'-ol tulakal a'-ixi'im-eh ...
     when-3-leave-INTRAN all DET-corn-TOP
     When all of the corn comes out,

62. k-u-kap-äl ti ch'iil. ...
     INC-3-begin-INTRAN SUB grow
     it begins to grow.

63. Ya nukuch, humb'uy chun che'-eh ...
     already big height trunk tree-TOP
     When it's big, at the height of the tree trunks (stumps),

64. k-u-kap-äl mak u-paak-t-eh. ...
     INC-3-begin-INTRAN person 3-weed-TRAN-SPM
     one begins to weed it.

65. Yan-u-paak-t-ik mak ma'lo' ...
     OBLIG-3-weed-TRAN-PPM person well
     One has to weed it well,

66. yok' u-lah-p'-at-äl hanil,
     SUB 3-all-remain-INTRAN clear
     so it all remains clear,

67. tulakal ich-il a'-kol-eh. ...
     all in-POS DET-milpa-TOP
     all inside of the milpa.

68. K-u-kap-äl ti[ii] ch'iil=k'o'. ...
     INC-3-begin-INTRAN SUB grow=tassel
     It begins to tassel.

69. K-u-ho'm-ol u-ch'iil=k'o' a'-kol-eh ...
     INC-3-end-INTRAN 3-grow=tassel DET-milpa-TOP
     When the milpa finishes tasseling,

70. [k-u-,] k-u-wach'-äl,
     [INC-3-] INC-3-burst out-INTRAN
     it bursts out,

71. k-u-wach'-äl [u-...] u-top'. ...
    INC-3-burst out-INTRAN [3Ppr-] 3Ppr-flower
    its flower bursts out.

72. K-u-ho'm-ol u-wach'-äl u-top'-eh,
    INC-3-end-INTRAN 3-burst out-INTRAN 3Ppr-flower-TOP
    When the flowers finish bursting out,

73. k-u-kap-äl [e,] ti hok'-ol u-yix k'ok'och-il. ...
    INC-3-begin-INTRAN SUB leave-INTRAN 3Ppr-FEM baby ear-POS
    the baby ears begin to come out.

74. Ix k'ok'och, he'-lo',
    FEM baby ear OST-DIST
    Those baby ears

75. k-u-kap-äl ti polok-tal,
    INC-3-begin-INTRAN SUB fat-INCHOAT
    begin to fatten,

76. ti polok-tal,
    SUB fat-INCHOAT
    to fatten,

77. aasta [u-...] u-tu'l-ul tulakal [u-...] u-koh et-eh, ixi'im. ,
    until [3-] 3-fill-INTRAN all [3Ppr-] 3Ppr-grain with-POS corn
    until all of the grains fill with corn.

78. Ya yäh,
    already ripe
    Then it's ripe,

79. k-u-yäh-tal. ...
    INC-3-ripe-INCHOAT
    it ripens.

80. Yaah ... k-u-k'och-ol u-k'in-il,
    already INC-3-arrive-INTRAN 3Ppr-day-POS
    Already, the day arrives

81. ke hach ma'lo' t-u-men-t-ik-al mak ix tz'it. ...
    that very good for-3-make-TRAN-PPM-SUB person FEM tamale
    that's very good for one to make *ix tz'it*.

82. Ix tz'it u-k'aba' ...
    PN 3Ppr-name
    Ix tz'it is the name

83. a'-b'ooyo [k-uu-,] k-u-men-t-ik mak
    DET-bun [INC-3-] INC-3-make-TRAN-PPM person
    of the tamales that one makes

et-el ix kuxu' ixi'im-eh. …
with-POS FEM young corn-REL
with tender corn.

84. K-u-huch'-b'-ul. …
INC-3-grind-PAS-INTRAN
It is ground.

85. [eeh,] K-u-huch'-b'-ul, et-e(l) moliino. …
INC-3-grind-PAS-INTRAN with-POS mill
It is ground with a mill.

86. Iih, k-u-tz'a-b'-äl tz'eek asuukar ich-il …
and INC-3-put-PAS-INTRAN little sugar in-POS
And a little sugar is put in,

87. i k-u-tz'a-b'-äl u-b'äk'-e(l) k'ek'en …
and INC-3-put-PAS-INTRAN 3Ppr-meat-POS pig
and pork is put in,

88. [i k-u-chäk-ik ix,]
[and INC-3-cook-PPM FEM]

89. i a'-lo' u-meyah ix ch'up. …
and DET-DIST 3Ppr-work FEM woman
and that is women's work.

90. K-u-chäk-b'-äl. …
INC-3-cook-PAS-INTRAN
It is cooked.

91. Ii, k-u-han-t-ik mak
and INC-3-eat-TRAN-PPM person
And one eats it

92. i hach ki' u-ix-tz'it-il …
and very good 3Ppr-FEM-tamale-POS
and *ix ts'it*s are very tasty,

93. (u-)ix-tz'it-il ix kuxu' ixi'im. …
(3Ppr-)FEM-tamale-POS FEM tender corn
*ix ts'it*s of tender corn.

94. I b'ay-loh,
and like-DIST
And thus,

95. k-u-pak'-t-ik mak,
INC-3-wait-TRAN-PPM person
one awaits

96. u-yäh-tal a'-näl-eh. …
3-ripe-INCHOAT DET-ear-TOP
the ripening of the ears.

97. A'-ka' yäh-ak a'-näl-eh,
    DET-when ripe-IRREAL DET-ear-TOP
    When the ears are ripe,

98. k-u-kap-äl mak ti watz'. ...
    INC-3-begin-INTRAN person SUB double
    one begins to double (the corn over).

99. Ho'm-ol a'-watz'-eh
    TERM-INTRAN DET-doubling-TOP
    When the doubling is finished,

100. k-u-p'ät-ik mak, ka' p'e mes,
     INC-3-leave-PPM person two INAM month
     one leaves it two months,

101. ya wätz'-a'an a'-kol-eh ...
     already double-PART DET-milpa-TOP
     the milpa already doubled,

102. yok' u-lah-[...]-tikin-tal ma'lo' ...
     SUB 3-all-dry-INCHOAT well
     for it all to dry well,

103. yok' u-p'at-äl säk a'-ixi'im-eh,
     SUB 3-remain-INTRAN white DET-corn-TOP
     so that the corn remains white

104. ma' u-p'at-äl k'än-chu'. ...
     NEG 3-remain-INTRAN yellow-?
     and doesn't remain yellowish-black.

105. Tumen a'-kol ma' tan-u-wätz'-b'-äl-eh,
     because DET-milpa NEG DUR-3-double-PAS-INTRAN-TOP
     Because the milpa that isn't doubled,

106. k-u-p'at-äl hach k'as u-ixi'im-il,
     INC-3-remain-INTRAN very ugly 3Ppr-corn-POS
     its corn is left very ugly,

107. k'än-chu' u[u,]-hok'-ol u-ixi'im-il. ...
     yellow-? 3-leave-INTRAN 3Ppr-corn-POS
     its corn comes out yellowish black.

108. Kil-u-men-t-ik mak [a'-, a'-,] a'-wah,
     when-3-make-TRAN-PPM person [DET- DET-] DET-tortilla
     When one makes the tortilla

109. ti han-b'-äl-eh,
     SUB eat-PAS-INTRAN-REL
     to be eaten,

110. ya ma' säk,
     already NEG white
     then it's not white,

111. ya b'ox u-wah-il. ...
     already black 3Ppr-tortilla-POS
     then the tortilla (of that corn) is black.

112. Mentäk-eh, [yan-,] yan-u-wätz'-ik mak
     therefore-TOP [OBLIG-] OBLIG-3-double-PPM person
     Therefore, one must double

     a'-kol-eh,
     DET-milpa-TOP
     the milpa

113. yok' u-p'at-äl hach yutzil u-ixi'im-il. ...
     SUB 3-remain-INTRAN very pretty 3Ppr-corn-POS
     so that its corn remains very pretty.

114. K-u-ho'm-ol a'-watz'-eh ...
     INC-3-end-INTRAN DET-double-TOP
     The doubling ends,

115. ya t-u-mes-[ii]ih ... oktuubreh,
     already in-3Ppr-month-POS October
     already in the month of October,

116. ya a'-[,]-kol-eh ya lah-wätz'-a'an. ...
     already DET-milpa-TOP already all-double-PART
     already the milpa is all doubled.

117. Ya t-u-mes-i(l) novieembre,
     already in-3Ppr-month-POS November
     Then in the month of November,

118. k-u-ch'u'um-paal u-mes-i(l) disieembre,
     INC-3-begin-INTRAN 3Ppr-month-POS December
     (or when) the month of December begins,

119. k-u-kap-äl mak u-hoch-o' a'-kol-eh. ...
     INC-3-begin-INTRAN person 3-harvest-SPM DET-milpa-TOP
     one begins to harvest the milpa.

120. K-u-b'et-ik mak u-makan. ...
     INC-3-make-PPM person 3Ppr-granary
     One makes his granary.

121. A'-makan-eh,
     DET-granary-TOP
     The granary

122. tus-b'i(l) che' …
      join-PART log
      is of joined logs,

123. tu'ux k-u[u,]-b'el u-lik'-es mak a'-ixi'im-eh. …
      where INC-3-go 3-raise-CAUS/SPM person DET-corn-TOP
      where one is going to raise up the corn (to protect it).

124. [a'- i a'-] A'-kol-eh,
      [DET- and DET-] DET-milpa-TOP
      The milpa,

125. kwaando k-u-ho'm-ol mak u-hoch-eh,
      when INC-3-end-INTRAN person 3Ppr-harvest-TOP
      when one finishes his harvest,

126. yan-u-yeh-t-ik mak tulakal a'-nukuch näl. …
      OBLIG-3-pick-TRAN-PPM person all DET-big ear
      one has to pick out all of the big ears.

127. A'-nukuch näl hach ma'lo' …
      DET-big ear very good
      The big ear is very good,

128. ii ma'an [uu-…] u[u]-hol-xux-il,
      and NEG/COP [3Ppr-] 3Ppr-hole-wasp?-POS
      and it doesn't have insect holes,

129. ma' hat-al u-ni' tak a'-holo'och-eh,
      NEG break-PART 3Ppr-tip to DET-cob-TOP
      it's not broken, from the tip to the cob,

130. tulis. ,
      whole
      it's whole.

131. Tulakal a'-nukuch näl tulis-eh,
      all DET-big ear whole-REL
      All of the big ears that are whole,

132. layti' a'-lo' k-u-b'el u-yeh-t-eh mak-eh
      3Ipr DET-DIST INC-3-go 3-pick-TRAN-SPM person-REL
      it's those that one is going to pick out

133. [uu-,] u-lik'-es.
      [3-] 3-raise-CAUS/SPM
      to protect.

134. Yan-u-tus-ik mak [a'-,] a'-nukuch näl he'-lo'-eh
      OBLIG-3-order-PPM person [DET-] DET-big ear OST-DIST-TOP
      One has to line up those big ears

135. yok' a'-makan b'i che',
      over DET-granary of wood
      over the granary of wood

136. k-u-b'et-ik mak-e(h)
      INC-3-make-PPM person REL
      that one makes,

137. yan-u-b'et-ik mak u-nah-il. …
      OBLIG-3-make-PPM person 3Ppr-house-POS
      one has to make its (the milpa's) house.

138. A'-kol …
      DET-milpa
      The milpa

139. naach ti kah-eh,
      far from town-REL
      that's far from town,

140. yan-u-b'et-ik mak u-nah-il. …
      OBLIG-3-make-PPM person 3Ppr-house-POS
      one has to make its house.

141. Ii yalam a'-nah he'-lo'
      and below DET-house OST-DIST
      And below (the roof of) that house,

142. te' k-u-b'el u-b'et-eh mak a'-makan-i'ih. …
      there INC-3-go 3-make-SPM person DET-granary-SCOPE
      there one is going to make the granary.

143. I kwaando natz' a'-kol-eh,
      and when close DET-milpa-TOP
      And when the milpa is close,

144. yan-u-put-ik mak,
      OBLIG-3-transport-PPM person
      one has to transport it

145. et-e(l) tzimin. …
      with-POS mule
      with mules.

146. Wa ma' pwes kuch-b'il. ,
      COND NEG well load-PART
      If not, then loaded (on a person's back).

147. Wa ma'an tzimin-eh kuch-b'il. …
      COND NEG/COP mule-TOP load-PART
      If there aren't mules, loaded (on a person's back).

148. Yan-u-kuch-ik mak tulakal [a'-...] a'-u-näl-eh,
OBLIG-3-load-PPM person all [DET-] DET-3Ppr-ear-TOP
One has to carry all of the ears

149. u-tal-es u-lik'-es t-u-yotoch. ...
3-come-CAUS/SPM 3-raise-CAUS/SPM in-3Ppr-home
to bring them to put them up in his home.

150. Ma' patal-u-p'ät-ik mak ich k'aax ...
NEG ABIL-3-leave-PPM person in forest
One can't leave it in the forest,

151. tumen, k-u-p'at-äl ich k'aax-eh,
because INC-3-leave-INTRAN in forest-TOP
because, (if) it stays in the forest,

152. yaah, hum p'e b'a'ax kee ...
already one INAM thing SUB
then, a thing is that

153. patal-u-yokol-b'-ol. ...
ABIL-3-rob-PAS-INTRAN
it could be stolen.

154. I mentäk-e(h) yan-u-känän-t-ik mak,
and therefore-TOP OBLIG-3-guard-TRAN-PPM person
And therefore, one must guard it,

155. tumen layti'[u-...] u-yich,
because 3Ipr [3Ppr-] 3Ppr-fruit
because that is the fruit

156. tulakal [a'-,] a'-meyah t-u-b'et-ah a'-mak-eh ...
all [DET-] DET-work COM-3-do-DPM DET-person-REL
of all of the work that the person did,

157. i layti' [k-u-?...] tu'ux k-u-b'el mak ti kux-tal. ...
and 3Ipr [INC-3-] where INC-3-go person SUB live-POSIT
and that is where one is going to live.

158. B'ay-lo' u-meyah-b'-äl a'-kol-eh. ...
thus-DIST 3-work-PAS-INTRAN DET-milpa-TOP
Thus is the milpa worked.

159. Iih, k-in-tzikb'al-t-ik t-a' nohoch winik-eh
and INC-1sg-tell-TRAN-PPM to-DET-big man-TOP
And I tell it to the gentleman

160. yok' u-yohel-t-ik,
SUB 3-know-TRAN-PPM
for him to know

161. b'ix u-meyah-b'-äl.
      how 3-work-PAS-INTRAN
      how it is worked.

21. Canicula

Told by Fernando Tesucún on July 31, 1988

1. In-k'ab'a',
    1sgPpr-name
    My name

2. Feliks Fernando Tesukun. …
    PN
    is Felix Fernando Tesucún.

3. Käh-a'an-en wa'ye' San Beniitoh. …
    live-PART-1sg here PN
    I live here in San Benito.

4. B'el-in-ka'ah in-tzikb'al-t-eh …
    go-1sg-go 1sg-tell-TRAN-SPM
    I am going to tell

5. ti'ih … Don Karlos Koflin …
    to PN
    Don Carlos Hofling

6. b'ix … u-yuch-ul … a'-meyah-oo' … wa'ye' …
    how 3-happen-INTRAN DET-work-PL here
    what happens to the jobs here

7. kil-u-k'och-ol a'-mes-ih agoostoh. …
    when 3-arrive-INTRAN DET-month-POS August
    when the month of August arrives.

8. A'-meyah-oo' … ki-b'et-ik wa'ye'-eh …
    DET-work-PL 1pl-do-PPM here-REL
    The jobs that we do here,

9. yan-ki-käx-t-ik ma'lo' u-k'in-il,
    OBLIG-1pl-seek-TRAN-PPM good 3Ppr-day-POS
    we have to seek a good day

10. ti'a'al ka' pat-ak u-b'et-ik. …
    SUB SUB able-IRREAL 3-do-PPM
    so that we can do it.

11. U-mes-i[iii]h huulyo …
    3Ppr-month-POS July
    The month of July,

12. chumuk t-u-mes-ih huulyo …
    middle of-3Ppr-month-POS July
    in the middle of the month of July,

13. [yan] … yan, hum p'e mes …
    [COP] COP one INAM month
    it is a month

14. ke yan-ki-känän-t-ik, ma'lo', ki-meyah,
    SUB OBLIG-1pl-guard-TRAN-PPM well 1plPpr-work
    that we have to attend well to our work

15. tumen a'-k'in-oo'-eh …
    because DET-day-PL-TOP
    because the days,

16. ma' ki' ti'ih u-ch'äk-b'-äl che',
    NEG good SUB 3-cut-PAS-INTRAN wood
    they are not good for wood to be cut,

17. t-u-ch'äk-b'-äl xa'an,
    SUB-3-cut-PAS-INTRAN thatch
    for thatch to be cut,

18. t-u-ch'äk-b'-äl ak' …
    SUB-3-cut-PAS-INTRAN vine
    for vines to be cut,

19. ti'ih pak'. …
    SUB plant
    to plant.

20. Wa yan-u-päk'-ik mak ha'as …
    if OBLIG-3-plant-PPM person plantain
    If one has to plant plantain,

21. tulakal a'-che'-oo' k-u-tz'ik-oo' ich
    all DET-tree-PL INC-3-give/PM-PL fruit
    all of the trees that give fruit

22. i ma'lo' ti han-b'-äl-eh …
    and good SUB eat-PAS-INTRAN-REL
    and are good to be eaten,

23. ma' patal-u-päk'-ik mak,
    NEG ABIL-3-plant-PPM one
    one can't plant them

24. tumen a'-k'in-oo' he'-lo'-eh,
    because DET-day-PL OST-DIST-TOP
    because those days

25. u-k'ab'a'-eh,
    3Ppr-name-TOP
    are called

26. tieempo kaniikulah. …
    time Canicula
    the time of Canicula.

27. A'-kaniikulah-eh …
    DET-Canicula-TOP
    The Canicula,

28. hach b'in chokoh. …
    very REPORT hot
    they say, is very hot.

29. A'-k'in-eh,
    DET-sun-TOP
    The sun,

30. k-u-choko(h)-tal. …
    INC-3-hot-INCHOAT
    it gets hot.

31. I k-u-tal nukuch ah [,] chaak-ih = ha'. …
    and INC-3-come big MASC thunder-POS = water
    And strong thunderstorms come.

32. K-u-man a'-ha'-eh,
    INC-3-pass DET-water-TOP
    The rain passes,

33. k-u-choko(h)-tal a'-k'in-eh
    INC-3-hot-INCHOAT DET-sun-TOP
    the sun gets hot,

34. pero chokoh ke, [k-u-t'äk-ik a'-,]
    but hot SUB [INC-3-?-PPM DET-]
    but hot so that

35. k-u-chäk-ik [a'-,] a'-b'a'ax-tak mum. …
    INC-3-cook-PPM [DET-] DET-thing-PL tender
    it cooks the tender things.

36. A'-päk'-aal-oo' tantoh-u-hok'-ol-eh,
    DET-plant-PART?-PL IMMED-3-leave-INTRAN-REL
    The seedlings that just came out,

37. k-u-lah-kim-il et-el u-chokoh-il a'-lu'um-eh. …
    INC-3-all-die-INTRAN with-POS 3Ppr-hot-POS DET-earth-TOP
    they all die with the heat of the earth.

38. A'-k'in-oo' he'-la'-eh ...
    DET-day-PL OST-PROX-TOP
    In these days,

39. wa mak tak-u-b'et-ik u-yotoch ...
    COND one DESID-3-make-PPM 3Ppr-home
    if one wants to make his home,

40. k-u-ch'äk-ik mak che',
    INC-3-cut-PPM one wood
    one cuts logs,

41. k-u-ch'äk-ik mak xa'an ...
    INC-3-cut-PPM one thatch
    one cuts thatch,

42. a'-max ma' u-yohel
    DET-who NEG 3-know
    the person who doesn't know

43. ke ma' ki'-eh ...
    SUB NEG good-REL
    that it isn't good,

44. k-u-b'et-ik. ...
    INC-3-do-PPM
    he does it.

45. I a'-meyah he'-la'-eh ...
    and DET-work OST-PROX-TOP
    And this work

46. ma' tan-u-xan-tal ...
    NEG DUR-3-last-INCHOAT
    doesn't last.

47. K-u-man ...
    INC-3-pass
    (When one month) passes

48. hum p'e mes,
    one INAM month

49. wa ka' p'e mes ...
    or two INAM month
    or two months

50. ho'm-ok u-b'et-ik mak u-yotoch-eh ...
    TERM-IRREAL 3-make-PPM one 3Ppr-home-TOP
    since one has finished making his home,

51. [k-u-to] k-u-top'-ol u-yix nok'ol-il a'-xa'an-eh. ,
    [INC-3-] INC-3-hatch-INTRAN 3Ppr-FEM worm-POS DET-thatch-TOP
    the worm of the thatch is hatched.

52. K-u-lah-han-t-ik u-le'. …
    INC-3-all-eat-TRAN-PPM 3Ppr-leaf
    It eats all of the leaves.

53. I k-u-p'ät-äl,
    and INC-3-remain-INTRAN
    And there remains

54. chen u-ch'ib'-il a'-xa'an-eh …
    only 3Ppr-stalk-POS DET-thatch-TOP
    only the stalk of the thatch

55. tumen, ix nok'ol he'-lo' k-u-top'-ol …
    because FEM worm OST-DIST INC-3-hatch-INTRAN
    because that worm is hatched,

56. tumen, ch'äk-b'-ih,
    because cut-PAS-3sg
    because it was cut

57. t-u-tieempo kaniikula. …
    in-3Ppr-time Canicula
    in the time of Canicula.

58. Ak' i che',
    vine and wood
    Vines and wood,

59. tulakal ma' ki' u-ch'äk-b'-äl,
    all NEG good 3-cut-PAS-INTRAN
    all are not good to be cut

60. tumen ma' tan-u-xan-tal. …
    because NEG DUR-3-remain-INCHOAT
    because they don't last.

61. [I,] I to'on komo ah meyah-ih=winik-o'on-eh …
    [and] and 1plIpr as MASC-work-POS=man-1pl-TOP
    And we, as we are men of work,

62. [ki-,] ki-b'el ti[ii,] meyah ich k'aax-eh,
    [1pl-] 1pl-go SUB work in forest-TOP
    we go to work in the forest,

63. yan-ki-känän-t-ik xan, ki-b'ah …
    OBLIG-1pl-guard-TRAN-PPM also 1plPpr-REFL
    we have to watch ourselves too,

64. tumen [a'-,] a'-tieempo he'-la'
    because [DET-] DET-time OST-PROX
    because (during) this time

65. ke u-k'ab'a'-eh kaniikula …
    SUB 3Ppr-name-TOP Canicula
    that is called Canicula,

66. tan-u-yalkä'=pach … kan. …
    DUR-3-run=back snake
    snakes are in rut. (male runs behind female)

67. Nukuch kan, k-u-yil-ik mak ich k'aax,
    big snake INC-3-see-PPM one in forest
    One sees big snakes in the forest,

68. u-lah-ch'ot-m-ah u-b'ah-oo',
    3-all-entwine-PERF-DPM 3Ppr-REFL-PL
    they have completely entwined themselves,

69. u-xib'-al i u-ch'up-al. ,
    3Ppr-male-POS? and 3Ppr-female-POS?
    the male and female.

70. Tan-u-yalkä'=pach-oo'. …
    DUR-3-run=back-PL
    They are in rut.

71. Layti' [u-,] u-tieempoh-il a'-la'
    3Ipr [3Ppr-] 3Ppr-time-POS DET-PROX
    This is the time

72. ke [ix,] ix ch'up u-kan-eh,
    SUB [FEM] FEM female 3Ppr-snake-TOP
    that the female snake

73. [yan-u-,] u-ka'a ti yan-tal u-yal. …
    [OBLIG-3-] 3-go SUB COP-INCHOAT 3Ppr-young
    is going to have her young.

74. I ti a'-tieempo tan-[u-,]-u-yalkä'=pach-oo'-eh
    and in DET-tiempo DUR-3-run=back-PL-REL
    And in the time they are in rut,

75. tz'iik-oo' …
    fierce-PL
    they are fierce,

76. porke u-lah-k'äx-m-ah u-b'ah,
    because 3-all-tie-PERF-DPM 3Ppr-REFL
    because they have tied themselves all up,

77. ah ton i u-ch'up-al-eh. …
    MASC male and 3Ppr-female-POS?-TOP
    the male and his female.

78. K-u-yil-ik-oo' mak,
    INC-3-see-PPM-PL person
    When they see a person

79. ke tan-u-b'el ich k'aax-eh,
    SUB DUR-3-go in forest-TOP
    that is going in the forest,

80. [k-u-tal-el,] k-u-tal-el
    [INC-3-come-INTRAN] INC-3-come-INTRAN
    they come

    u-[chuu]-yalkä'-t-oo' mak,
    3-[?]-run-TRAN-PL person
    running after the person,

81. tz'iik-oo'. ...
    fierce-PL
    they are fierce.

82. [A'-,] A'-k'in-oo' he'-la'-eh ...
    [DET-] DET-day-PL OST-PROX-TOP
    These days

83. [taay] hach ma'lo' xan
         very good also
         are very good too

84. ti'ih u-käxän-t-ik-al mak, tz'on. ...
    SUB 3-seek-TRAN-PPM-SUB person shoot
    for one to go out hunting.

85. K-u-b'el mak ti tz'on ich k'aax,
    INC-3-go person SUB shoot in forest
    One goes to shoot in the forest

86. k(a') a'-keeh-oo'-eh tan-u-yalkä'=pach-oo'. ...
    when DET-deer-PL-TOP DUR-3-run=back-PL
    when the deer are in rut.

87. I komo a'-[,]-kol-oo'-eh,
    and as DET-milpa-PL-TOP
    And as the milpas

88. mum,
    tender
    are tender,

89. mehen toh [u-,] u-näl-il. ...
    small still [3Ppr-] 3Ppr-corn ear-POS
    the corn ears are still small.

90. K-u-k'och-ol mak ich a'-kol-oo'-eh
    INC-3-arrive-INTRAN person in DET-milpa-PL-TOP
    (When) one arrives in the milpas,

91. te' k-u-man a'-keeh-oo'(-i'ih) [stumble]
    LOC INC-3-pass DET-deer-PL(-SCOPE)
    the deer walk there,

92. ah ton-oo' i u-ch'up-al-oo'-eh,
    MASC male-PL and 3Ppr-female-POS?-PL-TOP
    the males and their females,

93. t-u-man-oo' ti alkä'=pach. …
    DUR-3-pass-PL SUB run=back
    they are walking in rut.

94. [Ii,] I layt(i') a'-k'in-oo' he'-lo'-eh …
    [and] and 3Ipr DET-day-PL OST-DIST-TOP
    And those days,

95. mak-eh pwes …
    person-TOP well
    a person, well,

96. [k-u,] k-u-tz'on-ik mak …
    [INC-3] INC-3-shoot-PPM person
    a person shoots

97. i lub'-uk [a'-,] a'-ix ch'up u-keeh-eh,
    and fall-IRREAL [DET-] DET-FEM female 3Ppr-deer-TOP
    and (if) the female deer falls,

98. patal-u-tz'on-ik mak ka' tuul wa ox tuul,
    ABIL-3-shoot-PPM person two ANIM or three ANIM
    a person can shoot two or three

99. tumen a'-[,]-u-xib'-al-oo'-eh …
    because DET-3Ppr-male-POS?-PL-TOP
    because the males,

100. ma' tan-u-b'el-oo'
    NEG DUR-3-go-PL
    they aren't going

101. [porke,] tumen, u-ch'up-al-eh …
    [because] because 3Ppr-female-POS?-TOP
    because the female

102. [ya] ya lub'-al ti lu'um
    [already] already fall-PART on earth
    is already fallen on the ground

103. i ma' [?] tan-u-lik'-il …
      and NEG DUR-3-rise-INTRAN
      and it is not getting up,

104. i [stumble] mak-eh (k)-u-tz'on-ik,
      and person-TOP (INC)-3-shoot-PPM
      and one shoots

105. ka' tuul ox tuul u-xib'-al. …
      two ANIM three ANIM 3Ppr-male-POS?
      two or three males.

106. I layt(i') a'-k'in-oo' he'-la',
      and 3Ipr DET-day-PL OST-PROX
      And these are the days

107. hach ma'lo',
      very good
      that are very good

108. ti'(ih) a'-mak-oo' k-u-hok'-ol-oo'
      for DET-person-PL INC-3-leave-INTRAN-PL
      for the people that go out

109. ti käxän=ts'on ich k'aax-e'. …
      SUB seek=shoot in forest-REL
      to look for something to shoot in the forest.

110. A'-l(a') u-tzikb'al-il pwes …
      DET-PROX 3Ppr-talk-POS well
      This is the talk, then,

111. [eee,] u-tieempoh-i(l) kaniikula. …
          3Ppr-time-POS Canicula
          of the time of Canicula.

112. Ii, k-u-sas-tal tulaka(l) k'in-eh …
      and INC-3-light-INCHOAT every day-TOP
      And when every day dawns,

113. k-u-yub'-ik mak u-hum
      INC-3-hear-PPM person 3Ppr-sound
      one hears the sound,

114. b'ay u-hum chaak-eh. …
      like 3Ppr-sound thunder-TOP
      like the sound of thunder.

115. Hatzka', tantoh-(u)-sas-tal …
      early IMMED-(3)-light-INCHOAT
      Early, it's just dawning,

116. k-u-kap-äl [u-, u-,] u-hum a'-kaniikulah-e'
INC-3-begin-INTRAN [3Ppr- 3Ppr-] 3Ppr-sound DET-Canicula-TOP
the sound of the Canicula begins,

117. k-u-hum b'ay,
INC-3-sound like
it sounds like,

118. b'ay ah chaak-ih=ha' k-u-tal-eh. …
like MASC thunder-POS=rain INC-3-come-TOP
like a thunderstorm is coming.

119. I ma' ha'-i'ih
and NEG water-SCOPE
And it's not rain,

120. [chen u-,] chen u-hum. …
[only 3Ppr-] only 3Ppr-sound
just its sound.

121. Layt(i') a'-lo' k-u-ya'l-ik a'-nukuch,
3Ipr DET-DIST INC-3-say-PPM DET-great
It is that, that they said, the ancient

122. mak-oo' hach uch-ih-eh,
person-PL very happen-3sg-REL
people of long ago,

123. ke kaniikula.
SUB Canicula
that is Canicula.

22. Harvesting Chicle

Told by Fernando Tesucún on July 10, 1988

1. In-ten in-k'ab'a' …
EMP-1sgIpr 1sgPpr-name
Me, my name is

2. Feliks Fernando Tesukun. …
PN
Felix Fernando Tesucún.

3. Wa'yeh käh-a'an-o'on,
here live-PART-1pl
We are living here

4. ti hum p'e mo'nok … kah-tal-il
in one INAM small live-POSIT-POS
in a small town

5. u-k'ab'a',
    3Ppr-name
    whose name is

6. Ix Lu'. ...
    PN (fish species)
    Ix Lu'.

7. B'el in-ka'a in-tzikb'al-t-eh ...
    go 1sg-go 1sg-tell-TRAN-SPM
    I am going to tell

8. b'ix u-meyah-il ...
    how 3Ppr-work-POS
    how the work

9. chiikleh. ...
    chicle
    of chicle (is done).

10. In-ten-eh meyah-n-ah-een, hach yaab' haab'. ...
    EMP-1sgIpr-TOP work-DETRAN-DIST-1sg very many year
    I worked many years (at chicle).

11. U-meyah-il [a'-...] a'-chiikleh-eh ...
    3Ppr-work-POS [DET-] DET-chicle-TOP
    The work of the chicle,

12. k-u-b'el mak ...
    INC-3-go person
    people go,

13. yaab', winik-oo',
    many man-PL
    many men

14. u-meyah-t-oo'. ...
    3-work-TRAN-PL
    to work it.

15. Yan temporaada,
    COP season
    There are seasons

16. k-u-b'el treynta,
    INC-3-go thirty
    that thirty (men) go,

17. ventisiinko,
    twenty-five
    twenty-five,

18. kwareenta, winik …
    forty man
    forty men

19. u-meyah-t-oo'. …
    3-work-TRAN-PL
    to work it.

20. Tulakal a'-winik-oo' he'-la',
    all DET-man-PL OST-PROX
    All of these men

21. k-u-b'el-oo' ti meyah-eh …
    INC-3-go-PL to work-REL
    that go to work,

22. k-u-b'i s-äb-äl-oo' men u-tz'ul-il. …
    INC-3-go/CAUS-PAS-INTRAN-PL by 3Ppr-patron-POS
    are carried by their patron.

23. A'-tz'ul-eh …
    DET-patron-TOP
    The patron,

24. layti' u-yum-il a'-meyah-eh. …
    3Ipr 3Ppr-owner-POS DET-work-TOP
    he is the owner of the work.

25. Ayik'al. …
    rich
    He's rich.

26. Yaab' u-tzimin. …
    many 3Ppr-mule
    He has a lot of mules.

27. A'-tzimin-oo'-[,]-eh …
    DET-mule-PL-TOP
    The mules,

28. layti' k-u-b'el u-kuch-u'-oo',
    3Ipr INC-3-go 3-haul-SPM-PL
    they are going to haul

29. tuulakal, u-han-al a'-winik-oo' he'-la' k-u-b'el-oo',
    all 3Ppr-eat-NOM DET-man-PL OST-PROX INC-3-go-PL
    all of the food of these men that are going

30. ti käh-tal ich k'aax-eh. …
    SUB live-POSIT in forest-REL
    to live in the forest.

31. K-u-b'i s-äb-äl tuulakal a'-b'a'ax k'ab'eet-oo' ti'ih-eh,
    INC-3-go/CAUS-PAS-INTRAN all DET-thing need-PL 3IOpr-REL
    All the things that they need are carried in,

32. nok' …
    clothing
    clothing,

33. xana',
    shoe
    shoes,

34. han-al,
    eat-NOM
    food,

35. tz'ak,
    medicine
    medicine,

36. tuulakal a'-b'a'ax k'ab'eet,
    all DET-thing need
    all of the things that are needed

37. ti'ih mak ich k'aax-eh. …
    for person in forest-REL
    for people in the forest.

38. Yan-[u-…]-u-mem-b'-eh hum p'e b'odeega. …
    OBLIG-[3-]-3-make-PAS-INTRAN one INAM bodega
    They have to make a bodega.

39. T-a'-b'odeegah-eh,
    in-DET-bodega-TOP
    In the bodega,

40. te' k-u-lik'-s-äb'-äl tuulakal [a'-…]
    LOC INC-3-guard-CAUS-PAS-INTRAN all [DET-]
    there are guarded all

41. a'-b'a'ax k-u-[,]-täka'-t-ik [a'-, a'-…]
    DET-thing INC-3-send-TRAN-PPM [DET- DET-]
    the things that (the patron of the work) sends.

42. u-tz'ul-il a'-meyah-eh. …
    3Ppr-patron-POS DET-work-REL

43. I a'-tzimin-oo'-eh …
    and DET-mule-PL-TOP
    And the mules,

44. k-u-meyah-b'-äl. …
    INC-3-work-PAS-INTRAN
    they are worked.

45. Yan xan … winik-oo',
    COP also man-PL
    There are also men

46. k-u-meyah-t-ik-oo',
    INC-3-work-TRAN-PPM-PL
    that work them,

47. k-u-tz'ik-oo' u-kuch. …
    INC-3-put/PPM-PL 3Ppr-load
    they put on their cargo.

48. [Tumen a'-]
    [because DET-]

49. A'-winik-oo' he'-lo' k-u-meyah-t-ik-oo' a'-lo'-eh,
    DET-man-PL OST-DIST INC-3-work-TRAN-PPM-PL DET-DIST-REL
    Those men that work at that

50. [u-k'ab'a',] u-k'ab'a'-oo'-eh,
    [3Ppr-name] 3Ppr-name-PL-TOP
    are called

51. ařieeroh. …
    muleteer
    muleteers.

52. Ařieeroh-oo'-eh,
    muleteer-PL-TOP
    The muleteers,

53. yan-[u-,]-u-yohel-t-ik-oo',
    OBLIG-[3-]-3-know-TRAN-PPM-PL
    they have to know

54. u-nak'-äl-oo' …
    3-climb-INTRAN-PL
    how to climb

55. ti'(ih) oox. …
    to ramon
    the ramon tree.

56. A'-oox-eh hum p'e che' …
    DET-ramon-TOP one INAM tree
    The ramon is a tree,

57. ke layti' u-le' a'-che'-eh,
    SUB 3Ipr 3Ppr-leaf DET-tree-TOP
    that it is the leaves of the tree,

58. layti' u-han-al a'-tzimin-oo'-eh …
    3Ipr 3Ppr-eat-NOM DET-mule-PL-TOP
    they are the food of the animals,

59. tumen yan-u-wen-el mak ti beh. …
     because OBLIG-3-sleep-INTRAN person on road
     because one has to sleep on the road.

60. K-u-men-t-ik mak …
     INC-3-make-TRAN-PPM person
     One has

61. ka' p'e ak'ä',
     two INAM night
     two nights

62. oo, ox p'e ak'ä'
     or three INAM night
     or three nights

63. ke yan-u-wen-el mak ti beh …
     SUB OBLIG-3-sleep-INTRAN person on road
     that one has to sleep on the road,

64. asta', u-k'och-ol mak,
     until 3-arrive-INTRAN person
     until one arrives

65. a'-tu'ux … yan ha',
     DET-where COP water
     where there is water,

66. tu'ux yan yaab', (u-)che'-i(l) ya',
     where COP many (3Ppr-)tree-POS zapote
     where there are a lot of chicle zapote trees,

67. tu'ux k-u-b'el ti meyah-b'-äl a'-chiikleh-eh. …
     where INC-3-go SUB work-PAS-INTRAN DET-chicle-REL
     where the chicle is going to be worked.

68. I a'-winik-oo' he'-la',
     and DET-man-PL OST-PROX
     And these men,

69. k-u-b'el u-meyah-t-oo' a'-chiikleh-eh,
     INC-3-go 3-work-TRAN-PL DET-chicle-REL
     that are going to work the chicle,

70. u-k'ab'a'-oo'-eh,
     3Ppr-name-PL-TOP
     are called

71. chikleero. …
     chiclero
     chicleros.

72. A'-chikleeroh-eh ...
    DET-chiclero-TOP
    The chiclero

73. k-u-k'och-ol,
    INC-3-arrive-INTRAN
    arrives

74. a'-tu'ux k-u-b'el-oo' ti käh-tal ...
    DET-where INC-3-go-PL to live-POSIT
    where he is going to live

75. ox p'eeh,
    three INAM
    three

76. wa käm p'eeh, mes ...
    or four INAM month
    or four months

77. ti meyah-[,h]-eh. ...
    SUB work-TOP
    to work.

78. K-u-men-t-ik-oo', [u-,] u-mehen otoch-oo'. ...
    INC-3-make-TRAN-PPM-PL [3Ppr-] 3Ppr-small home-PL
    They make their little homes.

79. K-u-ch'äk-ik-oo' che'. ...
    INC-3-cut-PPM-PL tree
    They cut logs.

80. K-u-ch'äk-ik-oo' xa'an. ,
    INC-3-cut-PPM-PL thatch
    They cut thatch.

81. K-u-ch'äk-ik-oo' ak'. ...
    INC-3-cut-PPM-PL vine
    They cut vines.

82. K-u-meyah-t-ik-oo' ka' p'e k'in,
    INC-3-work-TRAN-PPM-PL two INAM day
    They work two days

83. t-u-wa'-kun-t-ik-al-oo' u-mo'nok otoch-oo',
    SUB-3-stand-CAUS-TRAN-PPM-SUB-PL 3Ppr-small home-PL
    in order to raise their little homes

84. tu'ux k-u-b'el-oo' ti kah-tal. ...
    where INC-3-go-PL to live-POSIT
    where they are going to live.

85. K(il)-u-ho'm-ol [u-,] u-yutz-kin-t-ik,
     when-3-end-INTRAN [3-] 3-good-CAUS-TRAN-PPM
     When they finish fixing

86. u-yotoch-oo' tu'ux k-u-b'el-oo' ti käh-tal-eh …
     3Ppr-home-PL where INC-3-go-PL SUB live-POSIT-REL
     their homes where they are going to live,

87. k-u-chun-ik-oo', u-meyah-oo'. …
     INC-3-begin-PPM-PL 3Ppr-work-PL
     they begin their work.

88. A'-yax meyah,
     DET-first work
     The first work

89. yan-u-b'et-ik-oo'-eh …
     OBLIG-3-do-PPM-PL-REL
     that they have to do,

90. k-u-b'el [u-…] u-ch'äk-ä'-oo' …
     INC-3-go [3-] 3-cut-SPM-PL
     they are going to cut

91. a'-yax, che'-oo' …
     DET-first tree-PL
     the first trees

92. k-u-[,]-b'el u-käx-t-oo'-eh …
     INC-3-go 3-seek-TRAN-PL-REL
     that they are going to seek

93. [u-hok'-s-ik-al,] t-u-hok'-s-ik-al-oo'
     [3-leave-CAUS-PPM-SUB] SUB-3-leave-CAUS-PPM-SUB-PL
     to get out

     u-yitz. …
     3Ppr-resin
     their resin.

94. U-yitz a'-che' he'-lo'-eh,
     3Ppr-resin DET-tree OST-DIST-TOP
     The resin of those trees,

95. k-u-ch'i-ik-oo'-eh,
     INC-3-take-PPM-PL-TOP
     they take it,

96. [t-u-] k-u-lah-b'on-ik-oo',
     [COM?-3] INC-3-all-paint-PPM-PL
     they completely paint

97. u-b'oolsah-oo' ...
    3Ppr-sack-PL
    their sacks,

98. o u-muchiilah-oo'. ...
    or 3Ppr-bag-PL
    or their bags.

99. A'-muchiilah-oo'-eh ...
    DET-bag-PL-TOP
    The bags,

100. [k-u,] dies,
     [INC-3] ten
     ten,

101. kiinseh,
     fifteen
     fifteen,

102. wa veinte muchiila ...
     or twenty bag
     or twenty bags,

103. yan-[u-,]-u-yutz-kin-t-ik mak,
     OBLG-[3-]-3-good-CAUS-TRAN-PPM person
     one has to fix,

104. k-u-tz'ik u-k'aan-il ...
     INC-3-put/PPM-TRAN 3Ppr-cord-POS
     put on their cords,

105. toh k'äx-b'il ...
     well tie-PART
     well tied,

106. i b'om-b'il ma'lo et-el u-miismo,
     and paint-PART well with-POS 3Ppr-same
     and painted well with the same

107. [u-y] u-yitz a'-che'-eh
     [3Ppr-] 3Ppr-resin DET-tree-TOP
     resin of the tree

108. i k-u-p'at-äl pim,
     and INC-3-remain-INTRAN thick
     and they remain thick (with resin)

109. yok' ma' u-hok'-ol. ...
     SUB NEG 3-leave-INTRAN
     so it (fresh resin) doesn't get out.

110. A'-muchiilah-oo' he'-lo'-eh
DET-bag-PL OST-DIST-PL
Those bags,

111. layti' k-u-b'el ti k'ab'eet-tal t-a'-chikleeroh-eh. …
3Ipr INC-3-go SUB need-INCHOAT to-DET-chiclero-TOP
they are going to be needed by the chiclero.

112. Tulakal k'in …
every day
Every day,

113. a'-muchiilah-oo' he'-lo',
DET-bag-PL OST-DIST
those bags,

114. yan-u-täk'-ik mak t-u-chun a'-che'-oo'-eh. …
OBLIG-3-stick-PPM person to-3Ppr-trunk DET-tree-PL-TOP
one has to attach them to the tree trunks.

115. K-u-täk'-ik mak-eh,
INC-3-attach-PPM person-TOP
One attaches them,

116. i k-u-nak'-äl mak et-e(l) sum. …
and INC-3-climb-INTRAN person with-POS rope
and one goes up with rope.

117. A'-sum, he'-lo'-e',
DET-rope OST-DIST-TOP
That rope

118. sum polok. …
rope thick
is thick rope.

119. K-u-yaal-b'-äl ti'ih-eh: "r̃op". …
INC-3-call-PAS-INTRAN 3IOpr-TOP rope
It is called: "rope."

120. Ii, tu'ux k-u-k'äx-ik u-b'ah a'-winik
and where INC-3-tie-PPM 3Ppr-REFL DET-man
And where the man ties himself

121. tu'ux k-u-b'el ti nak'-äl t-a'-che'-eh. …
where INC-3-go SUB climb-INTRAN to-DET-tree-TOP
is where he is going to go up the tree.

122. U-noh maskab'-eh,
3Ppr-big machete-TOP
His great machete,

123. hay,
      sharp
      it's sharp,

124. hay …
      sharp
      sharp,

125. b'ay u-yel xileeteh …
      like 3Ppr-edge razor
      like the edge of a razor

126. yok'ol-al ma' u-[,]-pa'-ik [u-,] u-pach a'-che',
      SUB-SUB NEG 3-split-PPM [3Ppr-] 3Ppr-bark DET-tree
      so that it doesn't split the bark of the tree

127. k-u-(b'e)l u-ch'äk-ä'-eh
      INC-3-go 3-cut-SPM-REL
      he is going to cut

128. porke te' [k] yan-u-[,]-chul u-b'ah,
      because LOC [INC?] OBLIG-3-drain 3Ppr-REFL
      because there it has to drain,

129. tulakal u-yitz a'-che',
      all 3Ppr-resin DET-tree
      all of the resin of the tree

130. k-u-(b'e)l u-ch'äk-ä'-eh. …
      INC-3-go 3-cut-SPM-REL
      he is going to cut.

131. I a'-lo' yan-u-k'och-ol,
      and DET-DIST OBLIG-3-arrive-INTRAN
      And that (the resin) has to arrive,

132. tulakal t-a'-muchiilah-eh. …
      all to-DET-bag-TOP
      all to the bag.

133. I ho'm-ol-[u-,]-u-meyah-t-ik-oo' a'-che'-eh …
      and TERM-INTRAN-[3-]-3-work-TRAN-PPM-PL DET-tree-TOP
      And (when) they finish working the tree,

134. k-u-yem-el,
      INC-3-descend-INTRAN
      he climbs down

135. i k-u-käx-t-ik u-laak'. ,
      and INC-3-seek-TRAN-PPM 3Ppr-other
      and seeks another.

136. I komo … ich k'aax-eh …
      and as in forest-TOP
      And as in the forest

137. [aaa' yan . . .] yan soona,
      [ahh COP] COP zone
      there are zones,

138. u-k'ab'a' soona [, ee,] chikleerah …
      3Ppr-name zone chicle
      they are called chicle zones,

139. tu'ux k-u-meyah-b'-äl a'-chiikleh-eh. …
      where INC-3-work-PAS-INTRAN DET-chicle-REL
      where the chicle is worked.

140. [Ii,] I hach yan u-ya'-il. …
      [and] and much COP 3Ppr-zapote-POS
      And they have a lot of zapote trees.

141. I tuulakal a'-winik-oo'
      and all DET-man-PL
      And all of the men,

142. a'-treynta wa a'-quareenta winik-oo',
      DET-thirty or DET-forty man-PL
      the thirty or forty men,

143. k-u-b'el [garbled] u-meyah-t-oo' a'-chiikleh-eh. ,
      INC-3-go 3-work-TRAN-PL DET-chicle-TOP
      go to work the chicle.

144. Layti' b'ay-lo' k-(u-b'el)-u-meyah-t-oo',
      3Ipr like-DIST INC-(3-go)-3-work-TRAN-PL
      They thus go to work it,

145. tuulakal-oo',
      all-PL
      all of them,

146. sansamal. ,
      every day
      every day.

147. Yan-u-lik'-il-oo' ak'ä'-u-sas-tal. …
      OBLIG-3-rise-INTRAN-PL night-3-bright-INCHOAT
      They have to get up at dawn.

148. K-u-b'et-ik-oo' u-han-al …
      INC-3-make-PPM-PL 3Ppr-eat-NOM
      They make their food,

149. [ii,] i k-u-b'i s-ik-oo' han-al ich k'aax,
[and] and INC-3-go/CAUS-PPM-PL eat-NOM in forest
and they bring food into the forest,

150. tumen ya layti'-oo'-eh,
because already 3Ipr-PL-TOP
because already they,

151. k-u-hok'-ol-oo'-eh ...
INC-3-leave-INTRAN-PL-TOP
when they leave,

152. ak'ä' =u-sas-tal. ...
night=3-bright-INCHOAT
it's at dawn.

153. Ii k-u-yok-ol-oo' t-u[u]-yotoch-oo'-eh,
and INC-3-enter-INTRAN-PL in-3Ppr-home-PL-TOP
And they enter into their homes,

154. k-u-tal-el-oo' ich k'aax-eh ...
INC-3-come-INTRAN-PL inside forest-TOP
they come from inside the forest,

155. las seis,
six o'clock
at six o'clock,

156. las siete ak'ä',
seven o'clock night
at seven at night

157. tan-u-k'och-ol-oo',
DUR-3-arrive-INTRAN-PL
they are arriving

158. u-b'et-oo' u-han-al. ...
3-make-PL 3Ppr-eat-NOM
to make their food.

159. Ii yan tz'ul ...
and COP patron
And there are patrons,

160. [eee] ke [a'-,] ah meyah-oo'-eh ...
SUB [DET-] MASC worker-PL-TOP
that, the workers

161. u-k'a't-oo' ka' xi'ik hun tuul ix ch'up,
3-want-PL SUB go/IRREAL one ANIM FEM woman
want a woman to go

162. u-men-t-eh u-han-al-oo'. ...
    3-make-TRAN-SPM 3Ppr-eat-NOM-PL
    to make their food.

163. [A'-] A'-ayik'al-eh k-u-käx-t-ik
    [DET-] DET-rich man-TOP INC-3-seek-TRAN-PPM
    The rich man seeks

    ix ch'up-eh
    FEM woman-TOP
    a woman,

164. a'-lo' u-k'ab'a' ix kosineera. ,
    DET-DIST 3Ppr-name FEM cook
    that one is called the cook.

165. Layti' k-u-(b'e)l u-chäk-ä',
    3Ipr INC-3-go 3-cook-SPM
    She is going to cook

166. tulakal u-han-al a'-winik-oo'-eh,
    all 3Ppr-eat-NOM DET-man-PL-TOP
    all of the food of the men,

167. (u-)p'o'-o' u-nok'. ...
    (3-)wash-SPM 3Ppr-clothes
    to wash their clothes.

168. A'-lo'-oo'-eh,
    DET-DIST-PL-TOP
    All of that (those things),

169. yan-u-b'o'ol-b'-ol u-meyah ix ch'up-eh. ...
    OBLIG-3-pay-PAS-INTRAN 3Ppr-work FEM woman-TOP
    the work of the woman, has to be paid for.

170. Ii, kada mes,
    and each month
    And each month,

171. yan-u-b'o'-t-ik a'-chikleeroh-eh u-meyah
    OBLIG-3-pay-TRAN-PPM DET-chiclero-TOP 3Ppr-work
    the chiclero has to pay for the work

    ix ch'up-eh. ...
    FEM-woman-TOP
    of the woman.

172. K-u-k'a't-ik-oo',
    INC-3-ask-PPM-PL
    She asks

173. oocho,
     eight
     eight

174. wa dies ketsal …
     or ten quetzal
     or ten quetzals

175. [yok'ol] yok', kaada, hun tuul winik …
     [for] for each one ANIM man
     for each man

176. [a'-,] a'-han-al k-u-b'et-ik ix ch'up-eh. …
     [DET-] DET-eat-NOM INC-3-make-PPM FEM woman-REL
     for the food that the woman makes.

177. Ii … wa ma'an ix ch'up,
     and COND NEG/COP FEM woman
     And if there isn't a woman

178. k-u-b'et-ik a'-han-al-eh
     INC-3-make-PPM DET-eat-NOM-REL
     that makes the food,

179. pwes, layti'-oo' yan-u-chäk-ik-oo' u-b'u'ul,
     well 3Ipr-PL OBLIG-3-cook-PPM-PL 3Ppr-bean
     well, they have to cook their beans,

180. u-b'äk',
     3Ppr-meat
     their meat,

181. u-[,]-ixi'im,
     3Ppr-corn
     their corn,

182. porke chen wah k-u-han-b'-äl ich k'aax,
     because only tortilla INC-3-eat-PAS-INTRAN in forest
     because only tortillas are eaten in the forest,

183. i ariina. …
     and flour
     and flour.

184. Ii, wa yan u-tz'on-oo'-eh
     and COND COP 3Ppr-gun-PL-TOP
     And if they have a gun

185. (k-)u-tz'on-ik-oo' b'a'al=che',
     (INC-)3-shoot-PPM-PL animal
     they shoot animals,

186. k-u-han-t-ik-oo' b'äk'. …
     INC-3-eat-TRAN-PPM-PL meat
     they eat meat.

187. Layti'-oo' yan-u-b'et-ik-oo' u-han-al-oo'. …
     3Ipr-PL OBLIG-3-make-PPM-PL 3Ppr-eat-NOM-PL
     They have to make their foods.

188. A'-meyah he'-la'-eh,
     DET-work OST-PROX-TOP
     This work,

189. k-u-xan-tal …
     INC-3-last-INCHOAT
     lasts

190. seys asta' siete, mes …
     six up to seven month
     six, up to seven months,

191. u-k'äl-m-ah u-b'ah a'-winik-oo' ich k'aax-eh. …
     3-keep-PERF-DPM 3Ppr-REFL DET-man-PL in forest-TOP
     the men have kept themselves in the forest.

192. Ii, k-u-ts'iib'-b'-il hum p'e kontraato. …
     and INC-3-write-PAS-INTRAN one INAM contract
     And a contract is signed.

193. A'-kontraatoh-eh …
     DET-contract-TOP
     The contract,

194. yan-u-men-t-ik mak. …
     OBLIG-3-do-TRAN-PPM person
     one has to fulfill it.

195. Dies, kiinseh, veynteh, aastaa … treynta kintal …
     ten fifteen twenty up to thirty quintal
     Ten, fifteen, twenty, up to thirty quintals

196. chiikle yan-u-k'ub'-ik-oo', [t-a'-,] t-a'-tz'ul-eh. …
     chicle OBLIG-3-deliver-PPM-PL [to-DET-] to-DET-patron-TOP
     of chicle they have to deliver to the patron.

197. [Ii…] i yan-u-meyah-b'-äl aasta u-hok'-ol [a'-…]
     [and] and OBLIG-3-work-PAS-INTRAN till 3-leave-INTRAN [DET-]
     And it has to be worked until

198. [aa] u-tz'o'k a'-kintal-eh,
     3Ppr-end DET-quintal-TOP
     the last of the quintals (comes out)

199. yok' u-pat-al u-yem-el a'-winik, t-u-yotoch-eh.
SUB 3-able-INTRAN 3-descend-INTRAN DET-man to-3Ppr-home-TOP
for the man to be able to come down to his home.

200. Wa ma' ma' tan-u-pat-al u-hok'-ol. ...
COND NEG NEG DUR-3-able-INTRAN 3-leave-INTRAN
If not, he isn't able to leave.

201. Yan-[u-, u-,]-u-muk'=yah-t-ik u-b'ah ich k'aax,
OBLIG-[3- 3-]-3-sustain-TRAN-PPM 3Ppr-REFL in forest
He has to sustain himself in the forest

202. aasta u-k'och-ol treyntay uuno, de maarso. ,
till 3-arrive-INTRAN thirty-one of March
until the thirty-first of March arrives.

203. Layt(i) u-k'in-il a'-lo'
3Ipr 3Ppr-day-POS DET-DIST
It is that day

204. [u-,] u-[,]-ho'm-ol a'-[,]-contraatoh-eh. ...
[3-] 3-end-INTRAN DET-contract-REL
that the contract ends.

205. I tulakal [a'-...] a'-[,]-mees-oo',
and all [DET-] DET-month-PL
And all of the months

206. ke yan a'-winik ich k'aax-eh,
SUB COP DET-man in forest-REL
that the man is in the forest,

207. wa yan yätan
COND COP 3Ppr/wife
if he has a wife

208. wa yan u-paal-oo'-eh ...
COND COP 3Ppr-child-PL-TOP
or if he has children,

209. a'-ayik'al he'-la',
DET-rich man OST-PROX
this rich man

210. ke layti' u-tz'ul-il a'-meyah-eh ...
SUB 3Ipr 3Ppr-patron-POS DET-work-REL
that is the one who is the patron of the work,

211. yan-[u-,]-u-man-s-ik ta'=k'in t-u-yätan
OBLIG-[3-]-3-pass-CAUS-PPM money to-3Ppr-wife
he has to pass money to the wife

a'-winik he'-la',
DET-man OST-PROX
of this man

212. k-u-meyah ich k'aax-eh. …
      INC-3-work in forest-REL
      that works in the forest.

213. A'-ta' = k'in he'-lo'
      DET-money OST-DIST
      That money

214. k-u-k'ub'-ik [a'-,] a'-ayik'al t-u-yätan
      INC-3-deliver-PPM [DET-] DET-rich man to-3Ppr-wife
      that the rich man delivers to the wife

215. [ah, a'-,] a'-winik ke'en ich k'aax-eh,
      [MASC DET-] DET-man be(?) in forest-REL
      of the man who is in the forest

216. (u-)k'ab'a'-eh,
      (3Ppr-)name-TOP
      is called

217. menswalidad. …
      monthly pay
      monthly pay.

218. Tulakal [u-,] u-tz'o'k a'-k'in,
      every [3Ppr-] 3Ppr-end DET-day
      All of the last days

219. k-u-ho'm-ol a'-mees-eh,
      INC-3-finish-INTRAN DET-month-REL
      that end the month

220. k-u-k'och-ol ix ch'up,
      INC-3-arrive-INTRAN FEM woman
      the woman arrives

221. u-ch'aa' u-ta' = k'in [t-u-yotoch a'-…]
      3-collect/SPM 3Ppr-money [at-3Ppr-home DET-]
      to collect her money

222. t-u-yotoch a'-ayik'al-eh. …
      at-3Ppr-home DET-rich man-TOP
      at the home of the rich man.

223. I b'ay-lo' aasta u-ho'm-ol a'-[,]-temporaadah-eh …
      and like-DIST till 3-end-INTRAN DET-season-TOP
      And thus, only when the season ends,

224. k-u-yem-el a'-[,]-winik-oo', ich k'aax-eh
     INC-3-descend-INTRAN DET-man-PL in forest-TOP
     the men come down from inside the forest,

225. k-u-k'och-ol-oo', t-u-yotoch
     INC-3-arrive-INTRAN-PL to-3Ppr-home
     they arrive at their homes

226. u-men-t-oo' u-meyah. ...
     3-do-TRAN-PL 3Ppr-work
     to do their work.

227. Ii [a'-, a'-,] tulakal [a'-, a'-...] a'-mees-oo' he'-la',
     and [DET- DET-] all [DET- DET-] DET-month-PL OST-PROX
     And all of these months

228. tan-u-meyah-b'-äl a'-chiikleh-eh ...
     DUR-3-work-PAS-INTRAN DET-chicle-REL
     that the chicle is being worked,

229. komo k-u-man-s-ik mak,
     as INC-3-pass-CAUS-PPM person
     as there come to one

230. hach yaab' [ee...] nesesidad ich k'aax,
     very many need in forest
     many needs in the forest,

231. tumen ... aveeses-eh yan, yan k'in
     because at times-TOP COP COP day
     because at times there are days

232. k-u-k'oh-a'an-tal mak,
     INC-3-sick-PART-INCHOAT person
     when one gets sick,

233. k-u-k'oh-a'an-tal,
     INC-3-sick-PART-INCHOAT
     he gets sick,

234. i komo naach yan mak tii [k],
     and as far COP person from
     and as a person is far from

235. tu'ux yan kah
     where COP town
     where there is a town

236. tu'ux yan doktor
     where COP doctor
     where there is a doctor

237.   tu'ux patal-u-tz'äk-ik u-b'ah mak-eh ...
       where ABIL-3-cure-PPM 3Ppr-REFL person-REL
       where one can cure oneself,

238.   yan-u-tz'äk-ik u-b'ah mak
       OBLIG-3-cure-PPM 3Ppr-REFL person
       one has to cure oneself

239.   et-el a'-tz'ak
       with-POS DET-medicine
       with the medicine

240.   k-u-täkä'-t-ik [a'-...] a'-tz'ul-eh. ,
       INC-3-send-TRAN-PPM [DET-] DET-patron-TOP
       that the patron sends.

241.   I wa ma' tun-ch'an-äl-eh,
       and COND NEG DUR/3-heal-INTRAN-TOP
       And if he isn't healing,

242.   yan-u-ta-s-äb'-äl yok' tzimin.
       OBLIG-3-come-CAUS-PAS-INTRAN on mule
       he has to be brought on a mule.

243.   Ii waa, ma'an tzimin a'-k'in he'-lo' k'ab'eet
       and COND NEG/COP mule DET-day OST-DIST need
       And if there isn't a mule that day it is needed,

244.   ke a'-winik hach, yah u-k'oh-a'an-il-eh,
       SUB DET-man very bad 3Ppr-sick-PART-POS-REL
       the man, whose sickness is very bad,

245.   yan-u-kuch-b'-ul,
       OBLIG-3-load-PAS-INTRAN
       he has to be loaded

246.   ti k'aan. ...
       in hammock
       in a hammock.

247.   [u-,] K-u-[,]-k'äx-b'-äl a'-k'aan-eh,
       [3-] INC-3-tie-PAS-INTRAN DET-hammock-TOP
       The hammock is tied

248.   ti hum p'e che'. ...
       to one INAM wood
       to a branch.

249.   I te' k-u-tal [a'-,] a'-[,]-k'oh-a'an-i'ih-eh ...
       and LOC INC-3-come [DET-] DET-sick-PART-SCOPE-TOP
       And there comes the sick one,

250. b'ay, [ti] ch'uy-a'an
     thus [?] hang-PART
     thus hung,

251. b'ay yuntun
     like sling
     like a sling

252. tu'ux k-u-ta-s-äb'-äl-eh. …
     where INC-3-come-CAUS-PAS-INTRAN-REL
     where he is carried.

253. I yan-u-xi'ma-t-ik mak ka' p'eeh,
     and OBLIG-3-walk-TRAN-PPM person two INAM
     And one has to walk two,

254. ox p'e k'in. …
     three INAM day.
     three days.

255. Kuch-b'il [a'-] a'-k'oh-a'an-eh
     haul-PART [DET-] DET-sick-PART-TOP
     The sick(ened) one is hauled

256. aasta u-k'och-ol tu'ux,
     until 3-arrive-INTRAN where
     until arriving where

257. ya [u-]patal-[u-…u-,]-u-yok-ol ich kaarro
     already [3-]ABIL-[3- 3-]-3-enter-INTRAN in car
     he can enter a car,

258. wa patal-u-yok-ol ich avion
     or ABIL-3-enter-INTRAN in plane
     or he can enter a plane

259. yok'ol k'och-ol,
     SUB arrive-INTRAN
     in order to arrive

260. [tak,] tak kah
     [to] to town
     at a town

261. tu'ux patal-u-tz'äk-b'-äl-eh. …
     where ABIL-3-cure-PAS-INTRAN-REL
     where he can be cured.

262. Peero, waa, yah,
     but COND bad
     But if it's bad,

263.   hach yah u-k'oh-a'an-il-eh,
       very bad 3Ppr-sick-PART-POS-TOP
       his illness is very bad,

264.   pwes ti b'eh,
       well on road
       well, on the road

265.   yan-u-kim-il. …
       OBLIG-3-die-INTRAN
       he has to die.

266.   I a'-tu'ux k-u-kim-il-eh,
       and DET-where INC-3-die-INTRAN-TOP
       And from where he dies,

267.   [pwe,] ka'ax kim-en-eh
       [well] although die-NOM-TOP
       although he's a corpse,

268.   yan-u-hok'-s-äb'-äl tak t-[u-,]-u-yotoch
       OBLIG-3-leave-CAUS-PAS-INTRAN till to-[3Ppr-]-3Ppr-home
       he has to be brought out to his home

269.   yok' u-yil-ik [u-,] u-na' wa u-yätan wa u-paal-oo',
       SUB 3-see-PPM [3Ppr-] 3Ppr-mother or 3Ppr-wife or 3Ppr-child-PL
       so that his mother or his wife or his children can see

270.   ke ya kim-ih u-tat-oo'-eh,
       SUB already die-3sg 3Ppr-father-PL-TOP
       that their father already died,

271.   i k-u-muk-b'-ul. …
       and INC-3-bury-PAS-INTRAN
       and he is buried.

272.   B'ay-lo' u-meyah-b'-äl a'-chiikleh-eh. …
       like-DIST 3-work-PAS-INTRAN DET-chicle-TOP
       Thus the chicle is worked.

273.   Ii, k-u-chu'úm-paal u-meyah-il …
       and INC-3-begin-INTRAN 3Ppr-work-POS
       And the work begins

274.   ti huulyo,
       in July
       in July

275.   i k-u-ho'm-ol,
       and INC-3-end-INTRAN
       and it ends

276. aasta [t-uu-,] chumuk u-mes-i(l) feb'reero. ...
     until [in-3Ppr-] mid 3Ppr-month-POS February
     (not) until the middle of the month of February.

277. [kuya', a',] A'-chiikleh-eh ...
     [?] DET-chicle-TOP
     The chicle,

278. k-u-lah-mol-b'-ol. ...
     INC-3-all-collect-PAS-INTRAN
     it's all collected.

279. K-u-mol-b'-ol. ,
     INC-3-collect-PAS-INTRAN
     It's collected.

280. Yan nukuch muchiila,
     COP big bag
     There are big bags,

281. u-k'ab'a'-e depoosito. ...
     3Ppr-name-TOP depository
     called depositories.

282. Tulakal [a'-,] a'-u-yitz a'-che' he'-lo'
     all [DET-] DET-3Ppr-resin DET-tree OST-DIST
     All of the resin of that tree

283. k-u-b'el [ti...]
     INC-3-go [SUB]
     that is going

284. ti tal-el ...
     SUB come-INTRAN
     to come

285. ti' ich k'aax ...
     from in forest
     from inside the forest,

286. k-u-ta-s-ik a'-chikleeroh-eh ...
     INC-3-come-CAUS-PPM DET-chiclero-REL
     that the chiclero brings,

287. te' k-u-(b'e)l u-[,]-hoch-oo'-i'ih. ,
     LOC INC-3-go 3-throw-PL-SCOPE
     there they go to throw it.

288. Te' k-(u-b'el)-u-hoch-oo'-i'ih,
     LOC INC-(3-go)-3-throw-PL-SCOPE
     There they go to throw it,

289. tulakal k'in,
      every day
      every day,

290. aasta u-tu'l-ul a'-noh muchiilah-eh. …
      until 3-fill-INTRAN DET-big bag-TOP
      until the big bag fills.

291. K-u-tu'l-ul-eh …
      INC-3-fill-INTRAN-TOP
      When it fills,

292. [k-u-, k-u-,] k-u-nutz'-ik-oo' k'aak'. …
      [INC-3- INC-3] INC-3-put together-PPM-PL fire
      they put together a fire.

293. Ii, k-u-tz'ik-oo' hum p'e noh paayla. …
      and INC-3-put/PPM-PL one INAM big caldron
      And they put on a big caldron.

294. T-a'-noh paayla' he'-lo'-eh
      in-DET-big caldron OST-DIST-TOP
      In that big caldron,

295. te' k-u-b'el ti chäk-b'-äl-i'ih. …
      LOC INC-3-go SUB cook-PAS-INTRAN-SCOPE
      there it is going to be cooked.

296. Ii … [toodos] (a'-ka') täk'-äk ma'lo'
      and [all] (DET-when) stick-IRREAL well
      And when it is well thickened,

297. [a'-,] a'-[,]-u-yitz a'-che' he'-lo'-eh
      [DET-] DET-3Ppr-resin DET-tree OST-DIST-TOP
      the resin of that tree

298. ya k-u-chich-tal. …
      already INC-3-hard-INCHOAT
      hardens.

299. Yan moolde,
      COP mold
      There are molds

300. [tu'ux k-uu…] tu'ux k-u-yutz-kin-t-ik-oo'
      [where INC-3] where INC-3-good-CAUS-TRAN-PPM-PL
      where they form it,

301. [?] (ya) k-u-hok'-ol-eh,
      (already) INC-3-leave-INTRAN-TOP
      then when it comes out,

302. markeetah. …
      block
      it's a block.

303. Ii ha',
      and water
      And it's liquid

304. k-u-yok-ol [ti,] ich a'-paaylah-eh,
      INC-3-enter-INTRAN [to] inside DET-caldron-REL
      that enters in the caldron,

305. tu'ux k-u-choko(h)-tal [a'-, a'-,] a'-u-yitz a'-[,]-che'-eh,
      where INC-3-hot-INCHOAT [DET- DET-] DET-3Ppr-resin DET-tree-TOP
      where the resin of the tree gets hot,

306. k-u-chich-tal [b'ay,] b'ay kib'-eh. …
      INC-3-hard-INCHOAT [like] like wax-TOP
      it hardens like wax.

307. Ya', kil-u-siis-tal-eh …
      already when-3-cold-INCHOAT-TOP
      Then when it gets cold,

308. [k-u-tz'ii] k-u-ch'i'-ik-oo' a'-mooldeh-eh,
      [INC-3-?] INC-3-take-PPM-PL DET-mold-TOP
      they take the mold,

309. k-u-men-t-ik-oo' markeetah. ,
      INC-3-make-TRAN-PPM-PL block
      they make blocks.

310. [stumble] K-u-b'on-ik-oo' yaab', hab'on …
                  INC-3-paint-PPM-PL much soap
                  They smear a lot of soap

311. ich a'-moldeh-eh
      in DET-mold-TOP
      in the mold

312. yok' ma' u-tak'-äl …
      SUB NEG 3-stick-INTRAN
      so it doesn't stick,

313. porke tä'-täk'-ki. …
      because INTENS-stick-ADJ
      because it's very sticky.

314. Ii … k-u-chich-tal-eh …
      and INC-3-hard-INCHOAT-TOP
      And when it gets hard,

315. k-u-k'och-ol [a'-,] a'-añeero,
     INC-3-arrive-INTRAN [DET-] DET-muleteer
     the muleteer arrives

316. et-el u-tzimin-oo',
     with-POS 3Ppr-mule-PL
     with his mules

317. tu'ux yan [a'-,] a'-kampameentoh-eh. …
     where COP [DET-] DET-camp-REL
     where the camp is.

318. Te' [k-uu a'-,) yan hun tuul nohoch-il,
     LOC [INC-3 DET-] COP one ANIM big-POS
     There, there is one chief

319. ich-il [a'-,] ah meyah-oo'-eh
     among-POS [DET-] MASC worker-PL-TOP
     among the workers,

320. yan hun tuul …
     COP one ANIM
     there is one

321. [u-,] u-nohoch-il,
     [3Ppr-] 3Ppr-big-POS
     who is the chief

322. i layti' [uu-… uu-…] u-ñepresentaanteh
     and 3Ipr [3Ppr- 3Ppr-] 3Ppr-representative
     and he is the representative

323. [a'-, a'-,] a'-tz'ul-eh. ,
     [DET- DET-] DET-patron-TOP
     of the patron.

324. Layti' b'ay layti' u-yum-il a'-meyah-eh. ,
     3Ipr like 3Ipr 3Ppr-owner-POS DET-work-TOP
     He, it's like he is the boss of the work.

325. Layti' k-u-k'ub'-ik [a'-,] a'-han-al-eh
     3Ipr INC-3-deliver-PPM [DET-] DET-eat-NOM-TOP
     He delivers the food,

326. layti' k-u-k'ub'-ik a'-[,]-tz'ak
     3Ipr INC-3-deliver-PPM DET-medicine
     he delivers the medicine

327. [t-a'-, ah] t-ah meyah-oo'-eh. …
     [to-DET-MASC] to-MASC worker-PL-TOP
     to the workers.

328. I layti' [k-u-] yan-u-lah-p'is-ik …
     and 3Ipr [INC-3-] OBLIG-3-all-weigh-PPM
     And he has to weigh all of it,

329. a'-chiikle he'-lo' k-u-k'ub'-ik a'-chikleeroh-eh. …
     DET-chicle OST-DIST INC-3-deliver-PPM DET-chiclero-REL
     that chicle that the chiclero delivers.

330. I a'-winik he'-lo'-eh
     and DET-man OST-DIST-TOP
     And that man,

331. u-k'ab'a'-e(h) enkargaado. …
     3Ppr-name-TOP agent
     he is called the agent.

332. I layti' a'-enkargaado yan-[u-,]-u-k'äm-ik,
     and 3Ipr DET-agent OBLIG-[3-]-3-receive-PPM
     And he who is the agent has to receive

333. tulakal a'-markeetah-oo',
     all DET-block-PL
     all of the blocks

334. ya chäk-a'an-eh. …
     already cook-PART-REL
     already cooked.

335. Ii, yan [u-,] u-p'is-oo'
     and COP [3Ppr-] 3Ppr-scale-PL
     And he has his scales

336. tu'ux k-u-p'is-ik-oo' b'oon u-'al-il. …
     where INC-3-weigh-PPM-PL how much 3Ppr-heavy-POS
     where he weighs how much its weight is.

337. [a'-b'o'] U-[,]-'al-il a'-chiikleh-eh …
     [DET-?] 3Ppr-heavy-POS DET-chicle-TOP
     The weight of the chicle,

338. k-u-tz'iib'(-t-ik-oo' ti hu'um) (tape change)
     INC-3-write(-TRAN-PPM-PL on paper)
     he writes it on paper

339. (b'oon) markeeta
     (how many) block
     how many blocks

340. k-u-k'ub'-ik … huhun tuul winik …
     INC-3-deliver-PPM each ANIM man
     each man delivers

341. i b'oon u-'al-il. …
      and how much 3Ppr-heavy-POS
      and how much its weight is.

342. I a'-lo' k-u-tz'iib'-t-ik-oo'
      and DET-DIST INC-3-write-TRAN-PPM-PL
      And those things he writes

343. yok' [u-b'i s-äb'-,] u-b'i s-äb'-äl ma'lo',
      SUB [3-go/CAUS-PAS-] 3-go/CAUS-PAS-INTRAN well
      so that (the accounts) are carried well

344. u-kweentah-oo', b'oon kintal …
      3Ppr-account-PL how many quintal
      of how many quintals

345. [eeh,] k-u-hok'-s-ik-oo' …
              INC-3-leave-CAUS-PPM-PL
              they take out

346. [ti'ih] ti'ih huhum p'e mes. …
      [in] in each INAM month
      in each month.

347. Aasta u-chuk-paal a'-dies,
      until 3-complete-INTRAN DET-ten
      (Not) until the ten

348. wa kiinse
      or fifteen
      or fifteen

349. wa veynte kintal u-kontraatoh a'- chikleeroh-eh,
      or twenty quintal 3Ppr-contract DET-chiclero-TOP
      or twenty quintals of the contract of the chiclero are completed,

350. entoonses ya patal-u-yem-el …
      then already ABIL-3-descend-INTRAN
      can he then come down,

351. ya ka'ax ma' u-k'och-ol
      already although NEG 3-arrive-INTRAN
      even if he doesn't arrive

352. [a'-, u-,) chumuk u-mees-il a'-febreeroh-eh. ,
      [DET- 3Ppr-] mid 3Ppr-month-POS DET-February-TOP
      until the middle of the month of February.

353. Ya patal-u-yem-el ti novieembre wa disieembre,
      already ABIL-3-descend-INTRAN in November or December
      He can already go down in November or December,

354. a'-mes t-u-chuk-b'-es-ah u-contraatoh-eh,
      DET-month COM-3-complete-?-CAUS-DPM 3Ppr-contract-REL
      the month that he completed his contract,

355. a'-k'in he'-lo' patal-u-hok'-ol t-u-kampameentoh-eh
      DET-day OST-DIST ABIL-3-leave-INTRAN from-3Ppr-camp-TOP
      that day he can leave his camp

356. i (u-)tal-el t-u-yotoch. ...
      and (3-)come-INTRAN to-3Ppr-home
      and come to his home.

357. B'ay-lo' u-meyah-il a'-chiikleh-eh. ...
      like-DIST 3Ppr-work-POS DET-chicle-TOP
      Thus is the work of chicle.

358. Ii [tan-] k-u-yaal-b'-äl xan ti'ih,
      and [DUR-] INC-3-say-PAS-INTRAN also 3IOpr
      And it is also called

359. cha',
      chicle
      cha', (the Mayan word)

360. [u-,] u-meyah-ih cha'.
      [3Ppr-] 3Ppr-work-POS chicle
      the work of *cha'*.

23. San José: Past and Present

Told by Domingo Chayax Suntecún on June 18, 1988[1]

1. B'ayoritah-eh ... [singsong]
    Now-TOP
    Now,

2. a'-mes tu'ux yan-o'on-eh,
    DET-month where COP-1pl-REL
    the month where we are,

3. u-mes-ih huunyo. ...
    3Ppr-month-POS June
    is the month of June.

4. Dies i oocho ...
    eighteen
    The eighteen(th)

---

[1] Don Domingo Chayax Suntecún, as suggested in his narrative, was proud of his Yucatecan heritage. This discourse reflects some Yucatecan influence, most notably in phonology. He was also a steward of the church, accounting for his thorough treatment of religious themes in this text.

5. yan-o'on b'a-la'-eh …
   COP-1pl TEMP-PROX-TOP
   we are on now

6. aaño mil novesieentos ocheenta i oochoh. …
   year 1988
   in the year 1988.

7. Tal-ih hun tuul nohoch winik …
   come-3sg one ANIM big man
   A gentleman came

8. eespaaña. …
   Spain
   from Spain.

9. Tal(-ih) u-sut-in-t-o'on,
   come-3sg 3-visit-?-TRAN-1pl
   he came to visit us

10. yok'ol=ka' wa'ye',
    over=world here
    from away in the world, to here

11. San Hoseh. …
    San José
    in San José.

12. U-k'ab'a'-eh
    3Ppr-name-TOP
    His name is

13. don Andres, …
    PN
    don Andrés,

14. peero ma' t-u-kun tak ten, apeyiido. ,
    but NEG INC-3-remain to 1sgIOpr last name
    but his last name didn't stay with me.

15. In-ten in-k'ab'a Domiingo Chayax Suntecun. … [singsong]
    EMP-1sgIpr 1sgPpr-name PN
    Me, my name is Domingo Chayax Suntecún.

16. Waye' ch'ih-een
    here grow-1sg
    Here I grew up,

17. way yan-ah-een-eh
    here COP-DIST-1sg-TOP
    here I was born,

18. waye' … ch'iih-een-eh …
    here grow-1sg-TOP
    here I grew up,

19. wa'ye', yan-en tak b'a-he-la'. …
    here COP-1sg till TEMP-OST-PROX
    here I am until now.

20. In-ten-eh …
    EMP-1sgIpr-TOP
    Me,

21. yan-ah-een,
    COP-DIST-1sg
    I was born,

22. aaño mil novesieentos katoorseh. …
    year 1914
    in 1914.

23. Ho'm-ih (in-)chuk-b'-es-ik seteenta i kwaatro aaño. …
    end-3sg (1sg-)complete-?-CAUS-PPM 74 year
    I finished completing 74 years.

24. Wa'ye' …
    here
    Here,

25. ch'iih-een
    grow-1sg
    I grew up,

26. ab'weela, in-ab'weelo …
    grandmother 1sgPpr-grandfather
    (my) grandmother, my grandfather,

27. in-na', in-tat, in-tiiah-oo' …
    1sgPpr-mother 1sgPpr-father 1sgPpr-aunt-PL
    my mother, my father, my aunts,

28. tulakal [in-…] in-famiilyah-(o)o' …
    all [1sgPpr-] 1sgPpr-family-PL
    all of my family,

29. way-(o)o'. …
    here-PL
    are here.

30. In-ab'weelah-eh …
    1sgPpr-grandmother-TOP
    My grandmother,

31. taan=kah-ih tal-oo' …
    Yucatán-POS come-PL
    they came from Yucatán,

32. ruumb'o kampech …
    direction Campeche
    in the direction of Campeche,

33. Yukatan. …
    Yucatán
    Yucatán.

34. Tal-oo' [,tib'] (u-)sut-in-t-eh Peten. …
    come-PL [?] (3-)visit-?-TRAN-SPM Peten
    They came to visit Petén.

35. Ki'-ah-ih t-u-yich-oo'-eh,
    good-DIST-3sg to-3Ppr-eye-PL-TOP
    It was good to their eyes (they liked it),

36. ka' kun-ah-oo',
    then remain-DIST-PL
    and then they remained

37. ti kah-tal wa'yeh. …
    SUB live-POSIT here
    to live here.

38. Waye', nohoch winik-ah-oo'-eh
    here big man-DIST-PL-TOP
    Here they became old men,

39. way(e') ix nuk-ah-oo'-eh …
    here FEM old lady-DIST-PL-TOP
    here they became old women,

40. aasta ka' kim-oo'. …
    until then die-PL
    until then they died.

41. Pues [u]uch-i(h) tan-in-ch'iil-eh …
    well happen-3sg DUR-1sg-grow-TOP
    Well, before, when I was growing up,

42. a'-kah-eh hach mo'nok. …
    DET-town-TOP very small
    the town was very small.

43. Ma'an mix b'a'al ma'lo'. …
    NEG/COP NEG thing good
    There wasn't anything good.

44. Ma'an mix k'aak', ti kaayeh. …
    NEG/COP NEG fire in street
    There weren't any lights in the street.

45. Ma'an mix … tu'ux k-u-tz'äk-b'-äl k'oh-a'an. …
    NEG/COP NEG where INC-3-cure-PAS-INTRAN sick-PART
    There wasn't anywhere the sick are cured (a clinic).

46. Mas chen nukuch kolel …
    more only great women
    Only great women

47. yohel-oo' …
    3/know-PL
    knew (curing)

48. et-el puuro tz'ak,
    with-POS pure medicine
    with pure medicine,

49. puuro pokche',
    pure herb
    pure herbs,

50. et-el [u-oras,] u-[,]orasion-oo',
    with-POS [3Ppr-] 3Ppr-prayer-PL
    with their prayers

51. k-u-b'et-ik-oo',
    INC-3-make-PPM-PL
    that they make

52. ti k'oh-a'an. …
    to sick-PART
    for the sick.

53. Et-el-oo' k-u-lik'-s-ik-oo', kolel-oo'-eh …
    with-POS-PL INC-3-raise-CAUS-PPM-PL woman-PL-TOP
    With them, the women raise (heal)

54. mehen paal-oo',
    small child-PL
    small children,

55. nukuch paal-oo'. …
    big child-PL
    (and) big children.

56. Yan xan nohoch kolel-oo',
    COP also great women-PL
    There were also great women

57. yohel …
    3/know
    knowing

58. u-cha'an-t-(eh) u-yan-tal mehen paal. …
    3-watch-TRAN-SPM 3-COP-INCHOAT small child
    to look after the birth of children (midwifery).

59. Pwees, uch-ih-eh …
    well happen-3sg-TOP
    Well, before,

60. a'-kah-eh hach, otzil ma' …
    DET-town-TOP very poor NEG
    the town was very poor, not,

61. ma' (he-b')ix yan-il b'a-la',
    NEG (OST-l)ike COP-POS TEMP-PROX
    not like it is now,

62. b'a'-he'-la' hach ma'lo'. …
    TEMP-OST-PROX very good
    now it's very good.

63. Yan, k'u=nah,
    COP god=house
    There is a church,

64. yan eskweela
    COP school
    there is a school,

65. yan … pweesto salud
    hay health station
    there is a health station

66. tu'ux k-u-[,]-k'och-ol k'oh-a'an-oo'. …
    where INC-3-arrive-INTRAN sick-PART-PL
    where the sick arrive.

67. [u-] hach … tal-a'an-oo', mak-oo' wa'ye', b'a-la'. …
    [3-] many come-PART-PL person-PL here TEMP-PROX
    Many people have come here now.

68. U-kaayeh-il-e hach ma'loo',
    3Ppr-street-POS-TOP very good
    The streets are very good,

69. tulakal. …
    all
    all of them.

70. Pwees … [u]uch-i(h) …
    well happen-3sg
    Well, before,

71. a'-tieempo [u]uch-i(h) a'-nukuch winik-oo'-eh
    DET-time happen-3sg DET-great man-PL-TOP
    in the times before, the great men,

72. u-tanah-oo' k-u-b'et-ik-oo'-eh,
    3Ppr-house-PL INC-3-make-PPM-PL-REL
    their houses that they make

73. puuro xa'an …
    pure thatch
    are pure thatch,

74. porke' k(-u-)y(a')al-ik-oo'-eh
    because INC-3-say-PPM-PL-TOP
    because they say that

75. hach b'in mas siis = 'ool. …
    very REPORT more fresh
    it is much more fresh, they say.

76. La'-laaminah-eh,
    DET-tin-TOP
    The tin

77. hach chokoh. …
    very hot
    is very hot.

78. Ma' ki' k-u-yub'-ik-oo'. …
    NEG good INC-3-feel-PPM-PL
    It doesn't feel good.

79. Peero b'e-he'-la'-eh,
    but TEMP-OST-PROX-TOP
    But now,

80. kaasi' la'-nah-oo'-eh …
    almost DET-house-PL-TOP
    almost, the houses,

81. puuro laaminah u-tanah a'-mak-oo'. …
    pure tin 3Ppr-house DET-person-PL
    the houses of the people are all tin.

82. Mas b'in k-u-xan-tal,
    more REPORT INC-3-last-INCHOAT
    They say it lasts longer,

83. pero hach ko(')oh b'a-he'-la. …
     but very expensive TEMP-OST-PROX
     but it's very expensive now.

84. B'iin a'-nukuch kolel-oo' uch-ih-eh …
     REPORT DET-big woman-PL happen-3sg-TOP
     They say that the great women in the past

85. ma' tan-u-män-ik-oo' …
     NEG DUR-3-buy-PPM-PL
     didn't buy

86. u-nu'uk-ul …
     3Ppr-kitchenware-POS
     their kitchenware,

87. u-traastoh-oo', t-u-kosiina. …
     3-dish-PL of-3Ppr-kitchen
     their dishes of the kitchen.

88. Layti' k-u-b'et-ik-oo' kum
     3Ipr INC-3-make-PPM-PL pot
     They make clay pots,

89. k-u-b'et-ik-oo' u-lak …
     INC-3-make-PPM-PL 3Ppr-plate
     they make their clay plates,

90. k-u-b'et-ik-oo' u-sarteen-oo',
     INC-3-make-PPM-PL 3Ppr-pan-PL
     they make their pans,

91. k-u-b'et-ik-oo' …
     INC-3-make-PPM-PL
     they make

92. tulak(al) a'-b'a'ax tu'ux k-u-han-al-oo'. …
     all DET-thing where INC-3-eat-INTRAN-PL
     all the things where they eat.

93. U-plaatoh-oo'-eh lak. …
     3Ppr-plate-PL-TOP clay plate
     Their plates are pottery.

94. Layti' k-u-b'et-ik-oo' et-el luk'. …
     3Ipr INC-3-make-PPM-PL with-POS clay
     They make them with clay.

95. I [stumble] tu'ux k-u-yuk'-ul-oo'-eh …
     and where INC-3-drink-INTRAN-PL-REL
     And where they drink,

96.   u-k'ab'a'-e(h) luch. …
      3Ppr-name-TOP calabash cup
      it is called *luch* (calabash cup).

97.   K-u-xot-ik-oo' …
      INC-3-cut-PPM-PL
      They cut them

98.   kwaando yäh-eh. …
      when in season-TOP
      when in season.

99.   K-u-sankochaar-t-ik-oo',
      INC-3-parboil-TRAN-PPM-PL
      They parboil them,

100. k-u-hoch'-t-ik—oo'
      INC-3-scrape-TRAN-PPM-PL
      they scrape them,

101. k-u-hay=k'in-t-ik-oo'. …
      INC-3-spread=sun-TRAN-PPM-PL
      they spread them out in the sun.

102. Layti' u-[,]-porsiiyo a'-mak-oo' uch-ih-eh,
      3Ipr 3Ppr-cup DET-person-PL happen-3sg-TOP
      That is the cup of people before,

103. ma'an porsiiyo mix baso. …
      NEG/COP cup NEG glass
      there weren't cups or glasses.

104. Layti' k-u-b'et-ik-oo'.
      3Ipr INC-3-make-PPM-PL
      They make them.

105. K-u-päk'-ik-oo' a'-che'-eh
      INC-3-plant-PPM-PL DET-tree-TOP
      They plant the tree,

106. k-u-tz'ik u-yich. …
      INC-3-give/PPM 3Ppr-fruit
      it gives its fruit.

107. Et-el u-yich-eh layti' …
      with-POS 3Ppr-fruit-TOP 3Ipr
      With its fruit, they

108. k-u-b'et-ik-oo' t-u-porsiiyoh-il. …
      INC-3-make-PPM-PL in-3Ppr-cup-POS
      make it into their cups.

109. K-u-b'et-ik-oo' nukuch haaroh-oo',
     INC-3-make-PPM-PL big pitcher-PL
     They make big pitchers,

110. nukuch … tinaahah
     big urn
     big water urns,

111. nukuch … p'uul,
     big jar
     big jars,

112. [inaudible] u-kaan. …
                 3Ppr-white clay
     [. . . ?]   their white clay.

113. Tulakal-oo' layti' k-u-b'et-ik-oo'. …
     all-PL 3Ipr INC-3-make-PPM-PL
     They make all of them.

114. K-u-b'et-ik-oo' la'-lak-oo'-eh …
     INC-3-make-PPM-PL DET-plate-PL-TOP
     They make the plates,

115. ix mehen sarteen-oo'-eh et-el u-maak-oo',
     FEM small pan-PL-TOP with-POS 3Ppr-lid-PL
     the little pans with their lids,

116. tulakal, layti' k-u-b'et-ik a'-nukuch kolel-oo'-eh. …
     all 3Ipr INC-3-make-PPM DET-great woman-PL-TOP
     everything, the great women make it.

117. Pwees … a'-tieempo b'in ha(ch) uch-ih t-in-ch'iil-eh …
     well DET-time REPORT very happen-3sg DUR-1sg-grow-REL
     Well, in the time long ago when I'm growing up, they say,

118. a'-nukuch kolel-oo'-eh …
     DET-big woman-PL-TOP
     the great women,

119. tu[uu]lakal-oo'-eh [k-u-,] k-u-na'at-ik-oo'
     all-PL-TOP [INC-3-] INC-3-understand-PPM-PL
     all of them, understand,

120. hach yan [u- … u-,] u-toh=ol-al-oo' kan dyoos. …
     much COP [3Ppr- 3Ppr-] 3Ppr-straight=soul-POS?-PL with God
     they have much contentment with God.

121. Ma'an (u-)laak' relihyoon,
     NEG/COP (3Ppr-)-other religion
     There wasn't any other religion,

122.   chen layt(i') a'-katooliko'o. ...
        only 3Ipr DET-catholic/PL?
        only that of the Catholics.

123.   Peero b'a-he'-la',
        but TEMP-OST-PROX
        But now,

124.   hach yan ... evanheliistah-oo'. ...
        many COP evangelist-PL
        there are many evangelists.

125.   Ya ma' tun ... ma' tun, ki' t-u-yich-oo' k'u=nah. ...
        already NEG then NEG then good to-3Ppr-eye-PL god=house
        Now, well it's not, well the church isn't good in their eyes.

126.   Apaarte tu'ux k-u-b'et-ik-oo',
        apart where INC-3-make-PPM-PL
        Apart is where they do

127.   u-orasioon-oo'. ...
        3Ppr-prayer-PL
        their prayers.

128.   Pwes kaasi, la'-kah-eh b'e-he'-lah ...
        well nearly DET-town-TOP TEMP-OST-PROX
        Well nearly, the town now,

129.   hach yaab' ... kreyeenteh-oo' yan-oo',
        very many believer-PL COP-PL
        there are very many believers,

130.   k-u-na't-ik-oo' u-laak', saantoh-oo',
        INC-3-understand-PPM-PL 3Ppr-other saint-PL
        they understand other saints,

131.   k-u-ya'al-ik-oo('). ...
        INC-3-say-PPM-PL
        they say.

132.   Peero, [stumble] yan xan mak-oo',
        but COP also person-PL
        But there are also people,

133.   kaasi [taan] taan=kooch-eh,
        nearly [half] half=?-TOP
        almost half,

134.   peero katooliko. ,
        but Catholic
        but Catholic.

135. B'e-he'-la' yan ma'lo' k'u=nah. …
     TEMP-OST-PROX COP good god=house
     Now there is a good church.

136. Yan paychi',
     COP prayer
     There are prayers,

137. k-u-men-b'-el miisa,
     INC-3-do-PAS-INTRAN mass
     mass is performed,

138. tulakal. …
     everything
     everything.

139. Pwees … tulakal a'-b'a'ax k-in-tzikb'a(l)-t-ik he'-lo'-e(h) …
     well all DET-thing INC-1sg-tell-TRAN-PPM OST-DIST-REL
     Well, all those things that I am telling,

140. k'och(-ih) t-u-k'in in-wil-ik. ,
     arrive(-3sg) in-3Ppr-day 1sg-see-PPM
     came in the time I saw.

141. Pwees b'e-he'-la' yah,
     well TEMP-OST-PROX already
     Well now, already,

     tun-k'och-ol u-k'in-il …
     DUR/3-arrive-INTRAN 3Ppr-time-POS
     the time is coming,

142. ya kaasi, chämach-en k-in-wu'uy-ik-eh. …
     already almost old man-1sg INC-1sg-feel-PPM-TOP
     now almost, I feel I am an old man.

143. Pweh tan-in-tzikb'a(l)-t-ik,
     well DUR-1sg-tell-TRAN-PPM
     Well, I am telling it

144. yok'ol u-yu'(uy)-ik a'-mak-oo'-eh …
     SUB 3-hear-PPM DET-person-PL-TOP
     so that the people hear

145. la'-k'in (t-)in-wil-ah-eh,
     DET-time (COM-)1sg-see-DPM-REL
     the time I saw,

146. hach t-u-hah-il. …
     very in-3Ppr-true-POS
     really truly.

147. Ii, a'-mak-oo' uch-ih-eh ...
and DET-person-PL happen-3sg-TOP
And the people before,

148. yan u-estiiloh-oo' k-u-b'et-ik-oo' ...
COP 3Ppr-custom-PL INC-3-do-PPM-PL
they have their customs they do

149. ti a'-[,]-tieempo ti'i(h), finaados ke ...
in DET-time for deceased that
at the time for the deceased (All Souls' Day) that

150. k-u-ya'al-ik-oo' k-u-tal [a'-,] a'-[,]-pixan-oo' ...
INC-3-say-PPM-PL INC-3-come [DET-] DET-soul-PL
they say that the souls come

151. u-sut-in-t-oo' u-yum-il a'-nah-eh. ...
3-visit-?-TRAN-PL 3Ppr-owner-POS DET-house-TOP
to visit the head of the house.

152. K-u-hok'-s-ik-oo' ...
INC-3-leave-CAUS-PPM-PL
They take out

153. hum p'ee(l) ... ho'ol, kristyaano, winik-oo'. ...
one INAM skull Christian man-PL
a skull of Christian men.

154. U-hach b'in ... t-u-[,]-tan-l-ah k'u=nah. ...
3-much REPORT COM-3-attend-?-DPM god=house
They say they really attended to the church.

155. U-k'ab'a'-oo'-eh,
3Ppr-name-PL-TOP
They are called

156. [prieero,] prioosteh-oo'. ...
               steward-PL
               stewards.

157. Ka' kim-i(h) b'in-oo'-e(h)
then die-3sg REPORT-PL-TOP
Then they died, they say,

158. ka' hok'-s-äb'(-ih) u-pol-oo'. ...
then leave-CAUS-PAS(-3sg) 3Ppr-head-PL
and their skulls were taken.

159. I b'a-he'-la' tun-eh,
and TEMP-OST-PROX then-TOP
And now, then,

160. kaada aaño ti' a'-primeero ti novieembre …
      each year at DET-first of November
      each year on the first of November

161. k-u-hok'-s-ik-oo' ti prosesioon …
      INC-3-leave-CAUS-PPM-PL in procession
      they take it out in a procession

162. hum p'e ak'ab' … (Yucatec form; Itzá = ak'ä')
      one INAM night
      one night,

163. a'-paychi'-oo' ti kaayeh-eh. …
      DET-prayer-PL in street-TOP
      the prayers are in the street.

164. I a'-mak-oo', hach yan … u-xul
      and DET-person-PL much COP 3Ppr-end
      And the people, they have their goal

      u-na'-t-ik-oo',
      3-understand-TRAN-PPM-PL
      to understand it,

165. [k-u-…?] (tu'ux) k-u-[…]-chun-ik-oo' u-[,]-puksik'al-(o)o',
      [INC-3] (where) INC-3-begin-PPM-PL 3Ppr-heart-PL
      where their hearts begin

166. t-u-b'et-ik-al [u-…] [hun kul prome', prome',]
      SUB-3-make-PPM-SUB [3Ppr-] [one CLASS promi(se) promi(se)]
      to make

167. u-devosioon-oo' ti' a'-mak-oo'-eh. …
      3Ppr-devotion-PL of DET-person-PL-TOP
      their devotions of the people.

168. K-u-[,]-k'a't-ik-oo',
      INC-3-ask-PPM-PL
      They ask

169. ka' tz'a-b'-äk-oo' ich liistah …
      SUB put-PAS-IRREAL-PL in list
      that they be put on the list,

170. i la'-[,]-prosesioon-e' k-u-b'el t-u-yotoch-e' …
      and DET-procession-TOP INC-3-go to-3Ppr-home-TOP
      and the procession goes to their house,

171. maax u-k'a't-ik-eh. …
      who 3-ask-PPM-REL
      of those who ask.

172. K-u-hok'-ol,
     INC-3-leave-INTRAN
     They go out,

173. nohoch kolel ti paychi'. ,
     great woman SUB pray
     great women, to pray.

174. U-laak', kolel-oo',
     3Ppr-other woman-PL
     The other women,

175. k-u-yaab'-tal mak t-u-pach. ...
     INC-3-much-come person at-3Ppr-back
     many people come behind.

176. K-u-k'och-ol t-a'-nah
     INC-3-arrive-INTRAN at-DET-house
     They arrive at the house

177. tu'ux k-u-[. . .]-b'el ti k'äm-b'-äl-eh. ,
     where INC-3-go SUB receive-PAS-INTRAN-REL
     where they go to be received.

178. K-u-hok'-ol yum-il ...
     INC-3-leave-INTRAN 3Ppr/owner-POS
     The owner comes out,

179. maax t-u-k'a't-ah-eh. ...
     who COM-3-ask-DPM-REL
     who asked for it.

180. K-u-mäch-ik-eh,
     INC-3-grasp-PPM-TOP
     He takes it,

181. k-u-b'en-s-ik [ti me ti me] ti meesah. ...
     INC-3-go-CAUS-PPM [to ta(ble) to ta(ble)] to table
     he takes it to the table.

182. K-u-t'äb'-(b')-äl kib'. ...
     INC-3-light-(PAS)-INTRAN candle
     The candle is lit.

183. K-u-tz'ä-b'-äl chumuk meesah-eh ...
     INC-3-put-PAS-INTRAN middle table-TOP
     (The following) are put in the middle of the table:

184. hum p'e lak-eh,
     one INAM plate-TOP
     a plate,

185. han-al … et ah kax,
     eat-NOM with MASC chicken
     food, with chicken,

186. hum p'e luch, sa'. …
     one INAM cup atole
     a gourd cup, of atole.

187. K-u-met=ixi'im-eh. …
     INC-3-wheel=corn-TOP
     They make a circle of corn.

188. K-u-hop'-ol ti reesa a'-mak-oo'-eh,
     INC-3-begin-INTRAN SUB pray DET-person-PL-TOP
     The people begin to worship,

189. ti paychi'. …
     SUB pray
     to pray.

190. Ho'm-ol a'-paychi'-eh …
     TERM-INTRAN DET-prayer-TOP
     After the prayer,

191. tulakal a'-mak-oo' k-u-man-äl-oo'-eh. …
     all DET-person-PL INC-3-pass-INTRAN-PL-TOP
     all of the people pass.

192. K-u-[…ha?]-man-s-äb-äl-oo' ich nah
     INC-3-[?]-pass-CAUS-PAS-INTRAN-PL in house
     They are passed into the house

193. u-yuk'-u', kafe
     3-drink-SPM coffee
     to drink coffee,

194. u-han-t-oo' b'ooyo. …
     3-eat-TRAN-PL tamale
     to eat bollos (tamales).

195. Yan konseerva,
     COP preserves
     There are preserves,

196. tulakal a'-b'a'ax k-u-si-ik a'-mak-(o)o'-e(h). …
     all DET-thing INC-3-give-PPM DET-person-PL-TOP
     everything that the people give.

197. Yan ak'ab' k-u-hok'-ol aasta …
     COP night INC-3-leave-INTRAN up to
     There are nights they come out of up to

198. kiinseh diesioocho nah. …
      fifteen eighteen house
      fifteen or eighteen houses.

199. Kaasi k-u-sas-tal a'-mak-oo' …
      almost INC-3-bright-INCHOAT DET-person-PL
      It almost dawns while the people

200. tun-man-(o)o' t-a'-prosesioon,
      DUR/3-pass-PL in-DET-procession
      are walking in the procession

201. t-u-pach a'-[,]-aanimas
      at-3Ppr-back DET-souls
      behind the, "souls"

202. kii a'-mak-oo' ti'ih-e(h). …
      say/3sg DET-person-PL 3IOpr-TOP
      the people call them (the skulls).

203. Pwes he'-lo' hach uch-ih …
      well OST-DIST very happen-3sg
      Well that was long ago,

204. i tak b'a-la'-eh,
      and till TEMP-PROX-TOP
      and until now,

205. k-u-k'ah-s-ik a'-mak-oo',
      INC-3-remember-CAUS-PPM DET-person-PL
      the people remember it,

206. u-b'et-ik-oo'. …
      3-do-PPM-PL
      they do it.

207. I ma' tun-tub'-s-ik-oo'. …
      and NEG DUR/3-forget-CAUS-PPM-PL
      And they don't forget it.

208. Peero, [hach…] ba-he'-la' [ma' tan-u-, u-…]
      but [very] TEMP-OST-PROX [NEG DUR-3- 3-]
      But now

209. ma' tan-u-ch'i'-ik-oo' a'-luch,
      NEG DUR-3-take-PPM-PL DET-calabash cup
      they aren't taking the calabash cup

210. [u-…] t-u-yuk'-ul-oo'-eh …
      [3-] SUB-3-drink-INTRAN-PL-TOP
      to drink,

211.   mix lak mas mix b'a'a(l)
       NEG plate more NEG thing
       nor the clay plates, nothing,

212.   [puuro …] chen, loosah-oo', peltreh-oo', [k-u-…]
       [pure] only imported dish-PL pewter-PL [INC-3-]
       only imported dishes, metal ones,

213.   k-u-ch'i'-ik-oo' b'e-he'-la'-eh.   ,
       INC-3-take-PPM-PL TEMP-OST-PROX-TOP
       they take now.

214.   Ya', [uch-] uch-ih-eh,
       already [happen-] happen-3sg-TOP
       Already (the way of) before,

215.   tan-u-tub'-s-ik a'-mak-oo'-e(h). …
       DUR-3-forget-CAUS-PPM DET-person-PL-TOP
       the people are forgetting it.

216.   Peero, komo a'-mak t-u-cha'an-t-ah-eh
       but as DET-person COM-3-witness-TRAN-DPM-REL
       But as the people that witnessed it,

217.   t-(u)-yil-ah-eh …
       COM-3-see-DPM-REL
       that saw it,

218.   k-u-k'ah-s-ik.   ,
       INC-3-remember-CAUS-PPM
       they remember it.

219.   Yaa, u-yich mak-eh
       already 3Ppr-eye person-TOP
       Now, the views of people

220.   ma' he-b'ix a'-uch-ih-eh. …
       NEG OST-how DET-happen-3sg-REL
       aren't like before.

221.   Uch-ih-eh pwes tun-cha'an-t-ik mak,
       happen-3sg-TOP well DUR/3-witness-TRAN-PPM person
       Before, well, people observed it

222.   kaada aaño,
       each year
       each year,

223.   kaada aaño,
       each year
       each year,

224. kaada aaño. …
     each year
     each year.

225. Pero b'a-ha'-la'-eh ma',
     but TEMP-OST-PROX-TOP NEG
     But now, no,

226. b'a-he'-la' ya …
     TEMP-OST-PROX already
     now, already,

227. hach hela'an k-u-yil-ik mak,
     very different INC-3-see-PPM person
     one sees it very differently,

228. ma', he-b'ix uch-ih-eh. …
     NEG OST-how happen-3sg-TOP
     not like before.

229. Pwes a'-nukuch winik-oo'-eh …
     well DET-great man-PL-TOP
     Well, the great men (of before),

230. aantes ka' k'och-ok a'-k'in-eh …
     before SUB arrive-IRREAL DET-day-TOP
     before the time (of the rite) came,

231. kwan(do), tu(n)-[…]-faaltar komo ka' p'e ox p'e semaanah …
     when DUR/3-lack like two INAM three INAM week
     when there lacked about two or three weeks,

232. k-u-hok'-ol a'-nukuch winik-oo'-eh,
     INC-3-leave-INTRAN DET-great man-PL-TOP
     the great men go out

233. ich k'aax …
     in forest
     into the forest

234. u-k'äxän-t-oo' kab' …
     3-seek-TRAN-PL honey
     to seek honey

235. t-a'-che'-oo'. ,
     in-DET-tree-PL
     in the trees.

236. (U-)k'ab'a', (a'-)che'-oo'-e(h)
     (3Ppr-)name (DET-)tree-PL-TOP
     The name of the trees is

237. ya'ax nik. …
     green ?
     ya'ax nik.

238. Tu'ux yan u-tu'uch-eh …
     where COP 3Ppr-knot-REL
     Where the (tree's) knot is,

239. k-u-wa'-tal-oo',
     INC-3-stand-POSIT-PL
     they stand

240. t-u-sak a'-k'in-eh. …
     in-3Ppr-brightness DET-day-TOP
     in the brightness of the day.

241. K-u-cha'an-t-ik-oo' ka'nal …
     INC-3-look-TRAN-PPM-PL above
     They look above,

242. tu'ux k-u-yil-ik-oo' k-u-hok'-ol [a'-…]
     where INC-3-see-PPM-PL INC-3-leave-INTRAN [DET-]
     where they see (the bees) leave

243. u-yum-il a'-kab' [t-u-…]
     3Ppr-owner-POS DET-honey [from-3Ppr]

244. t-u-hob'on a'-che'-eh. …
     from-3Ppr-hollow DET-tree-TOP
     from the hollow of the tree.

245. K-u-ya'al-ik-oo' kee,
     INC-3-say-PPM-PL that
     They say that

246. he'e-lo' yan kab'. …
     OST-DIST COP honey
     therc is honey theie.

247. K-u-pek-s-ik-oo' et u-macheeteh
     INC-3-hit-CAUS-PPM-PL with 3Ppr-machete
     They hit it with their machete

     t-u-chun a'-che'-eh. …
     at-3Ppr-trunk DET-tree-TOP
     at the base of the tree.

248. K-u-hok'-ol mas, yum-il a'-kab'-eh. …
     INC-3-leave-INTRAN more owner-POS DET-honey-TOP
     More bees come out.

249. (K-u-)käx-t-ik ka' p'ee(l),
     (INC-3-)seek-TRAN-PPM two INAM
     They look for two,

250. ox p'eeh,
     three INAM
     three,

251. kän p'ee(l),
     four INAM
     four

252. mas(-ih) t-a'-che'. ...
     more(-POS) in-DET-TREE
     more (hives) in the tree(s).

253. T-u-[,]-ox p'e k'in-eh
     on-3Ppr-three INAM day-TOP
     On the third day,

254. k-u-b'el u-[,]-pul-u' la'-che'-(o)o'-eh. ...
     INC-3-go 3-fell-SPM DET-tree-PL-TOP
     they go to fell the trees.

255. Te' k-u-ho(k)'-s-ik-oo' a'-kab'-i'ih. ...
     LOC INC-3-leave-CAUS-PPM-PL DET-honey-SCOPE
     There they take out the honey.

256. T-u-hob'on a'-che'-eh,
     in-3Ppr-hollow DET-tree-TOP
     In the hollow of the tree,

257. k-u-ch'i'-ik-(o)o' a'-mak-oo'-eh,
     INC-3-take-PPM-PL DET-person-PL-TOP
     the people get them,

258. [t-](k)-u-käh-(k)un-t-ik-oo'
     [DUR?-](INC)-3-town?-CAUS-TRAN-PPM-PL
     they domesticate

     la'-yum-il a'-kab-i('ih). ...
     DET-owner-POS DET-honey-LOC
     the bees there.

259. La'-kab'-eh
     DET-honey-TOP
     The honey,

260. k-u-ch'i'-ik a'-nukuch kolel-(o)o' he'e-lo'-eh,
     INC-3-take-PPM DET-great woman-PL OST-DIST-TOP
     those great women take it

261. t-u-b'et-ik-al konseerva t-a'-k'in(-il),
     SUB-3-make-PPM-SUB preserves on-DET-day(-POS)
     for making conserves on the day

262. ti'ih a'-[,]-finaados-eh. …
     for DET-deceased-TOP
     for the deceased.

263. I u-k'in-il-eh,
     and 3Ppr-day-POS-TOP
     And (on) their day,

264. a'-nukuch winik-oo'-eh,
     DET-great man-PL-TOP
     the great men

265. k-u-ch'i'-ik-oo'-eh. …
     INC-3-take-PPM-PL-TOP
     take it.

266. K-u-chäk-ik-oo',
     INC-3-cook-PPM-PL
     They cook it,

267. k-u-yoom-t-es-ik-oo'-eh. …
     INC-3-boil-TRAN-CAUS-PPM-PL-TOP
     they boil it.

268. Ho'mol-u-yoom-t-es-ik-oo'-eh …
     TERM-3-boil-TRAN-CAUS-PPM-PL-TOP
     After they boil it,

269. k-u-tz'i'-ik-oo' t-u-laak'. …
     INC-3-put-PPM-PL in-3Ppr-other
     they put it in another (container).

270. K-u-b'eet-ah wa t-u-[t]laak', tinaahah
     INC-3-make-DPM either in-3Ppr-other jar
     They make it either in another pottery jar

271. wa ti kuum. …
     or in pot
     or in a pot.

272. Te' k-u-hok'-ol
     LOC INC-3-leave-INTRAN
     There (a wheel of wax) comes out.

     hum p'e u-rueedah-il a'-kib'-(i')ih. …
     one INAM 3Ppr-wheel-POS DET-wax-SCOPE

273. Ma'lo' ma'lo' porke yan,
     good good because COP
     Good, good, because there are,

274. t-a'-kab'
     of-DET-honey
     of the honeys

275. yan, säk kab'
COP white honey
there is white honey,

276. yan a'-k'ekan
COP DET-type of honey
there is the *k'ekan* (a type of honey from black bees),

277. yan ... tulakal a'-kab'-oo' he'-lo'. ...
COP all DET-honey-PL OST-DIST
there are all of those honeys.

278. Kwaando [k-u-,]
when [INC-3-]
When,

279. ya meero (u-)k'och-ol u-k'in-il a'-finaados-eh ...
already mere (3-)arrive-INTRAN 3Ppr-day-POS DET-deceased-TOP
when the day of the dead really comes,

280. k-u-käx-t-ik-oo', k'uch. ...
INC-3-seek-TRAN-PPM-PL cotton thread
they seek cotton thread.

281. La'-k'uch he'-lo'-eh ...
DET-thread OST-DIST-TOP
That thread

282. ti'ih u-b'et-ik-al-oo' a'-kib'-eh. ...
SUB 3-make-PPM-SUB-PL DET-candle-TOP
is for making the candles.

283. (En)toon(s)es ke yan [u-...] u-sarten-oo'
then that COP [3Ppr-] 3Ppr-pan-PL
Then they have their pans

284. tu'ux k-u-[...]-tz'ik-oo'
where INC-3-put/PPM-PL
where they put it

285. ti', ib'-il a'-kib' ti k'aak'-eh. ...
SUB melt-INTRAN DET-wax in fire-REL
to melt the wax in fire.

286. K-u-ho(k)'-s-ik-oo'-eh,
INC-3-leave-CAUS-PPM-PL-TOP
They take it out,

287. k-u-hop'-ol [u-...]
INC-3-begin-INTRAN [3-]
they begin

288. u-t'ul-u'-oo'. [t-a'-...]
     3-drip-SPM-PL [on-DET-]
     to drip it.

289. T-a'-[...]-tämän-eh,
     on-DET-cotton-TOP
     On the cotton (thread)

290. k-u-kun-tal,
     INC-3-remain-POSIT
     remains

291. (u-)foorma hum p'e kib', polok. ...
     (3Ppr-)form one INAM candle thick
     the form of a thick candle.

292. Yan ti'ih, aanimas-eh-i'i(h).
     COP for soul-TOP-LOC
     They are for the souls there.

293. K-u-b'et-ik-oo' nukuch,
     INC-3-make-PPM-PL big
     They make big ones,

294. k'äs polok-oo'. ...
     little thick-PL
     medium thick ones.

295. Yan mehen kib',
     COP small candle
     There are little candles

296. ti('ih) ix-mehen, paal-al-oo'. ...
     for FEM-small child-POS?-PL
     for the little children.

297. Mehen aanhel-oo' k(iih) a'-mak-oo'(-eh)
     small angel-PL say/3 DET-person-PL(-TOP)
     Little angels, the people said,

298. nukuch winik-oo', aanimas ...
     big man-PL souls
     the great men (are called) souls,

299. ii, a'-mehen paal-oo'-eh ix-ch'up-al-oo',
     and DET-small child-PL-TOP FEM-girl-POS?-PL
     and the little children, the girls,

300. kiih-oo' a'-mak-oo'. ...
     say-PL DET-person-PL
     the people said.

301. Pwes ... tuulakal a'-mak-oo'-eh
      well all DET-person-PL-TOP
      Well, all of the people,

302. chen layt(i') a'-kib',
      only 3Ipr DET-candle
      it's only the homemade beeswax candle,

303. ma' tun-man-ik-oo' espeelma
      NEG DUR/3-buy-PPM-PL store candle
      they weren't buying store candles,

304. chen kib'. ,
      only beeswax candle
      only beeswax candles.

305. Uch-ih a'-kib'-eh,
      happen-3sg DET-wax-TOP
      Before, the wax,

306. k-u-ta-s-ik-oo' ti k'aax,
      INC-3-come-CAUS-PPM-PL from forest
      they bring it from the forest,

307. layti' k-u-b'et-ik-oo' [...u-,] u-kib'-oo'.
      3Ipr INC-3-make-PPM-PL [3Ppr-] 3Ppr-candle-PL
      they make their candles.

308. U-k'ab'a', espeelmah[?]-e(h) kib'-oo'. ...
      3Ppr-name store candle-TOP candle-PL
      The name of candles was *kiboo'*.

309. A'-kib'-eh,
      DET-candle-TOP
      The candle(s),

310. k-u-t'äb'-ik-oo',
      INC-3-light-PPM-PL
      (when) they light them

311. tan-(u-)-yuch-ul paychi'. ...
      DUR-(3-)-happen-INTRAN prayer
      the prayer occurs.

312. K-u-ho'om-ol a'-[,]-paychi'-eh ...
      INC-3-end-INTRAN DET-prayer-TOP
      (When) the prayer ends,

313. k-u-tup-ik-oo'. ...
      INC-3-extinguish-PPM-PL
      they extinguish them.

314. Ho'm-ol-eh …
TERM-INTRAN-TOP
Afterward,

315. i tulakal a'-mak tu'ux k-u-yuch-ul reesoh-eh
and all DET-person where INC-3-happen-INTRAN prayer-REL
and all of the people where the prayer happens,

316. chen puuro kib'-i('ih) yan t-a'-meesah. …
only pure wax-LOC? COP on-DET-table
only pure wax is there on the table.

317. Naach-i(l) k-u-tal mak-eh
far-POS INC-3-come person-TOP
From afar people come,

318. tun-yu'b'-ik u-b'ok a'-kib'
DUR/3-sense-PPM 3Ppr-smell DET-candle
smelling the aroma of the candles

      k-u-yel-el-eh. …
INC-3-burn-INTRAN-REL
burning.

319. Pwe(s) b'ay-lo', a'-mak-oo' uch-ih-eh,
well like-DIST DET-person-PL happen-3sg-TOP
Well, thus were the people before,

320. tuulakal. …
all.
all of them.

321. Lah-k'äh-a'an ten tak b'a-lah.
all-remember-PART 1sgIOpr till TEMP-PROX
I remember it all till now.

322. Ii … t-a'-k'u=nah tun-eh,
and in-DET-god=house then-TOP
And, in the church then,

323. heb'-a'an. …
open-PART
it was open.

324. Yan … nohoch winik-oo' …
COP great man-PL
There were great men

325. k-u-känän-t-ik a'-k'u=nah-eh. …
INC-3-guard-TRAN-PPM DET-god=house-REL
that guard the church.

326. Tun-pek-s-ik a'-kampaanaah,
DUR/3-ring-CAUS-PPM DET-bell
They ring the bell

327. tulakal a'-ak'ab'-eh. ...
all DET-night-TOP
all night long.

328. Te', k-u-b'el-s-äb'-äl [u-h,] u-yo'och b'ooyo,
there INC-3-go-CAUS-PAS-INTRAN [3-] 3-food ration tamale
There was carried their ration of bollos,

329. u-tamal. ...
3Ppr-tamale
their tamales.

330. K-u-b'el-s-äb'-äl xan u-xik-i(l)=ha' ...
INC-3-go-CAUS-PAS-INTRAN also 3Ppr-?-POS=water
Their liquor is carried also,

331. u-yuk'-u',
3-drink-SPM
to drink

332. yok'ol ma' u-wen-eh. ...
SUB NEG 3-sleep-INTRAN
in order not to sleep.

333. Asta' las trees las kwaatro ...
until three o'clock four o'clock
(Not) until three or four o'clock,

334. tun-sas-tal kab'-eh ...
DUR/3-bright-INCHOAT world-TOP
when it's dawning,

335. tan-u-k'och-ol ... la'-aanimas ti k'u=nah-eh. ,
DUR-3-arrive-INTRAN DET-souls to god=house-TOP
are the souls arriving to the church.

336. Tuulakal a'-mak-oo'-eh ...
all DET-person-PL-TOP
All of the people,

337. k-u-lah-'ok-ol-oo' u-yu(')b'-ih, a'-[,]-paychi'-eh. ...
INC-3-all-enter-INTRAN-PL 3-hear-SPM? DET-prayer-TOP
they all enter to hear the prayer.

338. [entoo',] A'-paadre k-u-tal las oocho las nweeve
[then] DET-father INC-3-come eight o'clock nine o'clock
The priest comes at eight or nine o'clock

339. u-b'et-eh u-miisa aanimas …
     3-make-SPM 3Ppr-mass souls
     to perform the mass of souls,

340. kii(h) a'-mak-oo'. …
     say DET-person-PL
     the people said.

341. Peero b'a'-la', b'a'-la' tun-eh
     but TEMP-PROX TEMP-PROX then-TOP
     But now, now well,

342. hach ma' tun-[b'et-,]-men-b'-e(l) he-b'ix uch-ih-eh. …
     very NEG DUR/3-[do-]-make-PAS-INTRAN OST-how happen-3sg-TOP
     it's really not done like before.

343. Hach hela'an tulakal …
     very different all
     Everything is very different,

344. tuulakal a'-b'a'ax-oo' he'-lo'
     all DET-thing-PL OST-DIST
     all of those things,

345. uuu, a'-nukuch winik-oo' uch-ih-eh …
     EXCLAM DET-great man-PL happen-3sg-TOP
     oh, the great men of before . . .

346. Pwes … [hach yan u-…] hach k-u-na't-ik-oo'
     well [much COP 3Ppr-] much INC-3-understand-PPM-PL
     Well, they understand a lot,

347. i hach … yan u-[tah](toh) = 'ool-al-oo', men dyoos,
     and much COP-3Ppr-[right] (right) = soul-POS?-PL by God
     and they have a lot of blessings (good health) from God,

348. hach k'äh-a'an dyoos u-yäknal-oo'. …
     much remember-PART God 3Ppr-with-PL
     God is much remembered with them.

349. A'-mak-(o)o' b'a-he'-la('),
     DET-person-PL TEMP-OST-PROX
     The people now

350. ma' tun-hach-k'a't-ik-(o)o' ma'lo'. …
     NEG DUR/3-much-ask-PPM-PL well
     aren't really asking (God) well.

351. Yan mak ma' tan-u-yub'-ik. …
     COP person NEG DUR-3-hear-PPM
     There are people that aren't hearing it.

352. Yan mak ki' t-u-yich. …
COP person good in-3Ppr-sight
There are people that like it.

353. Yan mak chen … chen u-k'och-ol u-ch'ema'-t-eh-eh
COP person only only 3-arrive-INTRAN 3-spy-TRAN-SPM-REL
There are people that only, that only come to spy,

354. k-u-luk'-ul yäknal-oo'. …
INC-3-be apart-INTRAN 3Ppr/with-PL
they are apart from them.

355. Peer(o) a'-uch-ih-eh,
but DET-happen-3sg-TOP
But before,

356. a'-nukuch kolel-oo'-eh,
DET great woman-PL-TOP
the great women,

357. aasta k-u-yok'-ol-oo' ti k'u=nah,
even INC-3-cry-INTRAN-PL in god=house
they even cried in the church

358. kwaando k-u-yu'b'-ik-oo'
when INC-3-hear-PPM-PL
when they heard

359. tan-[u-…]-u-paya(l)chi' a'-[,]-paadre,
DUR-[3-]-3-pray DET-priest
the priest praying

360. tu'ux yan a'-meesa [?]
where COP DET-table
where the table is,

361. (a'-)altar t-a'-k'u=nah-eh. …
(DET-)altar in-DET-god=house
the altar of the church.

362. Ii mix hun tuul mehen paal k-u-men=buuya,
and NEG one ANIM small child INC-3-make=noise
And not one child makes noise,

363. tuulakal-eh … chik-a'an, chik-a'an u-yuy-ub'-ul. …
all-TOP clear-PART clear-PART 3-hear-PAS-INTRAN
all of it, clearly, clearly it is heard.

364. I aasta u-ho'm-ol u-[,]-men-b'-el a'-miisa …
and till 3-end-INTRAN 3-make-PAS-INTRAN DET-mass
And until the mass is finished being performed,

365. la'-mak-oo' k-u-man-äl,
DET-person-PL INC-3-pass-INTRAN
the people pass

366. u-yutz'-in-t-oo' a'-[…]-kalabeera
3-kiss-?-TRAN-PL DET-skull
to kiss the skull,

367. aanimas yan t-a'-meesah-eh …
souls COP on-DET-table-TOP
souls that are on the table,

368. koomo, [k'i] la'-k'in he'-lo('),
as DET-day OST-DIST
as that day

369. u-k'in aanimas,
3Ppr-day souls
is the day of souls,

370. u-k'in aanimas kii(h) a'-nukuch kolel-oo'. …
3Ppr-day souls say DET-great woman-PL
the day of souls, the great women said.

371. K-u-b'et-ik-oo',
INC-3-make-PPM-PL
They make

372. a'-k'in,
DET-day
the day

373. a'-primeero novieembreh-eh …
DET-first November-TOP
the first of November,

374. ii a'-doose …
and DET-twelve
and the twelfth.

375. I k-u-b'et-ik-oo' oktaava. …
and INC-3-do-PPM-PL octave.
And they do the octave.

376. Oocho diias man-äk a'-noh k'in-eh
eight days pass-IRREAL DET-great day-TOP
(When) eight days have passed the great day

377. k-u-ka'-b'et-ik-oo' a'-[,]-oktaavah-e. ,
INC-3-REPET-do-PPM-PL DET-octave-TOP
they do the octave again.

378.   Aasta t-u-laak' año t-u-ka'ye' k-u-b'et-ik-oo'.
       till in-3Ppr-other year in-3Ppr-again INC-3-do-PPM-PL
       (Not) until the next year do they do it again.

IV. CONVERSATION

24. A Conversation between Don Julian and Don Domingo

Held on July 20, 1988

1. J: B'a'ax ki-bel ki-tzikb'al-t-ik ti'ih kompaadre? [laughter]
   what 1pl-go 1pl-tell-TRAN-PPM 3IOpr friend
   What are we going to say to/for him, friend?

2. D: Aah pwes ki-tzikb'al-t-ik ti'ih b'ix u-b'el ki-kol …
   EXCLAM well 1pl-tell-TRAN-PPM 3IOpr how 3-go 1plPpr-milpa
   Ah, well, we tell him how our milpas are doing,

3. b'a'ax meyah-il ki-b'et-ik …
   what work-POS INC/1pl-do-PPM
   what jobs we do,

4. (u-)laak' b'a'ax tzikb'al-il [?].
   (3Ppr-)other thing talk-POS
   other things of conversation.

5. J: Ma'lo', t-u-hah-il …
   fine in-3Ppr-true-POS
   Good, it's true,

6. b'ay-lo' in-ten-eh
   like-DIST EMP-1sgIpr-TOP
   thus I am,

7. ten-eh tan-[in]-in-han-t-es-ik
   1sgIpr-TOP DUR-[1sg]-1sg-clear-TRAN-CAUS-PPM
   me, I'm clearing

    in-kol
   1sgPpr-milpa
   my milpa,

8. tan-in-paak-t-ik tz'e-tz'(e)ek-tak. ,
   DUR-1sg-weed-TRAN-PPM INTENS-little-PL?
   I am weeding it little by little.

9. D: mhmm

10. J: Hach sup. …
   very overgrown
   It's very overgrown.

11. D: Pero ma'lo'? …
   but good
   But good?

12. J: Yutzil in-kol-eh yutzil. ,
   pretty 1sgPpr-milpa pretty
   My milpa is pretty, pretty.

13. D: Aa bweno [?]. …
        good
        Oh good.

14. J: Ho'leh-ih man-ih ik' ,
        yesterday-3sg pass-3sg wind
        Yesterday wind passed,

15.   k'a'am-ah-ih a'-ik'. ,
        strong-DIST-3sg DET-wind
        the wind was strong.

16. D: Hach t-u-hah-il.
        very in-3Ppr-true-POS
        That's very true.

17. J: K'a'am-ah-ih a'-ha'-eh
        strong-DIST-3sg DET-water-TOP
        The rain was strong,

18.   k'a'am-ah-ih a'-ik'-eh {D:hmm}
        strong-DIST-3sg DET-wind-TOP
        the wind was strong,

19.   ka' k'och-een sam-ih hatz'ka'-eh. …
        when arrive-1sg while-3sg early-TOP
        when I arrived this morning.

20. D: {J: ?} T-u-lah-pek-s-ah. ,
        COM-3-all-move-CAUS-DPM
        It blew (moved) everything around.

21. J: pek-s-ah. ,
        move-CAUS-DPM
        moved it.

22. D: mhmm …

23. J: [inaudible…] Uch-ak [u-,] u-ma'lo'-tal. …
        happen-IRREAL [3-] 3-good-INCHOAT
        Perhaps it will get well.

24. D: Pwes, Dyoos u-yohel-t-ik-eh …
        well God 3-know-TRAN-PPM-TOP
        Well, God knows

25.   u-lik'-il t-u-ka'ye'. …
        3-rise-INTRAN in-3Ppr-again
        if it (corn) will get up again.

26. J: Ma' wach'-äk? …
        NEG tassle-IRREAL
        It hasn't tasseled?

27. D: Mm, ma' pwes y(a) (h)ach [?],
           NEG well already very
        Hmm, no well it's still very,

28. J: hach {D: ?} <u>hach</u> mum. ,
        very very tender
        very tender.

29. D: hach mu'um. …
        very tender
        very tender.

30.   Peero u-noh ik' k-u-faltaar-e ti agoosto.
        but 3Ppr-big wind INC-3-lack-TOP in August
        But the great wind that lacks is in August.

31. J: Aay layti' a'-venti<u>kwatro de agoosto</u>. … {D: ?}
        EXCLAM 3Ipr DET-twenty-four of August
        Aye, the (wind) of August 24.

32.   San Bartolome. ,
        PN
        San Bartolomé. (Saint's day when big winds come)

33. D: mmhm … <u>Hach tz'iik</u> [?] … {J: ?}
           very fierce
           Very fierce …

34.   hach tz'iik a'-k'in he'-lo.
        very fierce DET-day OST-DIST
        that day is very fierce.

35.   Hach k-u-b'et-ik nohoch ik'. …
        much INC-3-make-PPM big wind
        It makes lot of big winds.

36. J: A'-lo' tulakal aaño b'ay-lo'.
        DET-DIST every year like-DIST
        That is that way every year.

37. D: mmhmm …

38. J: Pwes, k-u-tal a'-ha'-eh ,
        well INC-3-come DET-water-TOP
        Well, when the water comes,

39.   hach k-u-k'a'am-tal a'-ik'-eh. ,
        much INC-3-strong-INCHOAT DET-wind-TOP
        the wind becomes very violent.

40. D: Sii. …
        yes
        Yes.

41. J: Ii … hach swaave hach, hach ,
  and very soft very very
  And, very soft, very, very,

42. D: Tz'u'-tz'u'-ki a'-lu'um-eh ,
  INTENS-soft-ADJ DET-earth-TOP
  The earth is very soft/muddy,

43. [?] ya ch'ul mentäk-eh k-u-nay-äl. ,
  already wet so-TOP INC-3-side-INTRAN
  already wet, so it (the corn plant) goes on its side.

44. J: Puro säk=ni'is. ,
  pure white=?
  Pure soft white earth.

45. D: Säk=ni'is, ahh b'ay-lo …
  white=? EXCLAM like-DIST
  White earth, ahh, thus.

46. J: Mentäk-eh ma' [?]
  therefore-TOP NEG
  Therefore it doesn't…

47. D: Pero ma' witz tu'ux yan a-kol? …
  but NEG hill where COP 2Ppr-milpa
  But it isn't hilly where you have your milpa?

48. J: Ma' hach ka'nal, {D: aaa}
  NEG very high
  It's not very high,

49. mo'nok, tzel-ek. ,
  little side-?
  a little sloped.

50. D: Si, mmhmm …
  yes
  Yes, mmhmm.

51. Pwes b'ay-lo in-tia'al-eh.
  well thus-DIST 1sgPpr-own-TOP
  Well, mine is that way (too).

52. Chumuk-eh yan … mo'nok muul ah saay
  middle-TOP COP little mound MASC-ant
  In the middle of it there's a little ant mound

53. tu'ux … yutzil, yutzil
  where pretty pretty
  where it's pretty, pretty,

54.   komo, veynte treynta maatas,
        like twenty, thirty plants
        like about twenty, thirty plants

55.   nukuch b'a'ax [?],
        big thing
        are big things;

56.   u-mas-il-eh b'a'-tak-eh. ,
        3Ppr-more-POS-TOP thus?-PL-TOP
        the others are like this. (showing lower height with hand)

57. J: Aaa

58. D: Ka' k'och-een sam-ih-eh … tempraano …
        when arrive-1sg while-3sg-REL early
        When I arrived a while ago, early,

59.   t-u-lah-nay-b'-es-ah
        COM-3-all-side-?-CAUS-DPM
        it knocked them all on the side.

60. J: [laughter]

61. D: Ik' wal tal-ih mas k'a'am,
        wind DUB come-3sg more strong
        The wind came perhaps, stronger

62.   ik' t-u-b'et-ah wal-eh [?]. ,
        wind COM-3-do-DPM DUB-TOP
        wind did it perhaps.

63. J: K'a'am-ah-ih ik'.
        strong-DIST-3sg wind
        The wind was strong.

64. D: Si. ,
        yes
        Yes.

65. J: K'a'am-ah-ih {D: kom}
        strong-DIST-3sg
        It was strong,

66.   ho'leh k'a'am-ah-ih. ,
        yesterday strong-DIST-3sg
        yesterday it was strong.

67. D: Komo hach mehen-toh-eh
        as very small-still-TOP
        As it (corn) is still very small,

68.   ma' tun-hach-[,]-pul-ik. ,
        NEG DUR/3-much-throw-PPM
        it (the wind) is not knocking it down much.

69. J: Ma' tan. ,
  NEG DUR
  It isn't.

70. D: I ya a'-tan-u-wach'-äl-eh si. ,
  and already DET-DUR-3-tassel-INTRAN-TOP yes
  And that which is already tasseling, yes.

71. J: Aaa ya ma' tun-tz'ik mix b'a'al. ,
  EXCLAM already NEG-DUR/3-give/PPM NEG thing
  Ah, then it doesn't give (produce) anything.

72. D: Ma' tun-tz'ik mix b'a'al, pwes.
  NEG DUR/3-give/PPM NEG thing well
  It doesn't give anything then.

73. J: Ahaaa …

74. D: Wa dyoos k-u-yoo-t-ik-eh
  COND God INC-3-want?-TRAN-PPM-TOP
  If God wants it,

75. chak ma' u-b'et-ik noh ik' ,
  perhaps NEG 3-do-PPM big wind
  perhaps there won't be a big wind,

76. kwaando tan-u-wach'-äl,
  when DUR-3-tassel-INTRAN
  when it's tasseling,

77. uch-ak ma'. …
  happen-IRREAL NEG
  perhaps there won't.

78. Uch-ak ma' [u-…] u-ka'-k'a'am-tal. {J: mmhmm…}
  happen-IRREAL NEG [3-] 3-REPET-strong-INCHOAT
  Perhaps it won't get violent again.

79. J: Wa ma' si ma' tan-ki-b'el ki-mol-o' mix b'a'al [?]
  COND NEG yes? NEG DUR-1pl-go 1pl-harvest-SPM NEG thing
  If not, we're not going to harvest anything.

  {D: si pwes…}
  { yes well }
  {D: right}

80. U-lah-k'as-tal-eh.
  3-all-bad-INCHOAT-TOP
  It all becomes bad.

81. D: Aaa u-lah-k'as-tal pwes ,
  EXCLAM 3-all-bad-INCHOAT well
  Aah, it all becomes bad then,

82. k-u-lub'-ul-e
    INC-3-fall-INTRAN-TOP
    it falls

83. ya ma' tun-tz'ik mix b'a'al. ,
    then NEG DUR/3-give/PPM NEG thing
    then it isn't giving anything.

84. J: Ya ma' tan. ,
    then NEG DUR
    Then it isn't.

85. D: mhmm,

86. J: Kwando tan-u-wach'-äl-eh [?],
    when DUR-3-tassel-INTRAN-TOP
    When it's tasseling,

87. D: ahh si,

88. J: a'-tan-u-wach'-äl-eh
    DET-DUR-3-tassel-INTRAN-REL
    that which is tasseling

89. ya ma' tan-u-tz'ik mix b'a'al.
    then NEG DUR-3-give/PPM NEG thing
    isn't giving anything then.

90. D: Ma' tun-tz'ik mix b'a'al. ,
    NEG DUR/3-give/PPM NEG thing
    It isn't giving anything.

91. J: Ma' tan-a-wil-ik yaa,
    NEG DUR-2-see-PPM then
    You aren't seeing it (harvest) then,

92. ya tan-u-top'. ,
    then DUR-3-flower
    then it's flowering.

93. D: Si pwes. …
    yes well
    Right.

94. U-'al-il u-yi'ih k-u-b'et-ik
    3Ppr-heavy-POS 3Ppr-tassel INC-3-make-PPM
    The weight of the sprout makes

    u-'al-tal. ,
    3-heavy-INCHOAT
    it become heavy.

95. J: ahaaa

96. D: Layti' k-u-b'et-ik ti'ih. ...
    3Ipr INC-3-do-PPM 3IOpr
    It does it to it.

97. J: Haah. ,
    yes
    Yes.

98. D: mhmm ... [J clears throat]

99.   Pwes b'a-la' si tun-b'et-ik ha'. ...
    well TEMP-PROX yes DUR/3-make-PPM water
    Well, now it's raining.

100. J: B'a-la si tan-u-lub'-ul.
    TEMP-PROX yes DUR-3-fall-INTRAN
    Yes, now it's falling.

101. D: Mas, t-a'-aaño man-ih-eh. ,
    more in-DET-year pass-3sg-REL
    More than in the year that passed.

102. J: aah sii

103. D: T-a'-aaño man-ih-eh
    in-DET-year pass-3sg-REL
    In the year that passed

104.   ma' t-u-b'et-ah, ha' hach k'a'am
    NEG COM-3-make-DPM water very strong
    it didn't make very strong rain

105.   he-b'ix b'a-la'-eh. ,
    OST-how TEMP-PROX-TOP
    like now.

106. J: Ma'. ,
    no
    No.

107. D: Pero b'a'-la'-eh mas ma'lo'. ...
    but TEMP-PROX-TOP more good
    But now it's better.

108. J: Mas tz'eek.
    more little
    A little better.

109. D: Porke, t-a'-aaño man-ih-eh ...
    because in-DET-year pass-3sg-REL
    Because in the year that passed,

110.   a'-ha' t-u-b'et-ah-e' ti agoosto. ...
    DET-water COM-3-make-DPM-REL in August
    the rain that it made was in August.

111.   Wa ma' u-b'et-ik ha' t-a'-agoosto
      COND NEG 3-make-PPM water in-DET-August
      If it doesn't make rain in August

112.   ma' tun-yan-tal, näl-eh. …
      NEG DUR/3-COP-INCHOAT ear-TOP
      there aren't ears of corn.

113. J: Si. ,
       yes
       Yes.

114. D: Pero b'a-lah, uch-ak u-b'et-ik yax=k'in. …
       but TEMP-PROX happen-IRREAL 3-make-PPM first=sun
       But now, perhaps summer is starting.

115. J: Uch-ak. ,
       happen-IRREAL
       Perhaps.

116. D: mmmhmm …

117. J: B'a-lah ya demasiaado [?] {D: <u>si</u>} …
       TEMP-PROX already too much
       Now it's already too much (rain).

118.   Tz'o'k-(ih)-u-man k'in kaak. ,
      TERM-(3sg)-3-pass day thus?
      Days have finished passing that it is (raining).

119. D: mhmm …

120. J: Hum p'e [haah](haab')-ih ,
       one INAM year-3sg
       A year ago

121.   (t-a')-tieempo b'a-he'-la'-eh ma' toh (?). ,
      (in-DET)-time TEMP-OST-PROX-TOP NEG yet?
      at this timc it wasn't yet (raining).

122. D: Si <u>pwes</u>.

123. J: <u>Ma'</u> hach ma'lo'-ak , {D: <u>aha</u>}
       NEG very good-IRREAL
       It wasn't very good,

124.   <u>hach</u>, hach, tan-a'-yax=k'in-toh-eh. , {D: <u>si</u>.}
      very very DUR-DET-summer-still-TOP
      very, it was still very much summer.

125.   <u>Hu</u>hum pak, huhum pak, huhum pak, u-lub'-ul ,
      each time each time each time 3-fall-INTRAN
      Each time, each time, each time, it falls,

126. D: ahaa

127. J: i ma' tun-k'a'am-tal. ,
          and NEG DUR/3-strong-INCHOAT
          and it wasn't getting strong.

128. D: Ma' pwes ma' tun-ch'ul-ik a'-lu'um-eh. …
          NEG then NEG DUR/3-soak-PPM DET-earth-TOP
          Well no, it wasn't soaking the earth.

129. J: Hach tikin. …
          very dry
          It was very dry.

130. D: Hach tikin. …
          very dry
          It was very dry.

131. J: B'a-he'-la' mas ma'lo'.
          TEMP-OST-PROX more good
          Now it's better.

132. D: [inaudible…] Lub'-ih a'-ha' kon tieempoh-eh. …
          fall-3sg DET-water with time-TOP
          The water fell in time.

133. J: ahaa

134. D: [inaudible…] Man-ih t-a'-[,]-k'in-il a'-agoostoh-eh
          pass-3sg in-DET-day-POS DET-August-TOP
          It passed in the days of August (last year),

135.   ya, puro ha'. ,
          then pure water
          then pure rain.

136. J: Puro ha'. …
          pure water
          Pure rain.

137. D: Mhmm, puro ha'.
                   pure water
          Mhmm, pure rain.

138. J: Uch-ak ma' [u-,] u-wa'-tal a'-yax=k'in
          happen-IRREAL NEG [3-] 3-stand-POSIT DET-summer
          Perhaps the summer won't stand (stay)

          ti u-mes-il agoosto.
          in 3Ppr-month-POS August
          in the month of August.

139. D: Pwes, layti' a'-k-in-wa'l-ik-eh
          well 3Ipr DET-INC-1sg-say-PPM-REL
          Well, that is what I am saying,

140.   uch-ak ma', u-b'et-ik k'in.
             happen-IRREAL NEG 3-make-PPM sun
             perhaps there won't be summer.

141.   Wa ma' he'-u-[,]-yok-ol k'aak'-i'ih. …
             COND NEG ASSUR-3-enter-INTRAN fire-LOC
             If not, fire (plant blight) will enter there (in the leaves).

142. J: He'l-eh. , {D: hmm}
             ASSUR-TOP
             It will.

143.   Hum p'e haah-il-eh in-ti'a'al-eh
             one INAM year-POS-TOP 1sgPpr-own-TOP
             A year ago mine

             tan-u-wach'-äl ,
             DUR-3-tassel-INTRAN
             was tasseling,

144. D: hmm

145. J: ka' ti wa'-l-ah-ih [a'-y] a'-yax=k'in-e. ,
             when SUB stand-POSIT-DIST-3sg [DET-] DET-summer-TOP
             when summer stood (came).

146. D: mhmm …

147. J: Ok-ih k'aak'-i'ih {D: mmm}
             enter-3sg fire-LOC
             Fire entered there,

148.   k'och-ih u-ka'nal-il. …
             arrive-3sg 3Ppr-high-POS
             it reached the top (of the plant).

149. D: aahaa

150. J: T-u-lah-tikin-kun-t-es-ah ten. ,
             COM-3-all-dry-CAUS-TRAN-CAUS-DPM 1sgIOpr
             It dried everything on me.

151. D: aah ,

152. J: Ya puro (i)x-mehen-näl {D: clears throat} t-in-mol-ah-i'ih,
             then pure FEM-small-ear COM-1sg-harvest-DPM-LOC
             Then I harvested only little ears there,

153.   ma' nukuch-ah-ih. …
             NEG big-DIST-3sg
             they didn't get big.

154. D: Pwes b'ay-lo' uch-ih ten-eh. …
             well like-DIST happen-3sg 1sgIOpr-TOP
             Well thus it happened to me.

155. Igwal yutzil yutzi(l) pero ,
     same pretty pretty but
     The same, it was pretty, pretty, but

156. ka' wa'-l-ih a'-k'in-eh
     when stand-POSIT-3sg DET-sun-TOP
     when the sun stood

157. ka' ok-ih k'än alam-i'ih. …
     then enter-3sg yellow below-LOC
     then the yellow entered below there.

158. J: Layti' a'-he'-lo' k-u-yuch-ul-eh. {D: ?} …
     3Ipr DET-OST-DIST INC-3-happen-INTRAN-REL
     That is what happens.

159. D: Mia ha'li' oocho kostal näl t-in-hok'-s-ah-i'ih. ,
     DUB only eight bag ear COM-1sg-leave-CAUS-DPM-LOC
     I think I only got out eight bags of ears there.

160. J: Si? ,
     yes
     Yes?

161. D: Aalgo t-im-b'et-ah-i'ih
     something COM-1sg-do-DPM-LOC
     I did something (work) there

162. pero ma', t-u-tz'ah mix b'a'al. …
     but no COM-3-give/DPM NEG thing
     but it didn't give anything.

163. J: Hach tz'eek t-u-tz'ah.
     very little COM-3-give/DPM
     It gave very little.

164. D: mhmm …

165. J: A'-yax=k'in-eh k-u-k'as-kun-t-ik ,
     DET-summer-TOP INC-3-bad-CAUS-TRAN-PPM
     The summer makes it bad,

166. k-u-tikin-kun-t-es-ik. ,
     INC-3-dry-CAUS-TRAN-CAUS-PPM
     it dries it.

167. D: Si pwes. …
     yes well
     Right.

168. I b'ix u-b'el a-walak'-oo'? ,
     and how 3-go 2Ppr-animal-PL
     And how are your animals?

169. J: Ma'lo'-oo', ma'lo'-(o)o yutzil-oo'. ,
            good-PL good-PL pretty-PL
            They're good, good, pretty.

170.   Ho'leh-ih, ka'b'eh-ih t-im-b'en-s-ah …
            yesterday-3sg two days-3sg COM-1sg-go-CAUS-DPM
            Yesterday, day before yesterday I took them

171.   t-u-ka'ye' tak [tu,] tu'ux yan in-kol-eh. ,
            in-3Ppr-again to where COP 1sgPpr-milpa-REL
            again to where I have my milpa.

172. D: Aa bweeno. ,
                good
            Oh good.

173. J: Ahaa way [yan-in-,] in-wen-s-äm-ah-oo'
                   here [OBLIG-1sg-] 1sg-lower-CAUS-PERF-DPM-PL
            Uhuh, I have brought them down here,

174.   way paay(-il) Sik'u'-eh. {D: si} …
            here beach(-POS) PN-TOP
            here at the beach of La Trinidad.

175.   Ka'=b'eh-ih t-im-b'en-s-ah. ,
            two days-3sg COM-1sg-go-CAUS-DPM
            Two days ago I brought them.

176. D: mmm …

177. J: T-u-ka'ye'. ,
            in-3Ppr-again
            Again.

178.   B'a-la' ya k'och-oo'
            OST-PROX already arrive-PL
            Now then they have arrived

179.   tu'ux k-u-han-al-oo' {D: si pwes.} t-u-ka'ye'. ,
            where INC-3-eat-INTRAN-PL in-3Ppr-again
            where they can eat again.

180. D: [?] yan u-han-al-oo'. ,
                COP 3Ppr-eat-NOM-PL
            (?) they have their food.

181. J: Aa [yutz] hach yutzil a'-su'uk b'a-lah.
                     very pretty DET-grass TEMP-PROX
            Ah, the grass is very pretty now.

182. D: mhmm,

183. J: B'a-lah yutzil! …
            TEMP-PROX pretty
            Now it's pretty!

184. D: Tul wal a'-u-ha' tu'ux yan-oo'? ,
     full DUB DET-3Ppr-water where COP-PL
     Is the water full, perhaps, where they are?

185. J: Ya tan-u-tu'l-ul. ,
     already DUR-3-fill-INTRAN
     It's already filling.

186. D: mhmm,

187. J: Ya tan-u-tu'l-ul. …
     already DUR-3-fill-INTRAN
     It's already filling.

188. D: Ma' tan-u-sap'-äl ti yax=k'in? ,
     NEG DUR-3-dry-INTRAN in summer
     It's not drying up in the summer?

189. J: Ma' tan. ,
     NEG DUR
     It isn't.

190. D: Ma'lo'.
     good
     Good.

191. J: Ma' tan. …
     NEG DUR
     It isn't.

192.   T-u-muk'yah-t-ah tulakal a'-noh yax=k'in he'-la'
        COM-3-last-TRAN-DPM all DET-big summer OST-PROX
        It lasted all of this big summer

193.   man-ih-eh. ,
        pass-3sg-REL
        that passed.

194. D: Si. …
     yes
     Yes.

195. J: Ma' ti sap'-ih. ,
     NEG SUB? dry-3sg
     It didn't dry up.

196. D: Ma'lo' ma'lo' yan {J: ?} tu'ux u-ch'i'-ik ha' mak. …
     good good COP where 3-get-PPM water person
     Good, it's good there is a place where one can get water.

197. J: Yan. ,
     COP
     There is.

198. D: mhmm

199. J: Yan. …
          COP
          There is.

200.   Ya tan-[u-…]-u-mas-ch'iil,
          DUR-[3-]3-more-grow
          It's growing more,

201.   tz'e-tz'ek-tak tz'e-tz'ek-tak
          INTENS-little-PL? INTENS-little-PL?
          little by little, little by little

202.   tu'ux k-u-[,]-yalka'-eh
          where INC-3-run-REL
          where they run

203.   k-u-pan-t-ik
          INC-3-scrape-TRAN-PPM
          it wears it down,

204.   k-u-yalka'-eh {D: ahaa}
          INC-3-run-TOP
          they run,

205.   k-u-pan-t-ik. ,
          INC-3-scrape-TRAN-PPM
          it wears it down.

206. D: Si. …
          yes
          Yes.

207.   Yaab' wal su'uk-i'ih? ,
          much DUB grass-LOC
          Is there a lot of grass there?

208. J: Yaan. , {D: hm}
          COP
          There is.

209.   Ya b'a-la yan nohoch u-pach a'-su'uk-i'ih. ,
          already TEMP-PROX COP big 3Ppr-place DET-grass-LOC
          Already now there is a big place of grass.

210. D: Ya nohoch-ki. (?)
          already big-ADJ?
          It's already big.

211. J: ahaa ,

212. D: mhmm

213. J: U-laak' yan mas, ka'nal-eh
          3Ppr-other COP more high-REL
          The other (field) that is higher

214.   b'ay xan. ,
          like also
          is like it too.

215. D: Si. ,
          yes
          Yes.

216. J: Ya nohoch. …
          already big
          It's already big.

217. D: Uuu yan tu'ux u-han-al-oo' {J:?}
          COP where 3-eat-INTRAN-PL
          They have where (a place) to eat.

218. J: Yaan. …
          COP
          There is.

219.   Yan tu'ux u-han-al-oo'. {D:?} …
          COP where 3-eat-INTRAN-PL
          They have where (a place) to eat.

220.   B'a-he'-la' tan a'-ha'-eh
          TEMP-OST-PROX DUR DET-rain-REL
          Now that it's raining

221.   he-tu'ux-ak, [yan,] yan han-al. ,
          OST-where-IRREAL? COP COP eat-NOM
          there is food wheresoever.

222. D: Aa yan han-al yan ha'. {J: mhmm} , {J: mhmm} …
            COP eat-NOM COP water
          Ah, there is food, there is water.

223.   Layti' ma'alo' yan. ,
          3Ipr good COP
          There is that fine.

224. J: A'-tan a'-yax＝k'in-eh
          DET-DUR? DET-summer-TOP
          When there is summer

225.   hach, (k-u-)tikin-tal. ,
          very (INC-3-)dry-INCHOAT
          it gets very dry.

226. D: Tikin, {J:?}
          dry
          Dry.

227.   <u>Tikin</u> ma'an tu'ux. ,
       dry NEG/COP where
       Dry, there's nowhere (to get food and water).

228.   mmm …

229. J: Chen ich a'-su'uk ,
       only in DET-grass
       Only in the grass

230.   k-u-man-s-ik-oo'-eh. {D: mm} ,
       INC-3-pass-CAUS-PPM-PL-REL
       that they pass.

231.   I tak a'-su'uk-eh k-u-tikin-tal. ,
       and to DET-grass-TOP INC-3-dry-INCHOAT
       And even the grass dries.

232. D: Aa mentäk(-eh) a'-yax=k'in-eh …
         because of(-TOP) DET-summer-TOP
       Ah, because of the summer,

233.   (k-u-)tikin-kun-t-ik-oo'. ,
       (INC-3-dry-CAUS-TRAN-PPM-PL
       it dries it.

234. J: ahaa. …

235.   B'e-la' hach yutzil. …
       TEMP-PROX very pretty
       Now it is very pretty.

236. D: hmmhm,

237. J: A'-ha'-eh tulakal k-u-men-t-ik. ,
       DET-water-TOP all INC-3-do-TRAN-PPM
       The water does it all.

238. D: A[a]'-lo' si ma'lo'. …
       DET-DIST yes good
       That is good, yes.

239. J: Ma' ka'-ok-ok tzimin ich a-kol-eh? …
       NEG REPET-enter-IRREAL horse in 2Ppr-milpa-TOP
       Horses haven't entered your milpa again?

240. D: Pwes, b'in-een ho'leh-ih
       well go-1sg yesterday-3sg
       Well, I went yesterday,

241.   ma' ok-ok. …
       NEG enter-IRREAL
       they haven't entered.

242.   Komo t-in-wa'l-ah t-u-yum-il-eh
as COM-1sg-say-DPM to-3Ppr-owner-POS-TOP
As I said to its owner

243.   ka' u-k'äx-ä'
SUB 3-tie-SPM
to tie it,

244.   wa ma' in-ta-s-ik wa'ye'. ,
COND NEG 1sg-come-CAUS-PPM here
if not, I'd bring it here.

245. J: Aaa, ma'lo'. {D: ?} ,
          good
      Ah, good.

246. D: Chen halk'ä'-eh
only free-TOP
If it's free,

247.   u-ka'a u-käx-t-e(h) tu'ux u-han-al. ...
3-go 3-seek-TRAN-SPM where 3-eat-INTRAN
it's going to seek where to eat.

248. J: He'-tu'ux-ak-eh k-u-yok-ol.
OST-where-IRREAL?-TOP INC-3-enter-INTRAN
It enters wheresoever.

249. D: Pero ma' tun-käx-t-ik pok=che'
but NEG DUR/3-seek-TRAN-PPM weed
But it's not looking for weeds,

250.   k-u-käx-t-ik-eh
INC-3-seek-TRAN-PPM-REL
(it's not weeds) that it is looking for

251.   pero kol [?] {J: laughter} ...
but milpa
but milpa.

252. J: Layti' a'-lo' u-k'a't-ih. , {D: mm} ,
3Ipr DET-DIST 3-want-PM?
It is that it wants.

253.   Ma' tan-wil-ik a'-ixi'im-eh a'-näl-eh?
NEG DUR/2-see-PPM DET-corn-TOP DET-ear-TOP
Aren't you seeing the corn, the ears?

254.   [Tulakal u-ka',] Tulakal a'-b'a'al=che' k-u-han-t-ik.
[all 3-?] all DET-animal INC-3-eat-TRAN-PPM
All of the animals eat it.

255. D: K-u-han-t-ik. ,
          INC-3-eat-TRAN-PPM
          They eat it.

256. J: ahaa,

257. D: mm …

258. J: Layti' a'-he'-<u>lo'</u>
          3Ipr DET-OST-DIST
          That is . . .

259. D: <u>Ka'</u> layti' a'-he'-lo' a'-k'in ka'
          when 3Ipr DET-OST-DIST DET-day when
          It was that day when

          t-in-hok'-s-ah-eh …
          COM-1sg-leave-CAUS-DPM-REL
          I took it out,

260.   man-een in-wa'l-eh ti'ih u-yum-il ,
          pass-1sg 1sg-say-SPM to 3Ppr-owner-POS
          I went to say to the owner,

261.   k-u-men-t-eh a'-favoor-eh …
          SUB-3-do-TRAN-SPM DET-favor-TOP
          that he do the favor

262.   k-u-k'äx-ä'
          SUB-3-tie-SPM
          of tieing it,

263.   porke wa ma' in-ta-s-ik wa'ye' ti poosteh-eh. …
          because COND NEG 1sg-come-CAUS-PPM here to post-TOP
          because if not, I'm bringing it here to the post.

264.   "Aa ma' in-tia'al-i'ih" ki ten.
              NEG 1sgPpr-own-SCOPE say/3sg 1sgIOpr
          "Oh, it isn't mine," he said to me.

265.   "Komo no a-ti'a'al
          how NEG 2Ppr-own
          "How isn't it yours

266.   si, hun tuul winik t(-u-)ya'(al-ah) ten-eh
          if one ANIM man COM(-3-)say(-DPM) 1sgIOpr-TOP
          if a man told me

267.   ke a-ti'a'al, a-k'ab'a', b'ay-lo' ke" ,
          SUB 2Ppr-own 2Ppr-name like-DIST SUB
          that it is yours, your name, it is thus that,"

268. "Aaa [im-paa' (?)] (pak'-t-eh) k-im-b'el in-wil-a'
     [1sg-?] (wait-TRAN-SPM/IMP) INC-1sg-go 1sg-see-SPM
     "Oh, wait, I'm going to see

269. tu'ux k'äx-a'an t-im-men" kii. {J: laughter} ...
     where tie-PART DUR-1sg-do? say/3sg
     where I have it tied," he said.

270. Ka' b'in-een t-u-pach in-wil-a'. ...
     then go-1sg at-3Ppr-back 1sg-see-SPM
     Then I went behind him to see it.

271. Chen u-tus i ma'an mix u-sum-il ,
     only 3Ppr-lie and NEG/COP NEG 3Ppr-rope-POS
     It was only his lie and it didn't even have its rope,

272. halk'ä' u-man-äl [?]. [both laugh]
     free 3-pass-INTRAN
     it was walking loose.

273. J: Si ma'an tu'ux u-han-al
         if NEG/COP where 3-eat-INTRAN
         If there wasn't anywhere to eat,

274. mentäk-eh k-u-halk'ä'-t-ik.
     therefore-TOP INC-3-free-TRAN-PPM
     therefore he frees it.

275. D: [I,] i si ma' tun-käx-t-ik
         [and] and if NEG DUR/3-seek-TRAN-PPM
         And if he doesn't look for

276. tu'ux k-u-b'el ti han-al. ,
     where INC-3-go to eat-INTRAN
     where it is going to eat.

277. J: Sii. ,
         yes
         Yes.

278. D: Pwes k'och-ol t-im-b'et-ah-eh ,
         well arrive-NOM COM-1sg-make-DIST-TOP
         Well, when I made my arrival,

279. yan hun tuul winik [natz',] natz' t-in-kol , {J: aha} ,
     COP one ANIM man [near] near to-1sgPpr-milpa
     there was a man near my milpa,

280. tan-u-päk'-ik b'u'ul. ...
     DUR-3-plant-PPM bean
     he was planting beans.

281.   Tan-u-[,]-päk' = bu'ul-oo'
        DUR-3-plant-bean-PL
        They were bean-planting

282.   ka' t-u-cha'an-t-ah
        when COM-3-see-TRAN-DPM
        when he saw

283.   ok(-ih) a'-tzimin-eh. ...
        enter(-3sg) DET-horse-TOP
        the horse entered.

284.   Ka' t-u-täka'-t-ah u-paal u-hok'-es. ...
        then COM-3-send-TRAN-DPM 3Ppr-child 3-leave-CAUS/SPM
        Then he sent his child to get it out.

285.   In-ten k-in-k'och-ol
        EMP-1sgIpr INC-1sg-arrive-INTRAN
        Me, I was coming,

286.   a'-tzimin k-u-hok'-ol-eh.
        DET-horse INC-3-leave-INTRAN-TOP
        as the horse was leaving.

287.   Ma' (?) u-ch'i'-ik kabal-eh
        NEG 3-take-PPM below-TOP
        Instead of taking (the path) below

288.   t-u-ch'a'-ah ka'nal.
        COM-3-take-DPM above.
        it took it above.

289. J: Ka'<u>nal</u>. {D: <u>mhm</u>}
        above
        Above.

290. D: K-u-b'el-e' ,
        INC-3-go-TOP
        It goes,

291.   k-u-b'el t-u-pach ...
        INC-3-go at-3Ppr-back
        he goes behind (?),

292.   tatz' ich u-kol im-[,]-kompaadre Abraam.
        straight in 3Ppr-milpa 1sgPpr-friend Abraham.
        straight into the milpa of my friend Abraham.

293.   Ok-ih {D: laughter}
        enter-3sg
        It entered,

294. ka' ok-een in-hok'-es,
      then enter-1sg 1sg-leave-CAUS/SPM
      then I entered to get it out,

295. i te'e-lo' [tus,] (tun-)ch'i'-ik ka'nal. ,
      and LOC-DIST [?] (DUR/3-)take-PPM above
      and there it was taking (a path) above.

296. J: Tun-b'el ka'nal.
         DUR/3-go above
         It was going above.

297. D: A'-tieempo ka' [k'och-] te'-yan-e'ex
         DET-time when [arrive-] LOC-COP-2pl
         At the time when you all were there,

298. ka' t-u-sut(-ah) u-b'ah
      then COM-3-turn(-DPM) 3Ppr-REFL
      then it turned around,

299. k-u-tal (?). ,
      INC-3-come
      it was coming.

300. J: ahaa ,

301. D: Ka' t-in-hok'-s-ah tak ti b'eh. ...
         then COM-1sg-leave-CAUS-DPM till to road
         Then I got it out down to the road.

302. Ya tak b'a-lah k-in-wil-ik-eh
      already till TEMP-PROX INC-1sg-see-PPM-TOP
      Until now I see that

303. ma' ok-ok. ...
      NEG enter-IRREAL
      it hasn't entered.

304. J: I ma' t-u-han-t-ah a-kol? ,
         and NEG COM-3-eat-TRAN-DPM 2Ppr-milpa
         And it didn't eat your milpa?

305. D: Pwes chen t-u-huhum p'eel
         well only to-3Ppr-some INAM
         Well only some

306. i man-ih
      and pass-3sg

307. komo hach mehen toh a'-[?](näl). {J: aa} ...
      as very small still DET-(ear)
      as the ears are still very small.

308.   Chen u-k'o' ... [t-u-,] t-u-han-t-ah uu
                only 3Ppr-leaf [COM-3-] COM-3-eat-TRAN-DPM ?
                It only ate the top leaf . . .

309.   J: Ma'lo' wa [?](ma') , [?]
                good if NEG
                Good, if not…

310.   D: Komo tant-u-yok-ol
                as IMMED-3-enter-INTRAN
                As it just entered

311.   ka' [?] hok'-s-äb'-ih-eh ...
                when leave-CAUS-PAS-3sg-TOP
                when it was taken out,

312.   ma' t-u-b'et-ah mix b'a'al. ,
                NEG COM-3-do-DPM NEG thing
                it didn't do anything.

313.   J: ahaa ,

314.   D: Wa ma' [inaudible],
                COND NEG
                If not (if it wasn't removed),

315.   he'-u-han-t-ik-eh. ,
                ASSUR-3-eat-TRAN-PPM-TOP
                it would eat it.

316.   J: Ka' tuul-oo' [?]?
                two ANIM-PL
                Two (animals)?

317.   D: Ka' tuul pwes. ,
                two ANIM well
                Right, two.

318.   J: [laughter,] Aa ya ka' tuul ba'al=che' yan-u-han-al.
                         already two ANIM animal OBLIG-3-eat-INTRAN
                    Ah, two animals then have to eat.

319.   D: [inaudible]

320.   J: Todos wa'-l-ak-oo' ti han-al-eh
                all stand-POSIT-IRREAL-PL SUB eat-INTRAN-REL
                All that stop to eat

321.   he'-u-han-t-ik-oo'-eh. ,
                ASSUR-3-eat-TRAN-PPM-PL-TOP
                will eat (a lot of) it.

322. D: "'A'-kol he'-la' ma'an u-yum-il" ,
      DET-milpa OST-PROX NEG/COP 3Ppr-owner-POS
      "This milpa doesn't have an owner,"

      ki wal-eh. , [both laugh]
      say/3sg DUB-TOP
      perhaps it (animal) said.

323. J: "He'-la' yan a'-ki-ti'a'al-eh kiih-oo'. [both laugh]
      OST-PROX COP DET-1plPpr-own-TOP say-PL
      "This is ours," they said.

324. D: "Es meero." . . . . {J: laughter}
      is pure
      "It's pure (good)."

325.   Tak b'a-lah k-in-wil-ik-eh
      till OST-PROX INC-1sg-see-PPM-TOP
      Until now I see that

326.   ma' ok-ok. ,
      NEG enter-IRREAL
      it hasn't entered.

327. J: Ma'lo' entons(es) t-u-k'äx-ah
      good then COM-3-tie-DPM
      Good then, he tied it . . .

328. D: Komo, t-in-[,]-mo'nok-[,]-hil=pach-t-ah
      as COM-1sg-small-fence-TRAN-DPM
      As I fenced a little

      tulakal u-haal a'-b'eh-eh. ,
      all 3Ppr-edge DET-road-TOP
      all to the edge of the road.

329. J: Ya ma'
      already NEG
      Now then (they're) not...

330. D: Ya ma' tun-yok-ol. ,
      already NEG DUR/-3-enter-INTRAN
      Now then they aren't entering.

331.   De swerte a'-t-ah Peedroh-eh …
      of luck DET-of-MASC Pedro-REL
      Luckily, the (milpa) of Pedro,

332.   t-u-lah-hil=che'-t-ah tulakal u-vwelta. ,
      COM-3-all-fence-TRAN-DPM all 3Ppr-perimeter
      he fenced all of its perimeter.

333. J: Tulakal u-[?]
     all 3Ppr-
     All its…

334. D: Wa ma', t-u-ok(-ol) u-han-t-eh. …
     COND NEG DUR-3-enter-INTRAN 3-eat-TRAN-SPM
     If not, they would be entering to eat it.

335. J: Si pwes.,
     yes well
     Right.

336. D: mhmm …

337. J: Bay-lo' ha'li kot-b'il-eh,
     like-DIST only fence-PART-TOP
     Only fenced that way,

338. D: Ha'li b'ay-la'-eh.
     only like-PROX-TOP
     Only this way.

339. J: hil=che'-b'il u-haal-eh
     fence-PART 3Ppr-perimeter-TOP
     the perimeter being fenced,

340.   wa, ma'an tu'ux u-yok-ol-oo'. …
        COND NEG/COP where 3-enter-INTRAN-PL
        if they don't have anywhere to enter.

341.   A'-tzimin-eh ma' he-b'ix a'-wakax-eh. ,
        DET-horse-TOP NEG OST-like DET-cow-TOP
        The horse is not like the cow.

342. D: Ma' pwes. ,
     NEG well
     Well no.

343. J: A'-tzimin-eh yet-e(l) ka' p'e che'
     DET-horse-TOP 3Ppr/with-POS two INAM log
     The horse, with two logs

344.   ka' a-pul-u'-eh {D: aa si}
        SUB 2-throw-SPM-REL
        that you throw down,

345.   ya ma' tan-u-man. , {D: si,}
        then NEG DUR-3-pass
        then it doesn't pass.

346.   A'-wakax-eh ma'
        DET-cow-TOP NEG
        The cow, no,

347.   a'-wakax-eh ka'ax a-[,]-pul-u' ti'ih che'-eh, {D: ?}
DET-cow-TOP although 2-throw-SPM 3IOpr log-TOP
the cow, even if you throw down logs for it,

348.   (u-)chok'(-o') u-ho'ol-eh b'in-ih.
(3-)insert(-SPM) 3Ppr-head-TOP go-3sg
it puts its head in, it went.

349. D: [laughter] Ma'-ak tun. [both laugh]
            NEG-IRREAL? then
            Of course.

350. J: Layti' a'-lo' yan ti'ih. [both chuckle]
       3Ipr DET-DIST COP 3IOpr
       It has that (problem).

351. D: Es bweno, pero …
       it's good but
       Well yes, but …

352. J: Ma'lo' … [?] chan=b'el tan-u-ch'iil tz'e-tz'e-tak.
       fine slowly DUR-3-grow INTENS-little-PL?
       Fine, slowly it (milpa) is growing little by little.

353. D: Aa si. …
         yes
       Ah yes.

354. J: Si. ,
       yes
       Yes.

355. D: A'-kuch-ih, b'ay-la' dos años-eh …
       DET-before-3sg like-PROX two years-TOP
       It was like this before two years ago,

356.   a'-k'ek'en wal t-a'-mak-oo' …
DET-pig DUB of-DET-person-PL
the pigs, I think of the people

357.   t-a'-Nwee(va) tak ich in-kol
of-DET-PN til inside 1sgPpr-milpa
of New San José, even into my milpa

358.   [hu] k'och-oo' ti han-al-e.,
[?] arrive-PL SUB eat-INTRAN-REL
they arrived to eat.

359. J: Aa si. …
         yes
       Ah yes.

360. D: Ka' t-in-k'a't-ah ti'ih u-yum-il-oo'
          then COM-1sg-ask-DPM 3IOpr 3Ppr-owner-POS-PL
          Then I asked the owners

361.   maax t-a'-k'ek'en-oo'. ...
          who of-DET-pig-PL
          whose the pigs were.

362.   A'-[?]-k'ek'en k-u-man chen ti b'eh-eh ...
          Det-pig INC-3-pass only in road-REL
          The pigs that walk only in the road,

363.   ti'ih fulaanah-oo', [?]. ,
          3IOpr John Doe-PL
          belong to John Does.

364.   B'in-een in-wa'l(-eh) ti'ih u-yum-il-eh
          go-1sg 1sg-say(-SPM) to 3Ppr-owner-POS-TOP
          I went to say to the owners

365.   ka' u-k'äx-ä'
          SUB 3-tie-SPM
          that they should tie them

366.   wa k-u-k'äl-ä'.
          or SUB-3-enclose-SPM
          or enclose them.

367.   Wa ma' ... he'el-in-kin-s-ik k'ek'en-eh (?). , {J: laughter} ,
          COND NEG ASSUR-1sg-die-CAUS-PPM pig-TOP
          If not, I would kill some pigs.

368.   Pwes t-u-lah-kon-ah-oo'. ,
          well COM-3-all-sell-DPM-PL
          Well, they sold them all.

369. J: Ahaa. ,

370. D: Ka' xu'l-ih, u-b'el u-molestar a'-k'ek'en-oo'. ,
          then end-3sg 3-go 3-bother DET-pig-PL
          Then the pigs stopped going to bother.

371. J: Si pwes.
          yes then
          Right.

372. D: T-u-han-t-ah-oo' mäkäl
          COM-3-eat-TRAN-DPM-PL caladium
          They ate caladium,

373.   [?] (t-u-han-t-ah) kamut
          (COM-3-eat-TRAN-DPM sweet potato
          they ate sweet potatoes,

374. t-u-han-t-ah ixi'im
      COM-3-eat-TRAN-DPM corn
      they ate corn,

375. t-u-han-t-ah komo wätz'-a'an a'-[,]-näl-eh {J: ?}
      COM-3-eat-TRAN-DPM as double-PART DET-ear-TOP
      they ate it as the ears were doubled,

376. hmm pero si. ,
           but yes
      oh but yes (they ate it).

277. Ka' k'och-oo' hum pak-eh,
      then arrive-PL one time-TOP
      Then one time

378. komo oocho k'ek'en ich-il. , {J: ?}
      like eight pig inside-POS
      about eight pigs arrived inside.

379. Puro nukuch k'ek'en-oo', (k-u-)han-al-oo'. ...
      pure big pig-PL (INC-3-)eat-INTRAN-PL
      All big pigs, they were eating.

380. Si. ...
      yes
      Yes.

381. J: Ma'lo'.
      good
      Good.

382. D: Pwes ha'l(i') a'-[,]-b'es he'-lo' ok-ih-eh
      well only DET-time OST-DIST enter-3sg-REL
      Well, it's only that time that they entered,

383. ya ma' ka'-ok-ih. ...
      then NEG REPET-enter-3sg
      then they didn't enter again.

384. Ka' lah-kom-b'-ih men yum-il. ,
      then all-sell-PAS-3sg by 3Ppr/owner-POS
      Then all were sold by their owner(s).

385. J: [laughter] "Antes ka' u-han-t-eh" ki-wal-oo'-eh.
                before SUB 3-eat-TRAN-SPM say-DUB-PL-TOP
                "Before he eats them," perhaps they said.

386. D: Si pwes antes ka' u-han-t(-eh) ah ch'om.
      yes well before SUB 3-eat-TRAN(-SPM) MASC buzzard
      Right, before a buzzard eats them.

387. [both laugh heartily] [D: inaudible,]

388. J: Otzil a'-b'a'al=che'-oo'-eh, sii. ,
          poor DET-animal-PL-TOP yes
          The animals are wretched, yes.

389.   Yan mak xan u-k'a't-ih yan-tal ti'ih,
          COP person also 3-want-PM? COP-INCHOAT 3IOpr
          There are people that want to have them (animals)

390.   i [hach tz'eek] ma' tan-[u-,]-u-tzen-t-ik-oo'.
          and [very little] NEG DUR-[3-]-3-feed-TRAN-PPM-PL
          and they don't feed them.

391. D: [inaudible] u-han-al-oo'.
                        3Ppr-eat-NOM-PL
                        …their food.

392. J: Ma' tan-u-tz'ik u-han-al-oo'. ,
          NEG DUR-3-give/PPM 3Ppr-eat-NOM-PL
          They don't give their food.

393. D: hmm, Tan-u-han-al(-oo') ma'lo'-eh
               DUR-3-eat-INTRAN(-PL) well-TOP
               (When) they are eating well,

394.   ma' t-u-hok'-ol-oo' ti, molestar [inaudible]
          NEG INC-3-leave-INTRAN-PL SUB bother
          they don't go out to bother…

395. J: ahaa, A'-b'a'al=che' wi'ih, {D: ?}
               DET-animal hungry
               The animal is hungry,

396.   yan-u-käx-t-ik tu'ux u-han-al. …
          OBLIG-3-seek-TRAN-PPM where 3-eat-INTRAN
          it has to look for a place to eat.

397. D: Si pwes.
          yes well
          Right.

398. J: Layti a'-lo' yan-eh. ,
          3Ipr DET-DIST OBLIG-REL
          It is that that it must do.

399. D: Si. …
          yes
          Yes.

400. J: U-yum-il ma' tan-u-tz'ik u-han-al.
          3Ppr-owner-POS NEG DUR-3-give/PPM 3Ppr-eat-NOM
          The owner doesn't give its food.

401. D: Ma' t-u-tz'ik u-han-al (u-)k'ek'en. . . . {J: aa}
         NEG INC-3-give/PPM 3Ppr-eat-NOM (3Ppr-) pig
         He doesn't give his pigs their food.

402.   Pwes b'ay-lo' tak b'a-la' ma'. . . .
         well like-DIST till TEMP-PROX NEG
         Well it's that way until now, no.

403.   B'a-la' ma' k'och-ok, mix b'a'al,
         TEMP-PROX NEG arrive-IRREAL NEG thing
         Now, nothing has arrived

404.   ti molestarse [inaudible]
         SUB bother
         to bother . . .

405. J: Ma'lo'
         good
         Good.

406. D: mhmm . . .

407. J: Ma'lo'. . . .
         good
         Good.

408.   Ten k-in-wil-ik a'-mehen kol-oo' tzeel b'eh-eh yutzil. . . .
         1sgIpr INC-1sg-see-PPM DET-small milpa-PL side road-TOP pretty
         To me, the little milpas at the side of the road look pretty.

409. D: Ma'lo' ma-xa'?
         good NEG?-?
         Good, right?

410. J: Ma'lo' yutzil k-in-wil-ik.
         good pretty INC-1sg-see-PPM
         Good, they look pretty to me.

411. D: Pwes b'a-la' kasi tulaka(l) a'-mehen kol-oo' lah ma'lo'. . . .
         well TEMP-PROX almost all DET-small milpa-PL all good
         Well now, almost all of the little milpas are all good.

412.   [?] {J: ?} Layt(i') a'-ha'-eh t-u-b'et-ah . . .
          3Ipr DET-water-TOP COM-3-do-DPM
         It's the water that made them,

413.   u-lik'-il. ,
         3-raise-INTRAN
         raise up (grow).

414. J: ahaa,

415. D: Porke, ma'an ha'-eh ma'an,
         because NEG/COP water-TOP NEG/COP
         Because if there isn't water there isn't . . .

416. J: Ma'an mix b'a'al.
         NEG/COP NEG thing
         There isn't anything.

417. D: mix b'a'al ma'lo'. …
         NEG thing good
         anything good.

418.   Sii. (?) {J: mm} …
         yes
         Yes.

419. J: Hah a'-[k'i]-yax=k'in-eh hach yutzil pero hach otzil. …
         true DET-summer-TOP very pretty but very poor
         True, the summer is very pretty, but very poor.

420. D: Aaa ma'an mix b'a'al ti han-b'-äl. ,
         NEG/COP NEG thing SUB eat-PAS-INTRAN
         Ah, there isn't anything to be eaten.

421. J: Ma'an mix b'a'al. ,
         NEG/COP NEG thing
         There isn't anything.

422. D: Mhmm … t-u-hah-il. …
                        in-3Ppr-true-POS
         Mhm, it's true.

423. J: B'ay-lo'. …
         like-DIST
         Thus.

424.   Et a'-ha'-eh yan tulakal b'a'ax. ,
         with DET-water-TOP COP all thing
         With the water there is everything.

425. D: Si. …
         yes
         Yes.

426.   I tu'ux k-a-tak'-äl-eh
         and where INC-2-beach-INTRAN-REL
         And where you beach (your canoe)

427.   yaab' mak t-u-ka'ye', t-a'-mo'nok kah-eh.
         many person in-3Ppr-again in-DET-small town-TOP
         there are a lot of people again in the little town.

428. J: Aa ya tan-u-yaab'-tal-oo' t-u-ka'ye'. {D: mm} …
             already DUR-3-much-come-PL in-3Ppr-again
         Ah, already many are coming again.

429. B'a-he-la' ya' hach yaab' mak
     TEMP-OST-PROX then very many person
     Now already many people

     tan-u-k'och-ol-oo' t-u-ka'ye'-i'i(h)
     DUR-3-arrive-INTRAN-PL in-3Ppr-again-LOC
     are arriving again there,

430. tan-u-[,]-men-t-ik-oo' u-yotoch,
     DUR-3-make-TRAN-PPM-PL 3Ppr-home
     they are making their homes,

431. tan puuchah, tulakal-oo' yan … eeh,
     DUR EXCLAM all-PL COP?
     they are, wow! all are …

432. Tulakal a'-k-u-lah-men-t-ik-oo' u-yotoch-eh,
     all DET-INC-3-all-make-TRAN-PPM-PL 3Ppr-home-REL
     All of them that are completely making their homes,

433. tu'umben na(h) k-u-ka'-men-t-ik-oo'. ,
     new house INC-3-REPET-make-TRAN-PPM-PL
     are making new houses again.

434. D: mhmm

435. J: Tulakal [ix] ix lä' na(h)-oo'-eh ya lah [lu] lub'-oo'.
     all [FEM] FEM old house-PL-TOP already all fall-PL
     All of the old houses already completely fell down.

436. D: T-u-hah-il. … {J: ?}
     in-3Ppr-true-POS
     Truely.

437. T-u-lah-p'ät-ah-oo'
     COM-3-all-leave-DPM-PL
     They left everything,

438. b'a-la' t-u-ka'-sut-k'-aal-oo'
     TEMP-PROX DUR-3-REPET-return-CELER?-INTRAN?-PL
     now they are returning again

     ti käh-tal-i'ih.
     to live-POSIT-LOC
     to live there.

439. J: Yan mak, t-a'-[,]-tieempoh-oo' he'-lo'
     COP person from-DET-time-PL OST-DIST
     There are people from those times

440. ka' tal-oo'-eh. ,
     then come-PL-REL
     that came.

441. D: hmm ,

442. J: Tal-oo' b'in. …
           come-PL REPORT
           They say they came.

443. D: Si.
           yes
           Yes.

444. J: Te'-lo' ka' ka'-sut-k'-ah-oo'
           LOC-DIST then REPET-return-CELER?-DIST-PL
           Then they returned there again,

445.   ka' ka'-b'in-oo' t-u-ka'-pach. , {D: aa} ,
           then REPET-go-PL in-3Ppr-REPET-back
           then they went back again.

446.   Ma' ki'-ah-ih t-u-yich-oo' wa'ye'
           NEG good-DIST-3sg to-3Ppr-eye-PL here
           They didn't like it here,

447.   ka' ka'-b'in-oo'. {D: m<u>mm</u>}
           then REPET-go-PL
           then they went again.

448.   <u>I</u> b'a-lah tan-u-ka'-tal-oo'
           and TEMP-PROX DUR-3-REPET-come-PL
           And now they are coming again.

449. D: Tan-u-ka'-tal-oo'. …
           DUR-3-REPET-come-PL
           They are coming again.

450. J: Ay ma' patal. …
             NEG ABIL
           Ah, it's impossible.

451.   Ma' patal-u-na't-ik mak a'-mak-oo'-eh
           NEG ABIL-3-understand-PPM person DET-person-PL-TOP
           One can't understand the people,

452.   he-b'ix, yan k-u-tal-oo'(-eh)
           OST-how COP INC-3-come-PL(-REL)
           just as there are those who come,

453.   yan tun-b'el-oo'(-eh)
           COP DUR/3-go-PL(-REL)
           there are those who are going,

454.   yan k-u-tal-oo'(-eh)
           COP INC-3-come-PL(-REL)
           there are those who come,

455.   yan tun-b'el-oo'(-eh). …
           COP DUR/3-go-PL(-REL)
           there are those who are going.

456. D: I tu'ux mas ma'lo'?
           and where more good
           And where is it better?

457.   Ma' t-u-käx-t-ik-oo' ha'li wa'yeh. …
           NEG INC-3-seek-TRAN-PPM-PL only here
           They don't seek it (land) except here.

458. J: Ma'an tu'ux mas, {D: mm tulakal} chen wa'ye'. ,
           NEG/COP where more all only here
           There isn't anywhere else, only here.

459. D: Tulakal tu'ux b'ay-lo lah-yan yum-il. ,
           all where like-DIST all-COP 3Ppr/owner-POS
           All where it is like that, all has owners.

460. J: B'ayoorah-eh he-tu'ux-ak-eh {D: mm} hach yaab' mak. …
           now-TOP OST-where-IRREAL?-TOP very many person
           Now there are many people wheresoever.

461.   Hach yaab' mak. {D: winik-eh (?)} …
           very many person {man-TOP}
           There are a lot of people.

462.   He-tu'ux-ak-eh. , {D: mhmm}
           OST-where-IRREAL?-TOP
           Wheresoever.

463.   Wa'ye' mas ma'lo'
           here more good
           Here it is better

464.   porque k-u-ya'l-ik-oo'-eh
           because INC-3-say-PPM-PL-TOP
           because they say that

465.   mas natz' yan a'-,
           more near COP DET
           the (fields) are closer,

466. D: Aa yan a'-lu'um-oo'.
                COP DET-land-PL
           Ah, there are the fields.

467. J: a'-lu'um-oo' ti'ih u-meyah-t-oo'-eh.
           DET-land-PL SUB 3-work-TRAN-PL-TOP
           the fields for them to work.

468. D: I k'aax t-u-meyah-t-oo'. ,
         and forest SUB-3-work-TRAN-PL
         And forest for them to work.

469. J: ahaa,

470. D: Yan ha' yan tulakal.
         COP water COP all
         There is water, there is everything.

471. J: Yan ha' yan tulakal. , {D: mm}
         COP water COP all
         There is water, there is everything.

472.   Mentäk-eh k-u-ka'-tal-oo'
         therefore-TOP INC-3-REPET-come-PL
         For that, they come again

473.   u-käx-t-oo' wa'ye'. ,
         3-seek-TRAN-PL here
         to seek it here.

474. D: Si pwes.
         yes well
         Right.

475. J: Ma'an tu'ux mas u-b'el-oo'
         NEG/COP where more 3-go-PL
         There is no place else for them to go,

476.   he-tu'ux-ak ka' xi'ik-oo'-eh
         OST-where-IRREAL? SUB go/IRREAL-PL-TOP
         wheresoever they might go,

477.   [hach,] hach yaab' mak.
         [very] very many person
         there are many people.

478. D: Hmm mas peor wal-eh. ...
              more bad DUB-TOP
              Maybe worse.

479.   B'ay-lo' t-a'-Nweevah-eh. ,
         like-DIST in-DET-PN-TOP
         Thus it is in La Nueva.

480.   Hach yaab' mak b'in(-ih) Naraanho. ...
         very many person go(-3sg) PN
         Very many people went to Naranjo.

481. J: B'ay b'in.
         like REPORT
         Thus they say.

482. D: Pwes ma'lo' t-u-b'et-ah u-kol-oo'
    well well COM-3-do-DPM 3Ppr-milpa-PL
    Well, they made their milpas well

483.   pero tulakal u-[,]-päk'-aal-oo' [ma',] ma' ki'-ah-ih
    but all 3Ppr-plant-PART-PL [NEG] NEG good-DIST-3sg
    but all of their plants were not good,

484.   chen a'-näl b'in ma'lo'. ,
    only DET-ear REPORT good
    only the corn ears are good.

485. J: Asi?
    thus
    Thus?

486. D: Ha'li a'-kol b'in hach yutzil-eh. …
    only DET-milpa REPORT very pretty-TOP
    Only the milpa, they say, is very pretty.

487.   T-u-päk'-ah-oo' {J: humming} b'in sikil k'uum tulakal-eh. …
    COM-3-plant-DPM-PL REPORT squash seed calabash all-TOP
    They planted *sikil* (a squash), calabash, everything.

488.   Lah-tikin-ah-ih {J: ?} b'in. ,
    all-dry-DIST-3sg REPORT
    It all dried, they say.

489.   Hok'-ih pero …
    leave-3sg but
    It came out, but

490.   t-u-tz'utz'-ah chiinche. ,
    COM-3-suck-DPM insect
    bugs sucked (ate) it.

491. J: A'-lo' si hah,
    DET-DIST yes true
    Yes, that is true

492.   porke, ten xan t-in-päk'-ah tz'eek sikil, {D: hm}
    because 1sgIpr also COM-1sg-plant-DPM little squash seed
    because I too planted a little squash seed,

493.   i eee ka' chu'um-pah(-ih) a'-ha'-eh
    and EXCLAM when begin-INTRAN(-3sg) DET-water-TOP
    and oh, when the rains began

494.   k-a-wil-a'
    SUB-2-see-SPM
    you should have seen

495.   b'ix u-hok'-ol [stumble] ix ki=say t-u-chun-eh. ,
          how 3-leave-INTRAN FEM ?=ant at-3Ppr-base-TOP
          how the bugs came out of their bases.

496. D: Si. …
          yes
          Yes.

497. J: T-u-lah-tz'utz'-ah u-chun. …
          COM-3-all-suck-DPM 3Ppr-base
          They sucked (ate) all of the bases.

498.   T-u-<u>lah-tikin-kun-t-es-ah</u> u-yak'-il. {D: ?} ,
          COM-3-all-dry-CAUS-TRAN-CAUS-DPM 3Ppr-vine-POS
          It completely dried the vines.

499. D: <u>Ya</u> {J: ?} ma' tun-tz'ik u-yich. ,
          then NEG DUR/3-give/PPM 3Ppr-fruit
          Then it doesn't give its fruit.

500. J: Ma' tan. ,
          NEG DUR
          It doesn't.

501.   Ya b'ay-lo' k-u-lah-tikin-tal. …
          already like-DIST INC-3-all-dry-INCHOAT
          Already like that, it all dries.

502.   Komo ma' hach, lub'-uk a'-ha' ma'lo'-eh ,
          as NEG much fall-IRREAL DET-water well-TOP
          As the rain hasn't really fallen well,

503. D: Si pwes.
          yes well
          Right.

504. J: hach tikin-ah-eh. …
          much dry-DIST-TOP
          it really dried out.

          (The conversation continues on another theme.)

REFERENCES

Andrade, Manuel J. 1976. "Mopan" Notes (with Yucatec, Itzá, and Quekchí). Microfilm Collection of Manuscripts on Middle American Cultural Anthropology, 246. University of Chicago Library. (Gathered in Bacalar, Corozal, San Luis, San Antonio, Belize, in 1931).

Armas, Isaías. n.d. Vocabulario breve de la lengua maya 1897 recogido en el pueblo de San José y San Luis (Itzá). Middle American Research Institute, 5.265.

Blair, Robert W. 1964. Yucatec Maya Noun and Verb Morpho-Syntax. Ph.D. diss. Department of Linguistics, Indiana University.

Brasseur de Bourbourg, Charles E. 1865. *La Maya et ses dialects, lacandón, petén, mopán, chol.* Paris: Archives de la Commission Scientifique du Méxique, 127–29.

Bricker, Victoria R. 1974. The Ethnographic Context of Some Traditional Mayan Speech Genres. In *Explorations in the Ethnography of Speaking,* edited by Richard Bauman and Joel Sherzer, 368–88. Cambridge: Cambridge University Press.

———. 1981a. Grammatical Introduction. In *Yucatec Maya Verbs (Hocaba Dialect),* by Eleuterio Po'ot Yah, v–xlviii. Latin American Studies Curriculum Aids. New Orleans: Tulane University, Center for Latin American Studies.

———. 1981b. *The Indian Christ, The Indian King: The Historical Substrate of Maya Myth and Ritual.* Austin: University of Texas Press.

———. 1981c. The Source of the Ergative Split in Yucatec Maya. *Journal of Mayan Linguistics* 2(2): 83–127.

Bright, William. 1984. American Indian Linguistics and Literature. New York: Mouton.

Brody, Jill. 1986. Repetition as a Rhetorical and Conversational Device in Tojolobal (Mayan). *International Journal of American Linguistics* 52:255–74.

———. 1989a. Discourse Markers in Tojolobal Mayan. In *Papers from the 25th Annual Regional Meeting of the Chicago Linguistic Society,* part 2, *Parasession on Language in Context,* edited by Bradley Music, Randolph Graczyk, and Caroline Wiltshire, 15–29. CLS 25. Chicago: Chicago Linguistic Society.

———. 1989b. Conversation as the Matrix for Discourse Analysis. Ms.

Bruce, Robert. 1968. *Gramática del Lacandón.* Mexico City: Instituto de Antropologia e Historia.

Burns, Allan F. 1983. *An Epoch of Miracles: Oral Literature of the Yucatec Maya*. Austin: University of Texas Press.

Chafe, Wallace L. 1982. Integration and Involvement in Speaking, Writing, and Oral Literature. In *Spoken and Written Language: Exploring Orality and Literacy*, edited by Deborah Tannen, 32–53. Norwood, N.J.: Ablex.

Chase, Arlen F. 1985. Postclassic Peten Interaction Spheres: The View from Tayasal. In *The Lowland Maya Postclassic*, edited by Arlen F. Chase and Prudence M. Rice, 184–205. Austin: University of Texas Press.

Du Bois, John W. 1987. The Discourse Basis of Ergativity. *Language* 63:805–55.

Durbin, Marshall, and Fernando Ojeda. 1982. Patient Deixis in Yucatec Maya. *Journal of Mayan Linguistics* 3(2): 3–23.

Edmonson, Munro S. 1982. *The Ancient Future of the Itza: The Book of Chilam Balam of Tizimin*. Austin: University of Texas Press.

———. 1986. *Heaven Born Merida and Its Destiny: The Book of Chilam Balam of Chumayel*. Austin: University of Texas Press.

England, Nora. 1988. A Typology of Parallelism. Ms.

Farriss, Nancy M. 1984. *Maya Society under Colonial Rule*. Princeton: Princeton University Press.

Givón, T. 1984. *Syntax: A Functional-Typological Introduction*, vol. 1. Philadelphia: John Benjamins Publishing Co.

Hanks, William F. 1989. Elements of Maya Style. In *Word and Image in Maya Culture*, edited by William F. Hanks and Don S. Rice, 92–111. Salt Lake City: University of Utah Press.

Halliday, M. A. K. 1967. Notes on Transitivity and Theme in English, part 2. *Journal of Linguistics* 3:199–244.

Hofling, Charles A. 1982. Itza Maya Morphosyntax from a Discourse Perspective. Ph.D. diss. Department of Anthropology, Washington University.

———. 1984a. Irrealis Subordinate Clauses and Related Constructions in Itza Maya. In *Proceedings of the Tenth Annual Meeting of the Berkeley Linguistics Society*, edited by C. Brugman and M. Macaulay, 596–608. Berkeley: Berkeley Linguistics Society.

———. 1984b. On Proto-Yucatecan Word Order. *Journal of Mayan Linguistics* 4(2): 35–64.

———. 1987. Discourse Framing in Itzá Maya. *Anthropological Linguistics* 29:478–88.

———. 1989. Noun Phrase Referencing in Itzá Maya. Ms.

———. 1990. Possession and Ergativity in Itzá Maya. *International Journal of American Linguistics* 56:542–60.

Hymes, Dell. 1981. *"In vain I tried to tell you": Essays in Native American Ethnopoetics*. Philadelphia: University of Pennsylvania Press.

Jones, Grant D. 1982. Agriculture and Trade in the Colonial Period Southern Maya Lowlands. In *Maya Subsistence: Studies in Memory of Dennis E. Puleston*, edited by Kent V. Flannery, 275–93. New York: Academic Press.

_____. 1989. *Maya Resistance to Spanish Rule: Time and History on a Colonial Frontier*. Albuquerque: University of New Mexico Press.

Kaufman, Terrence. 1976. Archaeological and Linguistic Correlations in Mayaland and Associated Areas of Mesoamerica. *World Archaeology* 8:101–18.

Means, Philip A. 1917. *History of the Spanish Conquest of Yucatan and of the Itzas*. Papers of the Peabody Museum of American Archaeology and Ethnology, Harvard University, no. 7. Cambridge, Mass.

Rice, Don S. 1986. The Petén Postclassic: A Settlement Perspective. In *Late Lowland Maya Civilization, Classic to Postclassic*, edited by Jeremy A. Sabloff and E. Wyllys Andrews V, 301–44. A School of American Research Book. Albuquerque: University of New Mexico Press.

Schumann, Otto. 1964. El Origen del Mundo: Un Cuento Maya-Itzá. *Tlalocan* 4(4): 351–52.

_____. 1971. *Descipción Estructural del Maya Itzá del Petén, Guatemala, C.A.* Centro de Estudios Mayas, Cuaderno 6. Mexico City: Universidad Nacional Autónoma de México.

Sherzer, Joel, and Anthony C. Woodbury, eds. 1987. *Native American Discourse: Poetics and Rhetoric*. Cambridge: Cambridge University Press.

Sosa, Jose Maria. 1970. *Monografía del Departamento de El Petén*. 2 vols. Guatemala: Editorial "Jose de Pineda Ibarra."

Swann, Brian. 1983. *Smoothing the Ground: Essays on Native American Oral Literature*. Berkeley: University of California Press.

Tedlock, Dennis. 1983. *The Spoken Word and the Work of Interpretation*. Philadelphia: University of Pennsylvania Press.

_____. 1985. *Popol Vuh: The Mayan Book of the Dawn of Life*. New York: Simon and Schuster.

Thompson, J. Eric S. 1976. *Maya History and Religion*. Norman: University of Oklahoma Press.

_____. 1977. A Proposal for Constituting a Maya Subgroup, Cultural and Linguistic, in the Petén and Adjacent Regions. In *Anthropology and History in Yucatan*, edited by Grant D. Jones, 3–42. Austin: University of Texas Press.

Ulrich, Mathew, and Rosemary Ulrich. 1976. *Diccionario Bilingüe: Maya Mopán y Español; Español y Maya Mopán*. Guatemala: Summer Institute of Linguistics.